OTHER TITLES IN THE SMART

Taking the Red Pill
Science, Philosophy and Religion in The Matrix

Seven Seasons of Buffy
Science Fiction and Fantasy Writers Discuss Their Favorite Television Show

Five Seasons of Angel
Science Fiction and Fantasy Writers Discuss Their Favorite Vampire

What Would Sipowicz Do?
Race, Rights and Redemption in NYPD Blue

Stepping through the Stargate
Science, Archaeology and the Military in Stargate SG-1

The Anthology at the End of the Universe
Leading Science Fiction Authors on Douglas Adams' Hitchhiker's Guide to the Galaxy

Finding Serenity
Anti-heroes, Lost Shepherds and Space Hookers in Joss Whedon's Firefly

The War of the Worlds
Fresh Perspectives on the H. G. Wells Classic

Alias Assumed
Sex, Lies and SD-6

Navigating the Golden Compass
Religion, Science and Dæmonology in Philip Pullman's His Dark Materials

Farscape Forever!
Sex, Drugs and Killer Muppets

Flirting with Pride and Prejudice
Fresh Perspectives on the Original Chick-Lit Masterpiece

Revisiting Narnia
Fantasy, Myth and Religion in C. S. Lewis' Chronicles

Totally Charmed
Demons, Whitelighters and the Power of Three

King Kong Is Back!
An Unauthorized Look at One Humongous Ape

Mapping the World of Harry Potter
Science Fiction and Fantasy Authors Explore the Bestselling Fantasy Series of All Time

The Psychology of The Simpsons
D'oh!

The Unauthorized X-Men
SF and Comic Writers on Mutants, Prejudice and Adamantium

Welcome To Wisteria Lane
On America's Favorite Desperate Housewives

The Man From Krypton
A Closer Look At Superman

BOARDING THE ENTERPRISE

Transporters, Tribbles and the Vulcan Death Grip in Gene Roddenberry's *Star Trek*

BOARDING THE ENTERPRISE

EDITED BY
DAVID GERROLD
AND ROBERT J. SAWYER
WITH LEAH WILSON

BENBELLA BOOKS, INC.
Dallas, Texas
BENBELLA

BenBella Books, Inc.
6440 N. Central Expressway, Suite 617
Dallas, TX 75206
www.benbellabooks.com • Send feedback to feedback@benbellabooks.com

Printed in the United States of America
10 9 8 7 6 5 4 3 2 1

Library of Congress Cataloging-in-Publication Data

Boarding the Enterprise : transporters, tribbles, and the Vulcan death grip in Gene Roddenberry's Star trek / edited by David Gerrold and Robert J. Sawyer, with Leah Wilson.
p. cm.
Includes bibliographical references and index.
ISBN 1-932100-87-3 (alk. paper)
1. Star trek (Television program) I. Gerrold, David, 1944- II. Sawyer, Robert J.

PN1992.77.S73B63 2006
791.45'72—dc22

2006012225

Proofreading by Stacia Seaman and Princy Alexander
Cover design by Todd Michael Bushman
Text design and composition by John Reinhardt Book Design
Printed by Victor Graphics, Inc.

Distributed by Independent Publishers Group
To order call (800) 888-4741 • www.ipgbook.com

For media inquiries and special sales contact Yara Abuata at yara@benbellabooks.com

CONTENTS

INTRODUCTION
WELCOME ABOARD THE ENTERPRISE 1
Robert J. Sawyer

FOREWORD
THE TROUBLE WITH TREK 5
David Gerrold

STAR TREK IN THE REAL WORLD 17
Norman Spinrad

I REMEMBER STAR TREK . . . 33
D. C. Fontana

ALL OUR TOMORROWS 41
Allen Steele

THE PRIME QUESTION 57
Eric Greene

WE FIND THE ONE QUITE ADEQUATE 87
Michael A. Burstein

WHO AM I? 101
Lyle Zynda

WHAT HAVE YOU DONE WITH SPOCK'S BRAIN?!? 115
Don DeBrandt

LOST SECRETS OF PRE-WAR HUMAN TECHNOLOGY 125
Lawrence Watt-Evans

EXAGGERATE WITH EXTREME PREJUDICE 135
Robert A. Metzger

TO BOLDLY TEACH WHAT NO ONE HAS TAUGHT BEFORE 153
David DeGraff

WHO KILLED THE SPACE RACE? 163
Adam Roberts

ALEXANDER FOR THE MODERN AGE 169
Melissa Dickinson

HOW STAR TREK LIBERATED TELEVISION 185
Paul Levinson

BEING BETTER 197
Howard Weinstein

APPENDIX
EPISODE REFERENCE 211

Robert J. Sawyer

Introduction: Welcome Aboard the Enterprise

LAST FALL, I GOT INVITED to the Singapore Writers Festival, along with fellow science fiction authors Bruce Sterling and Norman Spinrad. Periodically, when we were out sightseeing in that beautiful city, people would notice our fancy name badges, or overhear us chatting about the festival, and ask who we were. At first we mentioned our books, but, of course, the titles elicited blank stares. And so I started simply pointing to Norman and saying, "This man wrote an episode of *Star Trek*."

"Oh, wow!" people always replied. "Which one?"

"'The Doomsday Machine,'" I said. And the appreciative nods began. Four decades on, and all over the planet, people still know and love *Star Trek*—indeed, they know it so well that they recognize individual episodes by their titles.

And of course, everyone is familiar with the catch phrases from the show: "Beam me up," "He's dead, Jim," "The Prime Directive," "Warp factor six," "At the time, it seemed the logical thing to do," "Phasers on stun," "Hailing frequencies open," "Live long and prosper" and the most famous split infinitive in human history, "To boldly go where no man has gone before."

Those last words, part of *Star Trek*'s opening narration, were first heard on September 8, 1966, when the debut episode was broadcast. In a way, that narration was hopelessly optimistic: it promised a five-year mission for the starship *Enterprise*, but *Star Trek* was taken off the air after only three seasons.

But in another way, the words also turned out to be enormously shortsighted. Forty years on—time enough for eight five-year missions—*Star Trek* is such a major part of our culture that it's almost impossible to imagine the world without it. More people today know who Mr. Spock is than Dr. Spock; the prototype of the space shuttle—still the most advanced spacecraft humanity has ever built—was named *Enterprise*; our cell phones flip open just like Captain Kirk's communicator; and the original fourteen-foot model of good old NCC-1701 is on permanent display at the Smithsonian.

To date, there have been five prime-time television *Star Trek* series, a Saturday morning animated *Star Trek* series, ten *Star Trek* motion pictures and hundreds of *Star Trek* books. And it all started when a former cop and airline pilot named Eugene Wesley Roddenberry decided that maybe, just maybe, television audiences were ready for some adult science fiction. His "*Wagon Train* to the stars," with its irresistible mix of gaudy sets, hammy acting and sly social commentary, has been warmly embraced now by two full generations of human beings.

Granted, for the first time in two decades, there's no new *Star Trek* TV series in production, and, yes, there are no new *Star Trek* movies currently in the works. But if we've learned anything from the voyages of the *Enterprise*, it's that even death is not permanent. *Star Trek*, no doubt, will live again.

And well it should: no TV series of any type has ever been so widely loved—or been so important. Yes, important: *Star Trek* was the only dramatic TV show of its day to talk, even in veiled terms, about the Vietnam conflict, and it also tackled overpopulation, religious intolerance and race relations. (Who can forget Frank Gorshin—*Batman*'s Riddler—running about with his face painted half black and half white?) As William Marshall, who played cyberneticist Dr. Richard Daystrom in the episode "The Ultimate Computer" (2-24),[1] said in an interview shortly before he passed away, it's im-

[1] We've used this format to notate episodes referenced throughout the book: (season number-episode number). In other words, the episode titled "The Ultimate Computer" (2-24) was season two, episode twenty-four. See the appendix for a complete episode list.

possible to overstate the impact it had in the 1960s when white Captain Kirk referred to the black Daystrom as "sir." Was it any surprise, two decades later, that NASA hired Nichelle Nichols, who played Lt. Uhura, to help recruit the first minority astronauts? *Star Trek* gave us an appealing vision of a tolerant future that included *everyone*.

And that future is still compelling. We may not be quite sure how to get there from here but, as Edith Keeler said in Harlan Ellison's episode "The City on the Edge of Forever" (1-28), *Star Trek* taught us that the days and the years ahead are worth living for. More than anything else, the series was about hope.

To celebrate four decades of exploring strange new worlds, of seeking out new life and new civilizations, we've commissioned these commemorative essays. Some are by the people who actually made *Star Trek*: Norman Spinrad is here, along with D. C. Fontana, Howard Weinstein and my coeditor, David Gerrold, all of whom penned adventures of Kirk, Spock and McCoy that actually aired on TV. Other essays are by people like me: the current crop of science fiction writers who were deeply influenced by *Star Trek*, and at least in part took up our profession because of it. Still others are by academics who have found in those original seventy-nine hour-long episodes much worth pondering. Together, in these pages, we celebrate *Star Trek* with all the over-the-top gusto of Jim Kirk, we analyze it with the cool logic of Commander Spock and we explore its fallible, human side with the crusty warmth of "Bones" McCoy.

The first-ever book about *Star Trek* was the phenomenally influential *The Making of Star Trek*, published in 1968 when the original series was still in production. Written by Stephen E. Whitfield and Gene Roddenberry, it made possible the *Star Trek* fan-following that exists today, providing us with photographs of the props that were only glimpsed on screen, official biographies of the characters, blueprints of the *Enterprise* and the Klingon battle cruiser and the first ever *Star Trek* episode checklist. That book ended with these words: "Whither *Star Trek?* It really doesn't matter. We have its legacy... all we have to do is use it."

After forty years, we still don't know where *Star Trek* is going. But one thing is sure: it'll be a wondrous journey. So, come on aboard—we're about to leave orbit. Mr. Sulu, ahead warp factor one!

Robert J. Sawyer won the Hugo Award for his novel *Hominids* and the Nebula Award for his novel *The Terminal Experiment*. In addition, he's won Canada's top SF award nine times, Japan's top SF award three times and Spain's top SF award three times, as well as best-short-story-of-the-year awards from *Analog* and *Science Fiction Chronicle* magazines and the Crime Writers of Canada. His latest novel is *Mindscan*. He lives in Toronto.

David Gerrold

FOREWORD: THE TROUBLE WITH TREK

IT WAS SUPPOSED TO BE just another television show. Really. Not even the folks who were making it had any idea that it might become something more. Not at the beginning—and not for a long time afterward, either.

The year was 1966, and NBC had just committed itself to broadcast all of its programs in color.

When television broadcasting began in 1949, all television was in black and white. The images were flickery and fuzzy, but Americans bought millions and millions of black-and-white television receivers for the privilege of watching Milton Berle in their own living rooms. Then, along about 1953, RCA invented color television. The pictures were blurry, but they were bright and they were in color.

Unfortunately, there weren't a lot of programs being broadcast in color, and without any programs in color, Americans wouldn't buy color sets to replace their old black-and-white boxes. So it took a while for color television to penetrate the market—about ten years.

By 1964, color television manufacturing had become profitable, but there were still a lot of shows on the air in black and white. RCA owned a television network, NBC. They decided that the network should go all color, all the time, to help sell more color television receivers.

And so it began.

The executives at NBC understood that color television was still something of an infant technology. The sets were tricky to tune, and if the viewer saw anything less than a perfect picture, he'd blame the set and the whole color television system. So the executives decreed that color shows should be bright and vibrant and pretty to look at. It wasn't time for subtlety of hue—they knew that the system really couldn't handle it.

One day this fellow, Gene Roddenberry, came knocking on their door. He had a different-looking show, and it was full of bright colors: gold shirts, green shirts, blue shirts, red shirts, bright gray walls. It looked pretty. The folks at NBC didn't really understand this science fiction stuff, they said it was "too cerebral",[1] but they did think that it might be good competition for that other show over on CBS, *Lost in Space*.

So they put it on the air. The rest is history.

About that history—

The official and unofficial histories of *Star Trek*, in all of its various incarnations, have been written so many times, and in so many places, and by so many people,[2] that there's little need to repeat it here. But for those of you who've been buried in caves or living in Antarctica, or who have just gotten back from a forty-five-year round-trip to Proxima Centauri, here's the recap:

Star Trek, the original series, was never a big hit in its original network run. Yes, I know that's hard to believe, but facts are facts. The ratings were consistently lackluster. The show hovered in the middle of the pack, not a good place to be for an expensive show—and certainly not high enough to justify renewal. Nevertheless, NBC kept it around for three years. That was very fortunate. Because that was sufficient time for the show to shoot seventy-nine episodes, just enough for the syndication market.

Here's how the folks on the set felt about the show: we knew it was different. We knew it was special. And we weren't worried about the ratings. We were going to do the best job we could, no matter what. Why? Because we knew the show was special. And we cared about it.

[1] Translation: The average NBC executive is too stupid to be trusted with a three-syllable word.

[2] Including yrs trly.

But at the time, we had very little idea how much everybody else also cared. What happened after NBC canceled the show was a surprise.

Almost immediately, Paramount began distributing *Star Trek*'s seventy-nine episodes to independent (non-network) stations—stations that couldn't afford to pay for new episodes but could easily afford to buy reruns. They "stripped" the episodes, putting them on at seven o' clock in the evening, Monday through Friday—and suddenly they began winning big ratings. Sometimes they even won the whole hour.

Those seventy-nine hours of *Star Trek* were very popular. Boy, was NBC embarrassed.

See, here's what happened: NBC had broadcast the show at 8:30 P.M. on Thursday during the first year, 8:30 P.M. on Friday the second year and 10:00 P.M. on Friday the third year. The loyal audience followed the show from time slot to time slot, but a large part of the demographic market for the show was already in bed by then.

But the local stations, the independent stations, needed prime-time quality shows for the early evening hours—that was the only way they could compete with the networks. So they put *Star Trek* on the air at 4:00 P.M. and 7:00 P.M. and 7:30 P.M., and suddenly a whole new audience discovered the show. It was more popular than ever. The episodes pulled big ratings—and vindicated a lot of people who knew that *Star Trek* was a better show than NBC had ever believed.

In syndication, the show made so much money that Paramount's accountants nicknamed the episodes the "seventy-nine jewels." In fact, those episodes were so profitable that they actually kept the studio going through some very dark days in the seventies (though you'll never get anyone at Paramount to admit that publicly).

Now, here's the other half of the history—the part that doesn't get acknowledged often enough.

Way back in the 1920s, there was a fellow named Hugo Gernsback who edited a science fiction magazine called *Amazing Stories*. Because he encouraged readers to write in to the magazine, he became the seed around which science fiction fandom crystallized. By the mid-fifties, science fiction fandom was a lively subculture. There were science fiction fan clubs in almost every major city. Fans wrote fanzines, attended conventions and handed out awards for the books and stories that amazed them the most. Many fans even went on to become professional authors. (Ahem.)

At the 1964 World Science Fiction Convention in Chicago, Irwin Allen previewed his new science fiction show, and Gene Roddenberry previewed his. The fans yawned through *Lost In Space*, but they gave the *Star Trek* pilot a standing ovation—a fact which puzzled Irwin Allen to no end. He couldn't see the difference between Roddenberry's show and his own.

When *Star Trek* began broadcasting on September 8, 1966, science fiction fans took it to heart. They wrote about it in fanzines, discussed it at conventions and awarded it a Hugo. Lots of new people started showing up at science fiction conventions because they thought they would hear a lot more about *Star Trek*. But science fiction conventions are about a lot of things, not just a single television show.

The average science fiction convention of the '60s had an art show, a masquerade, panels on science, panels on writing, panels on publishing, speeches by major authors, an awards banquet and lots of ancillary activities, like fanzines and dances and ice cream socials.

Very quickly a schism developed in the science fiction community. There were the "Truefen"—and there were the "Trekkies." Both groups looked at each other with some disdain. The Truefen couldn't understand why the Trekkies were so awestruck by a bunch of actors in velour shirts. The Trekkies couldn't understand why the Truefen weren't.

The underlying conversation was far more serious—just what is this thing called science fiction anyway? Is it about thoughtful extrapolation of ideas? Or is it about the sense of wonder? Or is it about the human adventure? Or is it about all of these things?

The great game of the '60s was defining science fiction. And a lot of authors, myself included, spent much too much time writing definitions of the field that we have since come to regret writing. (Embarrassingly cringe-worthy is probably the mildest way to describe some of those early thoughts.)

By the time *Star Trek* hit the syndicated market, some of the *Trek*-fans were chafing at their (perceived) second-rate status within the larger science fiction community, so they got the idea of putting on their own Star Trek convention.

The rest is history.

I missed the first convention, held in New York in 1972, but I made it to the second one, in 1973. Wow!

The program committee decided to have a panel on the science of *Star Trek*. There weren't a lot of science fiction authors in attendance at that convention, only three of us—so I found myself sitting on a panel between Isaac Asimov and Hal Clement, not just two men who had lived their entire lives as SF writers, not just two of the greatest authors of the Golden Age of Science Fiction, but two living legends in the community. And here was I, a mere child of twenty-something, a tadpole in the great lily pond, parked uncomfortably between them.

The little voice in my head immediately began wondering, "David! What the hell are *you* doing sitting between Isaac Asimov and Hal Clement?"

And the other little voice in my head (there's a whole committee) immediately replied, "Keep your damn mouth shut—or the audience will start asking the same question!"

Unfortunately, because this was a Star Trek convention, and since this was a panel on writing for *Star Trek*, the first question came to me. The question was something about scientific accuracy. I said, "Well, I believe it's important to be as accurate as possible, so if I don't know the answer, I pick up the phone and call Isaac Asimov, and if he doesn't know the answer, he picks up the phone and calls Hal Clement, so let's go directly to Hal for the answer to that one."

Whew.

During the '70s, most of the Star Trek conventions were organized by enthusiastic fans. Thousands of people turned up for these conventions and the convention committees often found themselves with tens of thousands of dollars in the bank. Much of the profits went to various charities, some went to finance future conventions and some went into the pockets of various promoters. Uh-oh. As it became apparent that Star Trek conventions could be very profitable, several enterprising folks went into the business of staging conventions. The fan-run Star Trek conventions couldn't compete, and except for small local events, most of them have since faded away.

Meanwhile, when the fuddled folks at Paramount Pictures began to recognize that this *Star Trek* thing was not going to go away, they actually started wondering if this meant that there might be enough audience to support a new series. They began negotiating with Gene Roddenberry. Unfortunately for them, Gene Roddenberry had now learned to negotiate back. (Negotiate is a euphemism here.) Several long frustrating years later... it was 1977. Do you remember what happened on May 25, 1977?

Star Wars premiered at Grauman's Chinese Theater.

Suddenly, in a matter of days, science fiction was not only fashionable, it was *profitable.*

So Paramount decided to make a *Star Trek* movie. And another. And another. And another. The even-numbered ones were the good ones. Mostly.

In 1986, Paramount entered into negotiations with Fox to produce a new *Star Trek* series for Fox's new television network. The more they negotiated, the more they realized that they didn't want to give up the jewel in their crown to anybody else. So they sold *Star Trek: The Next Generation* and *Deep Space Nine* directly to television stations as first-run syndicated shows, and when they started their own network, UPN, they put *Voyager* and *Enterprise* on that.

At the time of this writing, the *Star Trek* phenomenon is four decades old, comprising ten movies and (rough estimate) 700 hours of television. (I'm sure that some obsessive-compulsive *Trek*fan has already computed the number of hours of *Star Trek* on film.) Those 700 hours include six television series (if you include *Star Trek Animated*). Three of the series have been about a starship called the *Enterprise.* Two of the series have involved Kirk, Spock and McCoy. Six of the movies have been about Kirk, Spock and McCoy. The rest have been about characters from *Star Trek: The Next Generation.*

Now, at this point we could talk about the statistics of *Star Trek* at length, and this would be as illuminating as counting the number of stars in the sky or the number of grains of sand on the beach. It would be an interesting exercise, and the result would be an interesting number, but so what? Do you want to eat the candy bar—or do you just want to read the list of ingredients on the wrapper?

The real question, the one that comes up in many of the articles and books that have been published about *Star Trek*, and the one that few people have ever really attempted to answer *in depth*, is this one: why has *Star Trek* become such an enduring phenomenon in the popular culture of America, and indeed, the entire world?

The truth is, *Star Trek* is a very uneven television show.

(Oh, come on. I'm not telling you anything you don't already know. Most of the fans of the various series are already quite vocal about their disappointments with this aspect or that, mostly the writing. So this isn't news. The show is uneven. Get over it, okay?)

But to its credit—especially during the first two years of the original series—the show reached for some very ambitious goals. After that, when the show fell into the hands of less ambitious producers and writers, it devolved into something else.

The fans of the show take it personally. This isn't just a TV show; it's a large part of their identity. So they react strongly to surprises. Anything that a fan sees as a betrayal of the vision of the show is seen as...well, an assault. Some fans have complained that each subsequent incarnation of *Star Trek* has gotten farther away from the original imperative—that episodes are incestuously mining the past instead of boldly exploring the future. *Star Trek* is supposed to be an issues-oriented show that asks people to think about the way the world works and whether or not the way it is, is the way it has to be. *Star Trek* has always suggested that we can change things for the better. If we choose to.

If we choose to....

And I think that takes us directly to the real appeal of the whole phenomenon. It isn't the stories and it isn't the actors. It's the underlying premise that the final frontier is not space—it's the human soul.

When *Star Trek* premiered, the nation was in turmoil; the world was in turmoil. We were in the middle of a protracted civil rights struggle, the chronic nuclear threat of the Cold War, the unending quagmire of a war in Vietnam, a growing recognition of the limitations of national power, discontent with the leadership of the nation, the nascent stirrings of ecological awareness, the shift in society toward the imperatives of the "baby boomers," a genuine dismay at the festering violence in our cities as demonstrated by the assassinations of some of our most beloved leaders—plus a sexual revolution. Not to mention the first surreal beginnings of the information revolution that would make it possible for each and every one of us to feel as if we were drowning in bad news twenty-four hours a day, seven days a week.

Of course, today we have none of those problems, do we? No more nuclear threat, no quagmire of a war, no discontent with the leadership of the nation, no ecological worries, no violence in the cities, no sexual revolution, no unending torrents of bad news—

Right.

Here's a clue to the enduring popularity of *Star Trek*: it's a way of believing. *Star Trek* doesn't just say that there will be a future—it says that the future is full of possibility. *Star Trek* represents a promise that tomorrow can be better than today—if we are willing to design and build it. It doesn't matter what's on the news today. *Star Trek* promises that these problems are only momentary. We will do better.

But....

That's the easy answer. That's what people have been saying about *Star Trek* for the last four decades. (Shameless self-promotion: I was the first person to put this thought into print. *The World of Star Trek*, published by Ballantine Books in February of 1973.) But it's also an incomplete answer.

Here's the rest of it.

Star Trek has its literary antecedents in science fiction. Science fiction is the bastard child of philosophy and religion; it is a literature of speculation. It is a literature of inquiry.

The essential inquiry, the inquiry underlying all other inquiries, is this one: "What does it mean to be a human being?"

We could spend years considering that question. It may very well be the ultimate question.[3]

So what's the answer to the ultimate question? What *does* it mean to be a human being?

Who's asking?

Because only a human being would ask that question.

But underneath that...it's the *wrong* question to ask.

[3] The ultimate answer is *not* 42, despite Douglas Adams.

The question is not *what* we are searching for. The question is *why* we are searching. Why do we go climbing mountains, exploring continents, jumping off the planet?

One theologian of my acquaintance suggests that we search because we are looking for God, and that we look for God outside ourselves in the mistaken belief that we cannot find God within ourselves.

One anthropologist of my acquaintance suggests that we search because it's hard-wired into us—that when we were little more than apes living on the savannah, our survival depended on our ability to search for food, and that we wander because we are always looking for the metaphorical equivalent of the next meal.

One philosopher of my acquaintance suggests that human beings search because we are uncomfortable being in the here and now—that to be here now requires authenticity and intimacy; that when we are off searching, we get to avoid being present to the experiences of the moment.

One wag of my acquaintance puts it much simpler: we search elsewhere because we're bored *here*.

I offer a different possibility to consider: we search because we're curious—because we simply want to know. Because the asking of the question is insufficient, we want to know not just the answer that the question requires—we also want to know the possibilities that are opened up as a result.

My "answer"—and it's just as correct as all the others—is that we search because that's what we do, that's who we are, that's what it means to be human. We ask questions because we want to know what's on the other side.

That's the appeal of *Star Trek*. Or of any other science fiction show, for that matter. It's about considering the possibilities. It's about opening the door, looking to see what's on the other side and asking, "Is this the journey we want to begin?"

Gene Roddenberry was right about this. The way the world is today isn't the way it *has* to be. We can do better. We can design a better world, we can build a better world—but the first step in designing is asking the question, "What do we want to build?"

Do we want to build starships and androids and transporter beams?

All of those things sound like good ideas. They sound like fun ideas. But we won't really know if they're good ideas until *after* we build them and discover how to really use them. It's only after an invention becomes real that we discover what it's really good for. Once an invention is in the hands of the people, that's when we invent the rest of it—the synergistic possibilities that couldn't be forseen. (Example: Once upon a time, you could have predicted the automobile or the airplane or the television, but could you have predicted drive-through restaurants, frequent-flier miles and infomercials?) There are two parts to an invention; the first part is the invention. The second part is all the interesting new possibilities we invent once we have the device in hand. Generally, we find that we have no real idea what kind of societal transformations an invention or discovery will create until after we're already living with them.

Science fiction gives us a hint of what's next. It is predictive, prescriptive and prophylactic. It is the journey to the top of the ridge so we can look out at the landscape on the other side of the mountain. It is a literature of possibility. And after all is said and done, that's the real job of science fiction—to ask the next question. Not to answer it—because the real answers might not be knowable until *afterward*—but simply to ask the question in the first place so that we can approach the possibilities in front of us with rational and conscious deliberation.

This is the trouble with *Trek*. It hasn't lived up to its potential. It hasn't delivered on its promise.

Does *Star Trek* ask the questions it should be asking? Sometimes it does, but most of the time, it doesn't even raise its hand to get called upon. It's not enough to be in the classroom expecting a social promotion.

Star Trek promises excellence. It looks like excellence, it dresses up with excellence, it pretends to excellence, but—

The promise of excellence carries with it the obligation to take on the challenge, no matter what, whatever it takes—even if it demands a journey into dangerous and uncomfortable places. Excellence challenges itself. Excellence challenges the world. Excellence challenges the people who are committed to it.

And excellence always transforms those who take on the challenge. And then they transform the people around them. And then they transform the world.

As human beings, we search. That's who we are. We search, whatever the reasons, for more, better and different. *Star Trek*, whatever it is, however we define it or approach it, is one of the expressions of that search for meaning and answers.

But after all is said and done, if *Star Trek* doesn't fully satisfy us, if it doesn't take us as far as we want to go, if it doesn't challenge us or transform us—that's not the failure of *Star Trek*.

It's our failure—for not looking beyond *Star Trek*.

There's more. A lot more. If, once upon a time, *Star Trek* challenged us to get out of the box, get out of the comfort zone, then that challenge is still incumbent. Only this time, perhaps it's time to get out of the box defined by *Star Trek* and move on out beyond.

What else is on the bookshelf?

David Gerrold is the author of numerous television episodes including the legendary "Trouble With Tribbles" episode of *Star Trek*. He has also written for *Land of the Lost*, *Babylon 5*, *Twilight Zone*, *Sliders* and other series. He has published forty-three books, including two on television production. He taught screenwriting at Pepperdine University for two decades. He has won the Hugo, the Nebula and the Locus awards. A movie based on his autobiographical novel, *The Martian Child*, is now in production.

Norman Spinrad

STAR TREK IN THE REAL WORLD

Star Trek is considered a classic of SF, but it's very much of the old school. Ironically, the writers of two of its best-loved episodes were the most influential American authors involved in SF's new school, the 1960s New Wave, a move toward a literate exploration of inner space: Harlan Ellison wrote "The City on the Edge of Forever" and Norman Spinrad penned "The Doomsday Machine." Spinrad is one of SF's most insightful critics, and here he turns an incisive eye onto the series with all the force of an absolutely pure antiproton beam.

> Far too little attention has been paid to *Star Trek* as the pivotal work in the growth of SF cinema into a dominant force, and the concurrent growth of SF publishing into what it is today....
>
> The creation of the *Star Trek* concept...was a cunning and audacious stroke of genius that changed the relation of SF to popular culture forever....
>
> *Star Trek* imprinted the imagery of science fiction on mass public consciousness, where it had never been before, opening, thereby, the languages and concerns of science fiction to a mass audience for the very first time...so that years and a generation of Trekkies later, George Lucas could confidently begin *Star Wars* with a full-bore space chase and take the largest film audiences in history with him from the opening shot.
>
> —Norman Spinrad, *Science Fiction in the Real World*

YOU MUST PARDON ME for beginning this essay by quoting myself, but the above words were written long before I sat down to write this. They appeared, not in a piece on *Star Trek* itself, but as part of a chapter on cinematic science fiction in a critical book exploring the relationship of science fiction to the wider world around us, and, for purposes of this discussion, *that* is as important as the words themselves, or who happened to be the author thereof.

In science fiction, and in the real world, there has never been a phenomenon quite like *Star Trek*. One scarcely knows where to begin. Consider perhaps the most improbable event of all: *Star Trek*'s third and final season as a network prime-time show was nearly a decade in the past when the first test-bed model of a space shuttle was rolled out of the hanger.

Presiding at the roll-out ceremony of the space shuttle *Enterprise* was the President of the United States. Gerald Ford and his people had not planned to name the prototype shuttle *Enterprise*, in fact there was no little derision when the notion was first broached.

That was before the letters came pouring in.

And even when the inevitable decision was finally made, the Powers-That-Be insisted that, in the time-honored military tradition, this first true space-ship had been named in honor of a previous vessel, the aircraft carrier *Enterprise* of World War II fame.

Sure it was.

Nevertheless, when the space shuttle *Enterprise* was rolled out, there beside the President of the United States was the captain of what the whole nation knew as the real *Enterprise*, along with representatives of his bridge crew, and the music they played was the theme from *Star Trek*.

Trekkies made him do it.

Just as they had kept the show on the air in prime time for two and a half seasons after NBC had tried to cancel it after the first thirteen weeks.

By the network numbers, *Star Trek* was a flop. It never rose much above twentieth place in the weekly Nielsens. NBC decided to pull the plug and told Paramount and Gene Roddenberry that no new episodes would be ordered. After the thirteenth week, *Star Trek*, like hundreds of failed series before it, would be dead.

But Roddenberry did something utterly unprecedented. He refused to take no for an answer. He decided to fight the network, to save his show using tactics that Hollywood had never seen.

He contacted a number of well-known science fiction writers, myself among them, and asked us to join a committee to save *Star Trek*. All Gene really wanted was our permission to use our names on a letterhead, and so most of us readily agreed.

Armed with this letterhead, he hired Bjo and John Trimble, well-connected science fiction fans, to use the "writers' committee" to put together a campaign to convince science fiction fans to write letters to NBC and Paramount demanding that the show be allowed to continue.

He succeeded beyond what must have been even his own wildest expectations.

In those days, when a network received a couple of thousand letters in praise of a TV show, they sat up and took notice. If they got five thousand, they were mightily impressed.

Science fiction fans dumped upwards of 75,000 letters on Paramount and NBC in a few short weeks. Fans picketed the studio and the network. It became a TV news item. Dumbfounded by this totally unprecedented outpouring of public opinion, NBC capitulated.

They literally didn't know what had hit them.

Particularly since the ratings never really improved.

What did Gene Roddenberry know that the network and studio mavens didn't?

It had taken Roddenberry years to get *Star Trek* on the air. He himself had written a ninety-minute pilot that didn't sell. He didn't give up. He hired Samuel A. Peeples to write another script, changed Spock's makeup a bit, changed the ship's captain and the actor who played him, and shot another pilot that finally sold.

During this whole process, Roddenberry did what no other producer had ever done. He made the rounds of the science fiction conventions, made speeches, sat on panels, socialized with the writers and fans, treated the science fiction community to early screenings of both pilot films. He took the fans and the writers inside. He campaigned for support within the science fiction community, and he got it.

What Roddenberry knew that NBC and Paramount didn't was that while there were perhaps no more than ten or fifteen thousand committed science fiction fans in the United States, they were highly organized, literate and voluble in print. Scores of science fiction conventions were held every year. Fans published hundreds of amateur "fanzines" filled with articles and letters from readers.

By tapping into this existing network, he was able to generate far more letters than there were fans. What NBC and Paramount didn't know was that those 75,000 letters were written, for the most part, by a comparatively small universe of committed people.

But, contrary to popular belief, network and studio heads are not *complete* idiots. When the first season ratings didn't improve, they tried to cancel the show again, and when they were bombarded by another blizzard of letters, even they began to realize that something, in the immortal words of Mr. Spock, did not compute—especially when the second season ratings were no better.

Roddenberry, however, had boxed them into a corner. The numbers said "cancel this show." But the continued letter-writing campaigns and the attendant, well-managed publicity would have made them seem like high-handed, anti-democratic monsters if they did.

They were royally pissed off. They set out to assassinate *Star Trek* at the beginning of the third season, to make sure that the ratings would be so bad that no reasonable person could blame them for finally canceling it.

Their demographic studies told them that *Star Trek*'s main audiences were children, teenagers and young adults in their twenties. So they slotted the show at 10:00 P.M. on Friday night, when most of the kiddies had been put to bed, and most of the teenagers and young adults were out on weekend dates. As a bit of insurance, they hired a new producer whose lack of understanding of what science fiction was all about would later be proven by his work as the producer of *Space: 1999*'s disastrous final season.

This time, the Powers-That-Be finally had their way. The third season's ratings were so bad that no amount of letter writing could save the show again. *Star Trek* was canceled and no doubt, they thought that was the end of it.

How wrong they were.

Network and studio heads may not be idiots, but they're not exactly Einsteins either. In the case of *Star Trek*, they failed to understand the true implications of their own numbers.

True, *Star Trek* had always been a ratings failure by network prime-time standards. But in those days, before the advent of cable channels fragmented the prime-time audience, those ratings meant that this "failure" was still watched by *twenty million people* a week for three years.

Ironically enough, the fact that Roddenberry was able to beat the system for three full seasons ended up enriching Paramount enormously. Three seasons' worth of programs is what you need to sell a viable syndication package, and from the time of its cancellation as a prime-time show until the present day, *Star Trek* reruns have been a staple of local syndication markets.

A show that flopped in prime time became the greatest syndication success in television history. *Star Trek* wouldn't die. It was so successful in syndication that it finally spawned a series of high-budget motion pictures. Successful films had from time to time spawned TV series, but *Star Trek* was the first to have reversed the process.

Indeed, *Star Trek* now exists in multiple incarnations. Feature films, spin-off series, scores of novelizations, comic books and, with a little button-pushing on your remote, you can probably still tune in reruns of the original TV show too!

How could this possibly happen? After all, hundreds of TV series have run three seasons or more and gone into syndication, but none have taken on a life after prime-time death like *Star Trek*'s. Perhaps the Hollywood Powers-That-Be should be pardoned for failing to anticipate the incredible.

How could they have known?

The conditions that created this phenomenon didn't exist when it began. Before *Star Trek*, there *was* no mass audience for science fiction.

Star Trek created it.

At the time that Gene Roddenberry began putting together the *Star Trek* project, science fiction had long languished in cultural obscurity.

The genre had been born as an offshoot of the pulp adventure magazines in the 1920s, and in the middle of the 1960s there were a handful of science fiction magazines—none of them with a circulation much above 100,000, and less than two hundred science fiction books published annually. Five thousand copies was quite a nice sale for an SF hardcover, and 100,000 sales made a paperback a big winner.

There had been a few successful major SF films like *Metropolis*, *The War of the Worlds* and *The Day the Earth Stood Still*, and some artistically successful B-movies like *Forbidden Planet*, *This Island Earth* and *The Power*, but generally speaking, SF films, or "sci-fi flicks," as they were more generally known, were B-movies featuring tacky monsters from outer space or other venues, typified by *The Creature from the Black Lagoon* and *The Thing*, in which John W. Campbell's subtle masterpiece, *Who Goes There?*, was turned into a monster movie featuring James Arness as a savage, carnivorous carrot.

When it came to TV, *The Twilight Zone* had been a long-running success, though most of the episodes were only borderline SF, and *The Outer Limits*, while it had done some serious SF, had relied heavily on monsters.

True, the devoted core of regular readers knew that inside the sleazy covers of those magazines and paperbacks there existed a universe of literally infinite literary possibility, that some of the finest American writers had done their best work therein for decades, and that what passed for "sci-fi movies" was only a pale shadow of the real stuff.

But the general public, when it thought of science fiction at all, thought of mad scientists, crazed robots and bug-eyed monsters, and the Hollywood Powers-That-Be viewed SF as low-budget monster movies aimed at a modest-sized cult audience.

How this situation evolved could be, and has been, the subject of whole books, *Science Fiction in the Real World* being one of them, and is far too complex a story to go into here, but for present purposes the point is that, by the 1960s, science fiction had evolved into something largely impenetrable to anyone who was not a regular science fiction reader.

The real stuff dealt with alien civilizations, faster-than-light space travel, mutated consciousness, time travel, alternate universes, relativity theory, synthetic religions, outre biology, the frontiers of psychology, speculative science, political theory and cybernetics. And because it had been written for a limited, educated, in-group audience for so long, it had long since come to be written without compromise, without any real attempt to make it transparent to anyone unfamiliar with the conventions, imagery and secret language.

This, in a way, was a literary strength. Most science fiction writers felt they had no chance of reaching a general audience, so they felt free to write for a theoretical ideal audience—the fans and regular readers, who understood the conventions and the special language, for whom the recondite imagery held meaning, who were, generally speaking, scientifically literate, who did not have to be persuaded that space travel lay in the realm of the realistically possible, who were already convinced that there must be other intelligent beings out there somewhere. This enabled science fiction writers at their best to produce work without intellectual compromise.

But this literary strength was a commercial weakness. It made much of even the best SF largely incomprehensible to a general audience. And when writers *did* try to reach a wider audience, they usually did it by watering the stuff down, by simplifying it, by bringing it closer to the here and now; in a way, by patronizing the general public.

These were the conditions that Gene Roddenberry faced when he set out to do a science fiction TV series. And two further problems as well, which were interrelated.

The first problem was that the anthology series was a dead form as far as prime-time TV was concerned; that is, the series in which each episode was, was a self-contained story with its own cast of characters. Since science fiction is inherently a literature built around surprise, novelty and the attendant sense of wonder, the anthology series was the ideal form for televised SF, and indeed, the only two successful SF TV series, *Twilight Zone* and *The Outer Limits*, had been anthologies.

But what the networks wanted were series that used *familiarity* to retain and build audience share, episodic series in which the same main characters appeared each week in a familiar format and setting, characters who could not really be changed by the events of each week's episode, a requirement that would seem to be the esthetic antithesis of the central appeal of science fiction.

Then too, science fiction was expensive to film. Space ships. Other worlds. Alien civilizations. No problem when you're writing short stories and novels, but when you have to build the sets, create the costumes and the makeup and do the special effects processing, the budget becomes prohibitive when you're talking about a time when $200,000 was about the top for an hour-long show. Not to mention the problem of doing it all on a timetable that enables you to do twenty-six episodes a season on a six-day shooting schedule for each.

The genius of Gene Roddenberry was that he was able to look at these problems, these creative restrictions, and, by making one big leap of faith, let them determine a series format that turned them into strengths.

It would be futile to attempt a science fiction anthology series. The networks weren't buying anthologies, and besides, you simply couldn't create sets, makeup and special effects for a new science fiction setting every week at $200,000 an episode without descending to tacky sleaze. No, it had to be an episodic series, and it had to use mostly reusable standing sets. But then how could you create the sense of novelty and sense of wonder each week that was the core esthetic effect of science fiction?

The answer to that one was the solution to all the problems via the required leap of faith.

Set the whole thing aboard a single spaceship. You could then do most of your shooting on standing sets. Irwin Allen had done much the same thing with a futuristic submarine in the series *Voyage to the Bottom of the Sea*. Network executives love one-line descriptions of a new concept told in terms of old shows when it's time to pitch: "*Voyage to the Bottom of the Sea*—in outer space!"

Or better yet: "Captain Cooke in outer space." A starship on a long voyage of exploration, completely out of touch with the Earth to save you the trouble of showing the complex civilization of the far future, so that each week the same cast of characters can confront almost anything that the writers can dream up. You can set many of the stories entirely within the standing spaceship sets. You can use the same spaceship models over and over again, even a library of standard space shots and effects.

In retrospect, it all seems quite obvious, but to conceive it at all required one big leap of faith—namely that you *could* persuade a mass general audience to accept an interstellar space ship as the setting for a TV series.

Roddenberry approached this problem from two directions, one dramatic, the other purely cinematic.

Give a general audience familiar character types and well-worn traditional character relationships they can readily understand, and they'll swallow your setting, no matter how outre, for it is character relationships that draw an audience into a story, not the physical backdrop.

So.... The Heroic Captain—call him...Kirk. His sidekick, the Crusty Old Sea Doctor Bones—call him...McCoy. The Pragmatic Grumbling Engineer—call him...what else? Scotty.

Any audience would accept such characters, familiar as they were from tales of the sea, and from there it was not such a great leap to transfer them from a sailing ship to a ship of space.

As for the spaceship itself, well, seeing is believing; one picture is worth a thousand words, work off the familiar conventions, give them a spaceship they can understand, a transmogrified ship of the sea.

A bridge, of course, the main and most elaborate set, where most of the action will naturally take place. An engine room to serve as Scotty's domain. A sick-bay for Dr. McCoy. A captain's cabin. A wardroom that can easily be redressed into anything. A corridor set to provide a sense of the ship's complex interior.

Voila, the starship *Enterprise*, its five-year mission to seek out new worlds and new civilizations, to boldly go where no man and no TV series has gone before!

But not quite yet *Star Trek*.

Roddenberry could have stopped there and, having cracked the basic problems, probably gotten his science fiction series on the air. But it wouldn't have been *Star Trek*, and it wouldn't have become the phenomenon that created the present mass audience for science fiction, both literary and cinematic. It would have indeed been merely

Voyage to the Bottom of the Sea in Outer Space, a good format for a successful TV series maybe, but not something that would pass into the collective popular unconscious.

But Gene Roddenberry, unlike Irwin Allen, took science fiction seriously. He wanted *Star Trek* to appeal to a naive audience, but he wanted it to have credibility with the SF cognoscenti too. He wanted it to be a genuine work of science fiction.

The original series guide, the so-called "bible," makes that almost maniacally clear. Roddenberry consulted experts and the *Enterprise* was designed and even blue-printed down to the smallest niggling detail, to the point where NASA even took a look at his plans to pick up some tips on spaceship ergonomics. The ship was utterly real for Roddenberry, as I learned during the story conferences for "The Doomsday Machine" (2-6).

Similarly with the details of the rest of the Star Trek universe: the phasers, the communicators, the shuttlecraft, the chain of command and, of course, the implications of the famous Prime Directive, which by now has attained the real-world credibility of Asimov's Three Laws of Robotics. When the writers sat down to do their episodes, all of this was as predetermined as a street-map of contemporary New York, and if you got something wrong, you had to change it, even if it meant altering the story to make it fit "*Star Trek* reality."

The result was that the layout, hardware, capabilities and limitations of the *Enterprise*, the parameters of the Star Trek universe, remained consistent from episode to episode. Gene Roddenberry knew his ship and its universe, and if you watched enough episodes, so did you. It allowed this imaginary spaceship to become psychologically real, seemingly complex and seemingly familiar in every detail, even though all you really ever saw was less than a dozen sets. No fictional spaceship has ever surpassed the *Enterprise* for this kind of detailed solidity, and not much on the NASA drawing boards either.

As a result, over three seasons the *Enterprise* became, to twenty million regular viewers, as familiar as Dodge City or Gilligan's Island or Lucy Ricardo's living room. And over time, the reruns made it familiar to scores of millions more, to the point that, by the time the space shuttle *Enterprise* was rolled out, an overwhelming majority of the American people were as at home on the bridge of what they psychologically regarded as the *real Enterprise*, the one commanded by the James T. Kirk that half of them had known all their adult lives, as they were in their own living room.

Indeed, the *Enterprise* was an extension of the collective national living room, just as the battlefields of Vietnam had been for eleven long years, via the magic window of the tube.

Endless TV coverage had quite literally brought Vietnam home, given it a psychological reality that no war had ever had before, altering, over time, the national psyche by demystifying war, leeching it of glory, revealing the reality as the grubby horror that it truly was.

So too did endless exposure to the science fiction universe of *Star Trek*, via the familiar confines of the *Enterprise*, de-mystify science fiction, imprint its imagery on the public consciousness, make at least two entire generations feel at home in outer space, precisely because it brought outer space into the home.

Thus did *Star Trek* create a mass general audience for science fiction. The technology of the *Enterprise* and all that it implied—faster-than-light travel, matter transmission, alien beings, human colonization of other planets—had passed into folklore, had become familiar, had become as American as apple pie or Gerald Ford's desire not to offend the Trekkie voting bloc.

Thus was the beaming presence of Captain Kirk and the *Star Trek* theme music required to give NASA's new spaceship media credibility.

Thus could George Lucas open *Star Wars* with a simple type frame reading "A long time ago in a galaxy far, far away," cut to a space battle shot and take the largest film audience in history with him.

Thus did major science fiction films become a Hollywood staple, indeed for a time quite dominating the industry. Thus did literary science fiction come to crash the best-seller lists, and at its peak, come to represent about twenty percent of all fiction published in the United States.

Star Trek opened the way.

Or rather, the *Star Trek* phenomenon opened the way. If the show had died after three first-run seasons and the usual few years of syndication, none of this would have happened, and the world would probably be very different. It took time, a decade or more of reruns, for *Star Trek* to alter the attitude of the American mass audience toward science fiction.

Josef Goebbels had declared that even the biggest lie will come to be believed if it is repeated often enough, and then went on to prove it.

If lies, why not images of the future, which, by their very nature, are neither false nor true? It was the endless repetitive exposure to *Star Trek* that did the deed.

But why didn't *Star Trek* die after the show was canceled? It's easy enough to see how *Star Trek* created the mass audience for science fiction via decades of reruns, but *that audience didn't yet exist* when *Star Trek* went into syndication. How could a show that had flopped in prime time survive long enough in syndication to become the staple of popular culture that it is today? How did it create the mass public audience for itself in the first place?

By the time the show was finally canceled, the letter-writing campaign had already spawned *Star Trek* fan clubs and huge Star Trek conventions, fanzines, the whole Trekkie subculture. While there were never enough Trekkies to make the show successful in prime time, there were enough to keep the tie-ins going even after the show had died, something quite unprecedented.

Star Trek fans continued to buy the novelizations, *Star Trek* toys, games, comics. They continued to hold conventions, which actually got *bigger* after the show was canceled. They continued to publish fanzines, they started writing their own *Star Trek* stories, even whole novels. Even *Star Trek* religions sprang up.

In short, *Star Trek* transcended television. It was no longer defined as those seventy-nine episodes of a canceled TV show running over and over again. It had become a popular myth imprinted upon mass culture, as surely as Robin Hood, or Billy the Kid or Cinderella, a modern legend, a set of mythic archetypes, the dramatic material for books, a cartoon series, a film series, spin-off series, paintings, even a strange sort of underground pornographic literature.

To the point where any character in any contemporary story who finds himself in trouble can look skyward and cry, "Beam me up, Scotty," and everyone will know just what he means.

Clearly then, one cannot entirely explain the *Star Trek* phenomenon by detailing the process that gave it birth and the consequences.

That can tell you *how* it happened, but not *why*. Clearly one must deal with *Star Trek* as dramatic literature in order to understand the power of its appeal in the first place.

We have come a long way into this discussion without really considering Mr. Spock. Kirk, the Heroic Captain; Scotty and Bones, the loyal sidekicks; Uhura, Chekov and Sulu, the gallant crewpeople—these are a traditional cast of shipboard characters as old as the tale of the sea, individuated and made memorable really only by the scripts and the actors' interpretations.

But Spock was... something else.

Whereas the rest of the *Star Trek* format may be seen as Gene Roddenberry's clever reinterpretations and combinations of pre-existing elements into a coherent and successful whole, Mr. Spock was Roddenberry's act of literary genius, a character unlike any other: a new, mythic archetype, and an exceedingly complex one.

Physically, with his pointed ears, Spock evoked the image of Satan and, with his ability to mind-meld, his physical powers and his superior intellect, he certainly possessed power beyond those of mortal men.

But far from being an egoistic, Faustian power-tripper, a tempter or a figment of evil, Spock, at least on the surface, *had* no ego. As a creature of pure logic, he might have represented science, but with his total loyalty to the ship, his captain and his duty, he represented social virtue, not overweening intellectual pride. He was a kind of scientific angel in devil's clothing, a being of pure intellect serving the cause of good because it was the logical thing to do.

And that was only the surface. Beneath the surface, Spock's cold logicality was the product of his people's long, and finally, successful battle with their own savage nature. Vulcan dedication to pure logic was, paradoxically enough, ultimately a religious belief, not a genetic inevitability. Vulcans had *chosen* to suppress their emotional life, although not entirely, as was evident in their behavior when they came into sexual heat. Logical Vulcan society seemed rather ritualized and even mystical whenever we saw it, and perhaps it was no accident that Vulcan features evoke the Orient in Western eyes, with implications of Zen, Taoism and transcendent states of being achieved through spiritual discipline.

Nor is that the end of it. For Spock was half-human, though he disliked being reminded of it, and the two halves of his being were shown to be in continual conflict. Over and over again, Spock surrendered to human emotions against his will, but almost always when these emotions represented human virtues like loyalty, empathy and compassion rather than vices.

Surely Mr. Spock was the most complex character ever to appear in a prime-time TV series. And more than that, he was that science fictional rarity, a fully realized intelligent alien, with an inner life at least as complex as that of any human, but one that was truly *different*. A character that was, on many levels, and in Spock's own oft-repeated words, "quite fascinating."

William Shatner was hired as the star, but Kirk was never the central character in *Star Trek*, and never could be. Whether Roddenberry intended it or not, Mr. Spock was the central figure of *Star Trek*, and in the end, it was the character of Spock that enabled *Star Trek* to transcend television, to survive, in one incarnation and another for nearly half a century, to pass into the collective consciousness of popular culture as surely as Superman, and take science fiction with it.

Did Roddenberry really know what he was doing when he created the character of Spock? Somehow I doubt it, for Spock, in the end, was a collaborative creation, the parameters of his character outlined by Roddenberry, interpreted by Leonard Nimoy, elaborated by the writers of the individual episodes and given additional reality by the imagination of the audience.

Spock was many things to many people. To those of a certain scientific bent, he represented not merely the intellectual but the moral and even spiritual superiority of the logical, scientific viewpoint. To those of a more mystical inclination, he represented higher consciousness, mental and spiritual clarity achieved by a continuous, conscious act of will. To the humanist, he epitomized the struggle toward a balance between logic and intuition, emotion and intellect.

Finally, Mr. Spock was a sexual fantasy figure of great power and considerable complexity. Physically, he resembled Satan, Dracula, the Mysterious Dark Stranger, the Dark Side of the sexual force, the deliciously dangerous Dream Lover. Yet, unlike such Satanic sex symbols, Spock was controlled, logical, loyal, trustworthy, admirable, virtuous. As a sexual fantasy figure, Spock was like no other, allowing the frisson of dark danger within the safe limits of spiritual and moral virtue: Albert Einstein in Jim Morrison's tight black leather clothing, a Mick Jagger that a girl can bring home to meet Mother.

It was the presence of this great character which, in the end, elevated a canceled television series to the status of a modern myth, a contemporary legend, a new literary archetype which has entered the collective unconscious, opening thereby the way for science fiction itself.

And in the end, perhaps, this opening up of the mass public consciousness to the things of science fiction by *Star Trek* goes deeper than mere familiarization with the imagery and the formerly secret language.

For Mr. Spock, alien though he was, was admirable, not menacing: humanity's ally, not its nemesis. His friendship with Kirk represented the possibility of empathy between the Self and the Other, between our own evolving species and the very different beings we are likely to meet when we venture out into the Final Frontier. Even McCoy, who seemingly represented humanity's conservative reticence to love the Stranger, warmed up to Spock in his heart of hearts, though neither of them were about to admit it.

This positive emotional openness to the new and the strange, this empathy for the alien, defines the heart and soul of science fiction. And up until a certain stage in human evolution, this acceptance of the alien, the foreigner, the Other, ran counter to the emotional attitude of our mass culture, and perhaps it was this divergence, as much as the unfamiliar settings, bizarre imagery and secret language, that prevented the acceptance of science fiction as part of the literary and cinematic mainstream.

Ultimately then, *Star Trek*, despite the literary flaws of so many of its episodes, films, books and assorted spin-offs, has succeeded on a moral level. In some small (or perhaps not so small) way, it has served the cause of our spiritual evolution as a species.

Clever format, fanatically loyal fans, marketing strategies and letter-writing campaigns all explain how *Star Trek* has survived through four decades in all its many incarnations.

But when it comes to *why Star Trek* has survived to attain a kind of permanent place in our cultural life, in the end, perhaps it can be simply said that it deserved to.

Norman Spinrad is the author of some twenty novels and sixty stories published in fourteen languages, including *Bug Jack Barron*, *The Iron Dream*, *He Walked Among Us* and *Mexica*. He has also written feature films, television programs and songs. He is also a journalist, film critic, literary critic and political commentator. He has been a radio talk show host, vocalist, literary agent and president of the Science Fiction Writers of America and World SF.

He grew up in New York, has lived in Los Angeles, London, San Francisco and Paris, and traveled widely in Europe, less so in Latin America and Asia.

D. C. Fontana

I REMEMBER STAR TREK...

The first name on *Star Trek*'s opening credits wasn't that of its lead performer, but rather that of its creator, Gene Roddenberry. But although Roddenberry got the ball rolling, many others made huge contributions to the universe we know and love, none perhaps more so than D. C. Fontana, who gave us Spock's parents, Sarek and Amanda, as well as the Tellarites and Andorians, and so much more. Here, she shares some of her memories.

I WAS THERE, and it was never dull. Gene Roddenberry usually held the center of events, his inventive mind solving problems and, often, creating mischief. Everyone has heard about the pair of Danish-designed, futuristic-looking salt and pepper shakers our prop man, Irving Feinberg, brought in for Gene's approval. Gene designated them McCoy's handy-dandy surgical instruments (with some buttons and little lights added), instead. The props actually used in the scene looked like restaurant dispensers because, as Gene said, "Sometimes salt shakers should look like salt shakers." Another time the greensman brought in an exotic plant for approval as set dressing. Gene looked at it, pulled it out of the pot and stuck it back in upside down so the roots dangled grotesquely and announced, "Now *that* looks alien."

Gene had a different way of looking at things. Late in the second season, I did a rewrite on "By Any Other Name" (2-22), which Marc

Daniels was set to direct. The script had a problem: we couldn't figure out a way in which a small handful of aliens could capture and control a starship with a crew of 400 on board. We wrangled and wrestled with it and couldn't find an answer. Finally, we went in to Gene's office and told him our problem.

He listened, thoughtfully pushing a many-sided Mexican onyx paperweight around on his desk with his forefinger. At last, he looked up at us and said, "Suppose the aliens have a little gizmo that captures the 'essence' of a person and turns it into a block that looks like that?" He tapped the paperweight. Bingo! We posited that the gizmo had a wide range, could affect a number of people at a time and, if desired, could turn the block back into the individual(s) with no lasting harm. The prop department came up with numerous blocks, cut from Styrofoam and shaped just like the one on Gene's desk, and the aliens easily took over the ship, leaving Kirk and his bridge crew as the only people to deal with.

There were always practical jokes, of course—with Gene as the chief ringleader. In his first week as story editor, John D. F. Black was working in his office, blissfully unaware of the plot being hatched in Gene's office. Gene called John and asked if he could interview an actress in Gene's place that afternoon.

Gene was persuasive, as only the Great Bird of the Galaxy could be. He said he was very busy overseeing all the production aspects of the start-up of the series, but he had promised the lady's agent she would have an interview. John could certainly ask the appropriate questions, couldn't he? John innocently agreed that he could.

What he didn't know was the actress was Majel Barrett, who had played "Number One" in the first *Star Trek* pilot. Although he had seen that episode, John didn't know Majel's real hair was short and blonde (not long and dark like the wig she wore in the pilot), or that she could change her appearance quite easily with makeup. So the tall, leggy blonde in the short-skirted dress who showed up for the interview went totally unrecognized as she was escorted into John's office by his secretary, Mary Stillwell. Mary was in on it and didn't blink an eye as Gene, associate producer Bob Justman, Bob's secretary and I dashed into her office and listened at the closed door.

Majel told us afterward how she played it. She sat down opposite

John, displaying a lot of leg. John gamely ignored it, explaining that he was deputizing for Gene and would be happy to take her photo and resumé. Majel gave him a dazzling smile and said she hadn't brought a photo or resumé, but she'd be happy to show him her "credits." She started to unbutton the already low-cut front of her dress.

"Ah, no. That's not necessary," John said, starting to panic.

"But you wanted to see my credits," she replied.

On Gene's cue, Mary buzzed in on the intercom, announcing that John's wife was on the phone (she wasn't), and Gene began banging on the office door demanding to see John immediately. We fell through the door as Gene opened it and found Majel laughing her head off, with John as far behind his desk as he could get, red-faced and embarrassed. As soon as we burst in, he realized he'd been had. Fortunately, he was a writer and a gentleman; the language he used to express his opinion about the stunt was to the point—but clean.

When Steve Carabatsos joined the production team as story editor after John left to write a Universal movie, he was given a week or two to settle in. Then, of course, he had to be properly "welcomed." Gene elicited the aid of Jim Rugg, our special effects supervisor, on this one. Jim came up with a weather balloon, a long line of hose and an air pump. The balloon was placed in Steve's office on the far side of the building; the hose was then snaked across the hall through the production office and out the window to the pump stationed in the studio street. The motor pushed the air into the balloon, and it inflated inside Steve's office.

When Steve came in and tried to push open his office door—*it pushed back*. Somewhat startled, he pushed again. Same result. Finally, he managed to shove it open far enough to look around the door and see a huge, orange balloon with a happy face inked on it completely filling his office. Naturally, the culprits were hiding around the corner watching the joke play out.

When I was hired as story editor—Gene sent flowers. I was a nervous wreck for weeks, waiting for the rest of the joke. There wasn't any. Darn, I was disappointed!

The makeup department had its share of excitement as well, and the writers were usually the cause of the problems. After all, we wrote the scripts that called for the unusual makeup requirements. Something bizarre always had to be dealt with, usually with cleverness, creativity and a short budget.

Take ears, for instance. Spock's ears were designed specifically for Leonard Nimoy, but not every set fit precisely or blended believably. Fred Phillips, the chief makeup artist, had to cast them in molds and bake them, and he usually made several pairs at a time every few days. Still, there were a lot of rejects, which meant wasted time and money.

Imagine then an episode that required ears for a number of actors. "Balance of Terror" (1-14), written by Paul Schneider, introduced the Romulans, cousins of the Vulcans, who, of course, had the same ears as Spock. Costume designer Bill Theiss was able to get around some of the difficulty by designing helmets for several of the actors portraying the aliens, but two had to have ears that could be seen, including the guest star, Mark Lenard. Lots of fitting, lots of baked rubber, lots of rejects. Excellent episode, though.

The ear problem persisted, although Fred got very good with Leonard's ears. The second season saw "Amok Time" (2-1), by Theodore Sturgeon, with *a lot* of Vulcans. And a lot of Vulcan ears. The third season had "The *Enterprise* Incident" (3-2), which brought back the Romulans. That one was on my head—but I *really* liked those mysterious Romulans, and damn the ears!

Actually, the ear problem was the reason the Klingons got to be our most useful villains. Created by Gene Coon for the episode "Errand of Mercy" (1-26), their makeup made them very attractive, time-wise. Primarily consisting of dark skin coloring, facial hair and various hair styles, their makeup was fairly easily applied and relatively inexpensive—at least compared to ears.

Hair was also a pain at times. Bill Shatner, whose hair was thinning, had to resort to a toupee on every show. Walter Koenig, who came aboard in the second season as the Russian Ensign Chekov, was supposed to be our little nod to the popular Beatles, so he needed the Beatle cut. However, when cast, Walter's hair was short, and he had to wear a wig until his own hair grew long enough.

Wigs came off in stunt fights. They also tended to be pastel-colored, braided, teased and elaborately coiffed. Sometimes the women's hairdos—wigs or their natural hair enhanced with artificial braids and extensions—looked like wedding cakes on steroids. I occasionally wondered why the hair of supposedly professional, military women on a starship of the future should look like it took ten hours and three stylists to turn out.

And then there was wardrobe. In my opinion, Bill Theiss' costume designs were the most beautiful and the sexiest on television, bar none. That the sexy part was true did not exactly make NBC's Broadcast Standards Department turn handsprings of joy. Our Broadcast Standards person, Jean Messerschmitt, was tasked by the network to see that we did not overstep the bounds of decency, according to the tenets of the time. That included revealing costumes.

Well and good, except they didn't understand the "Theiss Theory of Titillation." Bill designed with the understanding that a great deal of non-sexual flesh—such as a woman's back or the side of the leg—could be revealed safely by industry standards, keeping everything else decently covered, and still be sexy as hell. Often he used the theory a different way: promise everything would be revealed, but *never* deliver. Many an actress on *Star Trek* found herself securely glued into a gorgeous Theiss creation that looked like it would slide off at any second but (of course) never did. The only battle Bill ever lost with Broadcast Standards was on "Space Seed" (1-22), written by Carey Wilber. The tight-fitting and low-cut costumes on both the men and women of the Botany Bay were so revealing, Jean Messerschmitt didn't just caution us; she insisted the shots of the revived people exercising their bodies had to be trimmed to the absolute minimum—something like a ten-second shot. If one looks carefully at that episode on tape or DVD, and freezes it at just that point, one can see why Jean was adamant on the issue. In 1966, no show could get away with showing that much obviously sexual flesh, even when it was tastefully covered.

Aliens were another major problem. *Star Trek* was handicapped (as was every other science fiction show of the period) by technological immaturity—and lack of budget. We just couldn't afford to put the time or the money into heavy-duty alien costuming or make-up, and Computer Generated Imagery was definitely a thing of the far future. Therefore, we tried to avoid stories with non-humanoid aliens. Where we could get away with blinking lights or clouds or a really impressive voice actor, we did.

Still, we had to have some aliens, and one of the best aliens we ever did was the Horta in Gene Coon's "The Devil in the Dark" (1-25). Janos Prohaska, a freelance stuntman and creature creator, came over to the studio one day wanting to show the two Genes and me a new critter he had invented. We went out into the studio street in front of the office where there lay a large orange, brown and black blob of rubber. Janos put a rubber chicken out in front of it, and then crawled inside the thing. The ugly creature began to bump along the street, advancing on the rubber chicken. As it crawled over the chicken and "absorbed" it, a little trail of chicken bones came out the back end. We burst out laughing, and Gene Coon said, "I have to do something with that!" Later, the Horta appeared as an apparently horrific, mindless killer of innocent miners—until the crew realized it was only a mother protecting its young.

That kind of story was what set *Star Trek* apart from its on-air rivals, *Voyage to the Bottom of the Sea* and *Lost in Space*. Privately, we called them "Voyage to the Bottom of the Sink" and "Last in Space," and I'm sure they had equally derogatory names for us. The fact remained, however, that we told different and far better stories because Gene Roddenberry called us to a higher level. We were not writing for kids; we never talked down to our audience; we didn't recognize an "average" audience. We wanted the best. We wanted the viewers of *Star Trek* to soar with us—and they did.

There was nothing wrong with *Voyage to the Bottom of the Sea* or *Lost in Space*. They just catered to different audiences and told different kinds of stories. My brother used to do a very funny riff on how every *Voyage* show had a "creature of the week." The creature always wanted the Seaview crew to send either the Captain or the Admiral into its arms so it could do terrible things to their minds and bodies. Every week.

Our tales weren't like that. Gene Roddenberry and the *Star Trek* writers were more interested in stories that reflected the issues and problems of our times. We were the only show on the air that managed not just one but several episodes that examined aspects of the Vietnam War during a time when networks had decreed the subject absolutely taboo for anyone else. Against a backdrop of science fiction, we talked about racial discrimination, determining one's own future, defending personal and national freedoms, compassion, love and friendship that held against all odds. *Star Trek* told stories of how Man could be far better than he was, how there could be a better future if we could only reach for it and build it.

One network executive, frustrated by our insistence on honesty in the science and truth in the stories we were telling, finally blurted out in a meeting, "You people think that ship is really up there!"

Bob Justman had the last word on that occasion. He said, "It *is*."

And maybe that's why—almost forty years on—people watch the original series, time and time again, in countries all over the world. We believed in that starship and in Man's future. Our audience still does.

D. C. Fontana has credits as a writer on such diverse television series as *Star Trek*, *Bonanza*, *The Waltons*, *The Streets of San Francisco* and *Dallas*. She has served as story editor on the original *Star Trek* series, *Star Trek Animated*, *Fantastic Journey* and *Logan's Run*, and as associate producer on *Star Trek: The Next Generation*. She has experience in writing children's shows, science fiction, Westerns, action adventure, mysteries, daytime specials, animation and interactive games. She is a member of Mystery Writers of America, Romance Writers of America and the Society of Children's Book Writers & Illustrators, as well as the Writers' Guild of America, West, and Writers' Guild of Canada.

Allen Steele

All Our Tomorrows: The Shared Universe of Star Trek

The *auteur* school of filmmaking tells us that the director is the author of a film, and so we see credits such as "A film by So-and-So" or "A So-and-So Movie." But in television, the writer is king—and the fans know it, even if the network executives don't. Allen Steele, Hugo-winning author of the Coyote novels, is one of the current crop of SF giants who grew up watching *Star Trek*, and to such people the names of the episodes' writers are much more important than who happened to be guest-starring any given week. These days, TV shows are often scripted by a committee of full-time staff members locked in "the writers' room," but *Star Trek*'s episodes were as individualistic as the men and women who authored them, and many of the best were by people who had already established serious reputations in the world of print science fiction.

If, by some quirk of fate, you were to find yourself in a strange part of the world where you don't know the native language and were cornered by hostile locals who meant you grievous bodily harm, the wisest thing to do would be to attempt to communicate that you're just an innocent bystander. In that case, you could do worse than to raise your right hand palm outward, divide your middle and ring fingers in a V-shape and gravely intone, "Live long and prosper."

By much the same token, if you were driving on the interstate with some friends and noticed oily smoke boiling out beneath from the hood, and you were trying to make it to the next exit where you could pull over at a service station, you might find yourself trying to ease the situation by affecting a Scottish accent and saying, "I'm doing all that I can, Captain, but I don't know much how long the engines will take the strain."

And likewise, if you were at a party and wanted to get a laugh out of someone—maybe a pal who'd had a hard day at work—then you might lightly place your hands on either side of his head, close your eyes and say, "I sense...strong emotion. Longing. Longing and endless...thirst. Beer...I need more...beer."

These lines, either exactly quoted or loosely paraphrased, have become so much a part of our culture—not only Western, but global as well—that just repeating them will provoke immediate recognition. Certain phrases from the show—"Beam me up"; "I'm a doctor, not a mechanic"; "There's some...*thing* out there"—have become so familiar that even those who claim to hate *Star Trek* know what they mean. Yet far fewer people are likely to identify Theodore Sturgeon as the author of the expression "Live long and prosper," or to recall that it was Norman Spinrad who had Scotty fix the warp engines just in the nick of time for the first of many occasions, or that the Vulcan (or rather, "Vulcanian," in its first reference) mind-meld routine wasn't invented by Mr. Spock, but rather by Gene L. Coon.

It's an unfortunate fact that a writer's creations are sometimes better remembered than the writers themselves. Who's more recognizable: Sherlock Holmes or Sir Arthur Conan Doyle? Superman, or Jerry Siegel and Joe Shuster? James Bond or Ian Fleming? Yet in the case of the *Enterprise* and its crew, the situation is more complex. Although Gene Roddenberry is rightfully credited as being the creator of *Star Trek*, he didn't accomplish this feat all by his lonesome self. What Roddenberry did was create the basic concept—a framework, really—for a television series, to which he then invited many other writers to add bits and pieces here and there until, over the course of three short years, they collectively developed a universe unlike any that had ever been seen before. In doing so, they not only ensured the show's survival but also established the basis for five spin-off series, ten movies and nearly countless novelizations, comic books, computer games, fanfictions and parodies.

It's the strength of that universe that has given *Star Trek* its staying power; without that foundation, it's doubtful that the show would have lasted more than a season or been remembered more fondly today than, say, *Time Tunnel*. So the time has come to rediscover what it was that made the original series so great in the first place...and, just perhaps, to suggest the means by which the Star Trek universe may return to its former glory.

In 1960, when Gene Roddenberry began pitching *Star Trek* to the major networks, there was very little in the way of mature science fiction on TV. Certainly, during the '50s there had been afternoon space operas like *Captain Video, Tom Corbett, Space Cadet* and *Space Patrol*, but they were intended as children's shows. *Men Into Space*, a half-hour drama that appeared on CBS for one season in 1959–1960, was a bit more sophisticated, yet it seemed mainly to consist of stock footage of Air Force missiles. *Doctor Who* had arrived on the BBC in England in 1963, but it was virtually unknown in the U.S. By the time *Star Trek* made its NBC debut in 1966, *Voyage to the Bottom of the Sea* was on ABC and *Lost in Space* was airing on CBS, but by their second seasons both shows had slipped into high-camp kitsch. Clearly the time had come for an *adult* science fiction show.

During the '50s and early '60s, one of the dominant forms of TV programming—along with the Western, the variety show and the prime-time soap opera—was the anthology series. Shows like *Playhouse 90*, *General Electric Theater* and *Alfred Hitchcock Presents* didn't have recurring characters, but instead a regular host who introduced that night's teleplay. These programs were very much script-driven, each episode standing on its own as an individual story with no connection to the ones that came before it. *The Twilight Zone* is best remembered as the show that took this format in the direction of science fiction and fantasy, though it was preceded by the short-lived *Tales of Tomorrow* and, later, the '60s program *The Outer Limits*.

So when Roddenberry began pitching *Star Trek* to the networks, he wisely cast it in terms of an anthology series. In his initial proposal, he laid out the concept: "*Star Trek* is a new kind of television science fiction *with all the advantages of an anthology, but none of the limitations.*" From the very beginning, he had in mind a show that would have many different kinds of stories, yet which would have the same cast of characters.

Although this wasn't a totally original concept in and of itself—Westerns like *Wagon Train* and *Gunsmoke* had already been doing much the same for quite a while—it was new so far as TV science fiction was concerned. And because most previous episodic SF shows had been aimed at the breakfast-cereal crowd ("Quick, Joan! Grab the ray-gun before the guards discover we're missing from our cell!"), it eventually helped him to convince executives at Desilu and NBC that *Star Trek* wouldn't be about space cadets chasing asteroid pirates.

So where do you get intelligent, mature science fiction scripts? Certainly Roddenberry already had capable writers on his staff—producer Gene Coon, associate producer John D. F. Black and script editor Dorothy (D. C.) Fontana—yet it's to his credit that he actively courted established SF writers. Some, like Harlan Ellison, Richard Matheson and Jerome Bixby, had already written for TV, while others, like Norman Spinrad and Robert Bloch, had not, and in hindsight it was a particular act of chutzpah to allow a young novice like David Gerrold, with no prior credentials, to contribute what would become one of *Star Trek*'s most memorable episodes.

Yet *Star Trek* wasn't simply an anthology series recast as episodic TV. In many ways, it also was the creation of something heretofore unseen in the annals of television and only seldom seen in science fiction: the shared-universe anthology.

SF writers often develop their own "universes," or timelines, in which they set their novels and stories; this saves them the task of having to create an entire new background, along with characters and settings, for every story they write. Although Edgar Rice Burroughs invented the form with his Mars novels, E. E. "Doc" Smith was probably the first to do this on an interstellar scale with his Lensman series, commencing with *Triplanetary* in 1934 and continuing through *Children of the Lens* in 1947, with the "prequel" novel *First Lensman* published in 1948. Robert A. Heinlein perfected the art with his Future History series, which he initiated in *Astounding Science Fiction* in 1938 with his first published story, "Life-Line," and would continue intermittently throughout his life. Isaac Asimov did much the same with his Foundation series, which he began in 1941 as a sequence of stories for *Astounding* that were roped together in the early '50s as *Foundation*, *Foundation and Empire* and *Second Foundation*, and continued later in life with four more full-length novels. And there are countless others, with Frank Herbert's Dune Cycle and Larry Niven's Known Space series being perhaps the best known.

These universes were almost always the sole province of one writer. If you wanted to read a new Dune novel, for instance, then the only author who could produce one was Frank Herbert; it wasn't until many years after his death that Brian Herbert and Kevin J. Anderson produced a string of prequel bestsellers based on the elder Herbert's notes.

Yet there had also been experiments here and there in which authors or editors had created a single world and then invited other writers to contribute stories that would flesh it out. The first of these was perhaps the world of Uller, created by Fletcher Pratt and John D. Clark and published in 1952 as the anthology *The Petrified World*. In 1975, Harlan Ellison led a seminar at UCLA in which several SF writers put together a world called Medea and then wrote stories for it; the resulting anthology, *Medea: Harlan's World*, was eventually published in 1985. Yet it wasn't until 1978, when Robert Asprin devised the Thieves' World series of anthologies and novels, that the term "shared universe" was coined. Other shared-universe anthology series soon followed, such as George R. R. Martin's Wild Cards and David Drake and Bill Fawcett's The Fleet, until the concept gradually lost popularity in the early '90s (with the exception of Larry Niven's Man-Kzin Wars series, which was spun off from his Known Space stories).

Nonetheless, the best-known "shared universe" has remained with us for forty years. Gene Roddenberry came up with a simple scenario—a large starship, its crew mainly from Earth yet representing a loosely defined alliance of planets, with a small but diverse cast of characters as its core ensemble—and then put it in the hands of writers who filled in the blanks over the course of seventy-nine episodes.

And there were plenty of blanks that needed to be filled. In universe-building, there are two basic methods, which one may call "top-down" and "bottom-up." In the "top-down" approach, the writer (or writers) creates the entire world from the beginning—its history, culture, geography, races, technologies, perhaps even individual characters—and then uses this as the background for stories and novels. This was the classic methodology used by Heinlein for his Future History series, and was employed to a lesser extent by the authors participating in the 1975 UCLA seminar to create the background for the Medea stories.

The problem with the "top-down" approach is that it's inflexible; although relatively easy to devise, once the chronology is firmly locked in place, it becomes increasingly difficult to change. This is why Heinlein eventually had to resort to the multiple-universe theory to write latter installments of the Future History series, and one possible reason why Medea resulted in only a single collection of short stories.

The better approach, although more complex, is the "bottom-up" approach: the writer (or writers) begins with a rather basic concept and then continues to add to it, filling in the details one story at a time. It's time consuming, invites contradictions and always has the danger of blowing up in one's face... but when it works well, it has the possibility of nearly endless stories, one branching off from another.

The Star Trek universe is the "bottom-up" approach writ large. Although the show had a writer's guide, or "bible," that was updated at least twice over the course of the series, it's clear from watching the first season that the series background wasn't fully developed when the show went on the air. In "The Corbomite Maneuver" (1-10), written by Jerry Sohl and originally intended to be the first episode, the *Enterprise* was identified as the "United Earth Ship *Enterprise*": there would be no mention of the United Federation of Planets until "Arena" (1-18), written by Gene Coon and based on a short story by Frederic Brown, or Starfleet until "Court Martial" (1-20), written by Don M. Mankiewicz and Stephen W. Carabatsos. In "Mudd's Women" (1-6), written by Stephen Kandel from a treatment by Gene Roddenberry, Mr. Spock was referred to as a "Vulcanian," and although we discovered in "The Naked Time" (1-4), written by John D. F. Black, that Spock's father was a diplomat and his mother a schoolteacher, little else was known about him. We were also told in "Mudd's Women" that the *Enterprise* derived its power from "lithium" (not "dilithium") crystals.

There are a dozen reasons why *Star Trek* shouldn't have lasted more than one season, thereby making it little more than an interesting footnote in TV history. Yet what elevated the show above rivals like *Lost in Space* was the sophistication of its scripts. Under crushing deadlines, budget restraints and the almost constant threat of cancellation, the writers would create a fictional universe that would not only hold up for an entire generation, but which would also become one of the most recognizable cultural artifacts of the twentieth century.

Aside from Gene Roddenberry himself, probably the most influential of the *Star Trek* writers was D. C. Fontana. Along with acting as story editor during the first two seasons, Fontana also wrote or co-wrote eight episodes of the original series (along with two treatments under the pseudonym "Michael Richards"). Although producer Gene Coon penned more scripts, Fontana's contributions were considerable; beginning with "Charlie X" (1-2), she sought for a humanistic tone that raised the show above the average monster-of-the-week or the outer space shoot-'em-up.

Fontana was clearly intrigued by the idea of an alien who was also part-human. She tested this dichotomy with "Charlie X" (based on a treatment by Gene Roddenberry), in which she presented a seventeen-year-old boy who'd been raised by aliens, given near-infinite power to transmute matter and energy and yet remained an innocent, with the inevitable tragic results. This successfully accomplished, she moved her attention to a figure closer at hand: the *Enterprise*'s first officer. In "This Side of Paradise" (1-24), a script based on a treatment co-written by Jerry Sohl under the pseudonym "Nathan Butler," she pulled aside Spock's cool facade to expose the romantic who wasn't reluctant to make love to a woman or swing from a tree (she also revealed that Spock had a first name but that it was unpronounceable; I suspect that it was "Arnold," but that he was just too embarrassed to admit it). Much later, in the third-season episode "The *Enterprise* Incident" (3-2), she further explored Spock's romantic side by having him seduce a female Romulan commander while remaining both a Vulcan and a loyal Starfleet officer (although it should be noted that this aspect of the script was changed despite her protests).

Yet Fontana's greatest long-term contribution to the Star Trek universe was the second-season episode "Journey to Babel" (2-10). Not only were we introduced to Spock's parents, Sarek and Amanda, and given more of Spock's back story (he had a pet as a child, and was also taunted by other Vulcan children for being half-human), but for the first time we also get a real sense of the Federation as including not just humans and Vulcans, but treacherous Andorians, hairy and argumentative Tellarites and little copper-skinned guys who like to drink bath soap drenched in fruit juice. In the course of a single episode, we were shown a Federation that quarreled, negotiated and had high-level diplomatic meetings. "Journey to Babel" would go far to establish the depth of the Star Trek universe for many years to come.

The most prolific writer was the series producer, Gene Coon. Although Coon wrote or co-wrote more scripts than Fontana—nine in all—his work generally lacked her depth of character. If he's to be condemned for anything, it should be for bulldada like "Spock's Brain" (3-1), which he wisely credited under the pseudonym "Lee Cronin," or for oddball stories like "A Piece of the Action" (2-17) and "Bread and Circuses" (2-25), both of which seem to have been concocted solely to take advantage of the props department. Yet Coon was also capable of great work. His adaptation of Frederic Brown's novella "Arena" (first published in *Astounding* in 1944) was one of the high points of the series; one can only wonder what else could have been done if other classic SF stories had been similarly adapted for the *Star Trek* format (Murray Leinster's "First Contact" and Sir Arthur C. Clarke's "The Star" come to mind).

In other scripts, he laid down many of the fundamentals of the Star Trek universe. The Vulcan mind-meld in "The Devil in the Dark" (1-25) and the introduction of the Klingons, along with the Organian peace treaty in "Errand of Mercy" (1-26) established story elements that would play important roles in future episodes and spin-offs. And two characters he created—Khan Singh, instigator of the twentieth-century Eugenics Wars (in "Space Seed," 1-22) and

Zefram Cochrane, humankind's inventor of warp-drive technology (in "Metamorphosis," 2-9)—would reappear many years later in *Star Trek II: The Wrath of Khan* and *Star Trek: First Contact*. Both would figure into the last (as yet) spin-off series, *Star Trek: Enterprise*.

And yet, the contributions of Roddenberry, Fontana, Coon and Black notwithstanding, some of the most significant *Star Trek* scripts would come from those who weren't on the set every day: the science fiction writers who Gene Roddenberry enlisted to produce the type of stories he wanted for his new TV series.

Theodore Sturgeon wrote only two teleplays for *Star Trek*, yet both were responsible for major additions to its shared universe. Sturgeon, of course, had been a major voice in science fiction since the late '30s; although periodically hampered by writing blocks that would render him silent for years on end, he still managed to produce several classic novels (*More Than Human*, *Venus Plus X* and *To Marry Medusa* among them), along with scores of short stories and novellas. To get Sturgeon aboard the good ship *Enterprise*, at least for a while, was a major coup, and he didn't let anyone down.

Sturgeon's trademark was the depth he brought to his characters and, true to form, his first *Star Trek* script, "Shore Leave" (1-15), went a long way toward giving James Kirk a past life. For the first time, we found out that the captain had attended Starfleet Academy—the existence of which had been previously mentioned but never really detailed—where he had been mercilessly hazed by an upperclassman named Finnegan. Starfleet Academy and its military school-like environment—appearing in "Shore Leave" as one part Annapolis, one part West Point—would henceforth remain a staple of the Star Trek universe. But more significantly, we also discovered that Kirk once had a love affair with a young woman named Ruth—perhaps the same girl mentioned in "Where No Man Has Gone Before" (1-3; written by Samuel A. Peeples), although we don't know this for certain—whom he'd left behind. By the end of the story, Kirk had settled old scores with Finnegan and revisited an old flame... and we had discovered that Kirk wasn't always the man he is now.

Sturgeon upped the ante with "Amok Time" (2-1), arguably the best episode of the entire series. It encompassed everything that was great about the original show, and one of the things that made it so great was the elegant way in which Spock's home world of Vulcan was depicted. In the course of less than fifty minutes, through means of the oldest and most basic story ever devised—boy meets girl, boy wins girl, boy loses girl—we were introduced to an entire culture that was both alien and yet recognizably human. From the moment that Spock reluctantly told Kirk the secrets of Vulcan mating rituals to the moment when he raised his hand in a now-familiar salute and said, for the first time, "Live long and prosper," we were immersed in everything that *Star Trek* promised: new worlds, and new civilizations. And the Star Trek universe would never be the same again.

A little more prolific than Sturgeon, yet no less extraordinary, was Robert Bloch, another author with a long track record as a novelist and short story writer, with his novel *Psycho* (the basis for the Alfred Hitchcock movie) and his Hugo-winning novella "That Hell-Bound Train" among his best-known work. Bloch's forte wasn't SF, but dark fantasy and horror, and he brought those elements with him to *Star Trek*. Although the show had already ventured into *noir* terrain before, with "The Man Trap" (1-1), and "The Enemy Within" (1-5), Bloch introduced an element of Halloween spookiness to the Star Trek universe with "What Are Little Girls Made Of?" (1-7) in the first season, and "Catspaw" (2-7) and "Wolf in the Fold" (2-14) in the second season. As a result, he made it possible for fantasy to mix freely with science fiction, though never without stepping over the line of plausibility.

Harlan Ellison was already a veteran TV scriptwriter by the time he came to *Star Trek*, having previously written for *The Man from U.N.C.L.E.*, *The Outer Limits* and (under the pseudonym Cordwainer Bird) *Voyage to the Bottom of the Sea*. He was also a rising star in the SF literary scene, with several award-winning short stories to his name. In "The City on the Edge of Forever" (1-28), his one and only *Star Trek* script, Ellison managed to combine his talents as both a scenarist and as a short-story writer.

Time travel had already been done twice before in *Star Trek*. Although "The Naked Time" (1-4) demonstrated that it was possible for the *Enterprise* to travel in time, and "Tomorrow Is Yesterday" (1-19) further explored the ramifications of doing so (the method Fontana used in this episode would be replicated in *Star Trek IV: The*

Voyage Home), the dangers of causing a temporal paradox had never before been shown to the degree depicted by Ellison's teleplay. Like Sturgeon's scripts and the best of Fontana's work, "The City on the Edge of Forever" (1-28) brought new depth to Kirk's and Spock's characters. Although Ellison was infuriated by the final result, which departed from what he wrote on several key points—a not-uncommon complaint among *Star Trek*'s writers—"The City on the Edge of Forever" nonetheless earned a Hugo award for best dramatic presentation, while the original script earned the Writers' Guild of America Award for Most Outstanding Dramatic Teleplay.

Another influential writer was Jerome Bixby. A short story writer before he went to work in Hollywood, his best-known story is "It's A *Good* Life," originally published in the *Star 2* paperback anthology and later adapted into one of *The Twilight Zone*'s most famous episodes. As "Jay Lewis" he'd written teleplays for *Men Into Space*, and among his screenplays were the original treatments for *Fantastic Voyage* (as Jay Lewis Bixby, co-written with Otto Klement) and *It! The Terror from Beyond Space*, which several SF film historians cite as being the inspiration for *Alien*.

Bixby didn't begin work on *Star Trek* until midway through the second season, yet two of his four teleplays contributed elements to the Star Trek universe. In "Mirror, Mirror" (2-4), which competed with "The City on the Edge of Forever" for a Hugo award, he introduced a parallel timeline in which the *Enterprise* was a warship representing a malign Federation bent on galactic conquest; this would be revisited nearly thirty years later in *Star Trek: Deep Space Nine*, and further in *Star Trek: Enterprise*. And in "Day of the Dove" (3-7), he instilled in the Klingons—who, up until that point, had been little more than thugs with heavy suntans—a warrior's code of honor, a trait that would become a major factor in subsequent *Star Trek* spinoffs during the '80s and '90s.

Other SF writers did their part to expand the universe. Norman Spinrad—who, during the '60s was, like Ellison, another brash young Turk, with his controversial novel *Bug Jack Barron* just ahead of him—contributed "The Doomsday Machine" (2-6), the fourth act of which featured Scotty racing the clock to save the *Enterprise*, something that would become an often-emulated staple of *Star Trek* spin-offs to come. George Clayton Johnson, who'd already co-written the treatment for *Ocean's 11* and, who would collaborate a few years later with William F. Nolan on the novel *Logan's Run*, contributed "The Man Trap" (1-1), which took the monster-aboard-ship story to a higher level. And David Gerrold—stepping up to the plate for the first time—hit a solid home-run with "The Trouble With Tribbles" (2-15), which took the premise of "The Man Trap" and, by deftly flipping it on its ear, introduced comedy to the show.

Yet by the time *Star Trek* entered its third season—after a last-minute reprieve from cancellation, due in large part to the now-legendary letter-writing campaign by its fans (including this writer, who was a mere fourth-grader at the time)—changes in the production staff caused a drop in quality of the scripts. Although Gene Roddenberry remained aboard as executive producer, he'd been replaced as line producer by Fred Freiberger; D. C. Fontana continued to contribute scripts, but Arthur H. Singer had taken her job as story editor. So while the third season would have memorable episodes—Fontana's "The *Enterprise* Incident"; Coon's "Spectre of the Gun" (3-6), under the byline Lee Cronin; Rick Vollaerts' "For the World Is Hollow and I Have Touched the Sky" (3-8); and Judy Burns and Chet Richards' "The Tholian Web" (3-9)—it lost most of its overall depth and quality when it lost most of its top-drawer SF writers like Sturgeon, Bloch and Ellison who'd helped shape the first two seasons. Among them, only Jerome Bixby would remain; David Gerrold's treatment for "The Cloud Minders" (3-21), co-written with Oliver Crawford, was scripted by Margaret Armen.

As a result, many of the third-season episodes were mediocre at best, while some—such as the infamous "Spock's Brain" (3-1) and the ludicrous "The Way to Eden" (3-20), both of which looked like leftovers from *Lost in Space*—bordered on self-parody. Under the circumstances, perhaps it may have been best that the original series ended with the third season. Better a quick execution than slow death.

Yet *Star Trek* didn't die, and neither did the anthology series concept it pioneered.

In 1973, four years after its prime-time demise, *Star Trek* returned as a Saturday morning cartoon produced by Filmation. Featuring the voices of most of the original cast—although Walter Koenig was notably absent—it lasted one and a half seasons as a half-hour program on NBC. Hindered by the limitations imposed by cel animation, this series has often been dismissed as little more than a footnote in Star Trek's forty-year history, but had a few good scripts, some by those who'd written for the original series.

The most notable were the series pilot, "Beyond the Farthest Star," written by Samuel A. Peeples (who'd also written the second original-series pilot, actually shown as the third episode, "Where No Man Has Gone Before"); "Yesteryear" (*StarTrek: AnimatedSeries* 1-2), in which D. C. Fontana continued her exploration of Spock's past, this time incorporating the time portal introduced by Harlan Ellison in "The City on the Edge of Forever"; and "More Tribbles, More Troubles" (*ST:AS* 1-5), David Gerrold's sequel to "The Trouble With Tribbles." Possibly the most intriguing episode was "Slaver Weapon" (*ST: AS* 1-14), written by Hugo and Nebula-award winning author Larry Niven; Niven rewrote his short story "The Soft Weapon," much in the spirit of the first season's loose adaptation of Fredric Brown's "Arena," and in doing so introduced—at least for a brief time—the Kzinti and Slaver races of his Known Space series to the Star Trek universe.

The animated *Star Trek*'s limited life was typical of most Saturday morning cartoons of the time, but by then Paramount executives had realized that they had a profitable commodity in this dead '60s TV show and had taken steps to revive it. During the mid-'70s, plans were made to launch a new series—alternately called *Star Trek II* or *Star Trek: Phase II*—that would reunite the original cast (although Leonard Nimoy, then struggling to avoid being typecast as Spock, would refuse to rejoin the show).

Though never produced, *Star Trek: Phase II* did eventually lead to the production of *Star Trek: The Motion Picture*. Yet during the brief period in which a new original-cast TV series was in pre-production, Gene Roddenberry once again courted major SF writers to contribute script proposals. Those who responded were Theodore Sturgeon ("Cassandra") and Norman Spinrad ("To Attain the All"), but the most surprising contributor was Richard Bach, the author of the bestseller *Jonathan Livingston Seagull*, who submitted a treatment titled "Practice In Walking." Yet only Alan Dean Foster's treatment for "In Thy Image" would see the light of day; drastically rewritten by Roddenberry and Harold Livingstone, "In Thy Image" would eventually find its way to the big screen as *Star Trek: The Motion Picture*...and in this way, the Star Trek universe was revived.

Following the success of three more original-cast movies, Paramount decided to launch a new syndicated series. Yet it wasn't long before it became plain that the *Star Trek* of the '80s would be different from the *Star Trek* of the '60s.

Although the two-hour pilot for *Star Trek: The Next Generation*, "Encounter at Farpoint," was co-written by Roddenberry and Fontana, and the first season featured a few scripts written by veteran original-series writers and a couple of SF authors, once the new show went into its second season it relied almost entirely upon scripts supplied by a staff of scriptwriters who'd previously written about cops, lawyers and doctors. Once Gene Roddenberry's role had been reduced to that of a figurehead, SF writers were seldom allowed to set foot on the *Enterprise*, save for a brief moment in 1992 when producer Rick Berman sent an open letter to the *SFWA Forum*, the in-house publication of the Science Fiction and Fantasy Writers of America, inviting its members to submit story proposals. If any were ever accepted, or even seriously considered, though, this writer never heard of it.

Subsequent spin-offs—*Deep Space Nine*, *Voyager* and *Enterprise*—would continue the trend. No longer would there be the surprise of finding a ground-breaking episode by someone who'd first written for SF magazines or had a novel or two under their belt (a friend who worked as a UCLA film-school intern on *Deep Space Nine* reported that his treatments were nitpicked to death by the writing staff and subject to Byzantine internal politics; none were ever produced). Not surprisingly, the shows became increasingly stale, coming to resemble upgraded versions of *Tom Corbett* or *Space Patrol* and only recapturing their creativity and vision when they revisited terrain developed during the original series, such as when an episode of *Deep Space Nine* used CGI re-imaged footage from "The Trouble With Tribbles," or when *Enterprise*, in its final season, devoted itself to prequels to "Amok Time," "Journey to Babel" and "Mirror, Mirror."

By then, Star Trek had become commonly referred to as a "franchise" even by its most devoted fans, much as if it were a fast-food chain. You can just picture someone pulling up to a drive-through with a pair of Vulcan ears on either side of the menu board. *Uh, yeah, I'll take a Romulan double-cheese... hold the onion and pickle, please... and a side of Tholian rings... oh, and a Federation extra-value meal for my kid. Does a starship come with that?*

As of this writing, the Star Trek universe is now on hold. *Enterprise* was canceled in May 2005 after four seasons of struggling to find its own identity. Yet it's doubtful that Paramount will let the "franchise" go the way of the dinosaur. Two generations have grown up watching Star Trek, in one form or another; there's no reason why it shouldn't be revived once more.

If Star Trek is to be continued, though, it must return to its roots. Using the latest generation of CGI special effects or putting another fashion model in a skintight uniform won't do the trick. The strength of the original series lay in its diversity. *Star Trek* was a science fiction anthology series; it needs science fiction writers in order to survive.

"Live long and prosper." Always remember that an SF writer came up with that.

REFERENCES

Asherman, Alan. *The Star Trek Compendium* (revised edition). New York: Pocket Books, 1986.

Ellison, Harlan. "Cosmic Hod-Carriers." *Medea: Harlan's World* (edited by Harlan Ellison). New York: Bantam, 1985.

Gerrold, David. *The World of Star Trek* (first edition). New York: Ballantine, 1973.

Okuda, Michael and Denise, and Debbie Mirak. *The Star Trek Encyclopedia* (first edition). New York: Pocket Books, 1994.

Reeves-Stevens, Judith and Garfield. *Star Trek Phase II: The Lost Series*. New York: Pocket Books, 1997.

Whitefield, Stephen E., and Gene Roddenberry. *The Making of Star Trek*. New York: Ballantine, 1968.

Allen Steele encountered *Star Trek* when he was eight years old, when one of his sisters gave him James Blish's first novelization of the series as a Christmas present. Because the show's first season wasn't aired in his hometown of Nashville, Tennessee, he didn't actually see an episode of *Star Trek* until a year later. Since then, he has become a Hugo-winning science fiction writer with a dozen novels and four collections of short stories to his credit. His most recent novels are the Coyote trilogy: *Coyote*, *Coyote Rising* and *Coyote Frontier*. He lives in Western Massachusetts with his wife and two dogs.

Eric Greene

THE PRIME QUESTION

Eric Greene played the alien child Loki on the 1977 Saturday morning SF series *Space Academy*, which also starred Pamelyn Ferdin and Brian Tochi, who had guest starred in the *Trek* episode "And the Children Shall Lead." He went on to write the brilliant critical study *Planet of the Apes as American Myth: Race, Politics and Popular Culture*, and to work for the American Civil Liberties Union. We could think of no one better qualified to look at *Star Trek*'s relationship to the real world of the 1960s.

> We had the overarching authority of science fiction and we could go anywhere with that and under that guise we could also talk about the issues of the day.... The war in Vietnam...no one was allowed to talk about on television if you had a contemporary show, but under science fiction we were able to get in commentary on Vietnam.
>
> —D. C. Fontana, *Star Trek* Story Editor

> Has a war been staged for us, complete with weapons and ideology and patriotic drum beating? Even...race hatred?
>
> —Captain James Kirk, "Day of the Dove" (3-7)

IN ITS FORTY YEARS *Star Trek* has become a legend. As the legend would have it, *Star Trek* derives its popularity from its positive view of the future, a future in which humanity has overcome poverty, prejudice and war, reached out to alien species and joined with them in a United Federation of Planets to explore the stars in peace and friendship.[1] Camelot in outer space.

More than an exciting concept for a series, this is an inspiring prospect for humanity. Like any mass media project, *Star Trek* was many things: entertainment, a livelihood, art, product. But it was also a bold attempt, conceptually, to burst open an unoccupied space—the future—and shape its contours. It was a bid to create that future by suggesting what it might look like, how it might function and what values it should embrace. That must be why the show struck such a nerve, right? Yes. But there was more to it than that. There always is.

Like Arthur's Camelot, or, more to the point, Kennedy's Camelot, the legend of *Star Trek* and the history of *Star Trek* overlap but also diverge. The legend represents an appealing and important piece of *Star Trek*'s success but overlooks other essential truths. *Star Trek* was not only a vision of a utopian future; it emerged from, described and addressed a fractured, violent present.

I by no means want to dismiss the positive vision that was such an important element of *Star Trek*. In my own case, for example, as a kid watching *Star Trek* in the '70s, the image from the show that most excited me—more than the colorful bridge, the magical transporter or even the elegant starship—was the briefing room. That's right, the briefing room. Just a table and some chairs. "The *briefing* room," you might ask yourself, "a table and some chairs? That certainly doesn't *sound* exciting. What could possibly be so exciting about *that*?" But I remember taking the worn copy of Stephen Whitfield and Gene Roddenberry's *Making of Star Trek* paperback that I shared with my older brother Jeff (the person who earned my everlasting gratitude for introducing me to *Star Trek*—and all that came with it), staring at the picture of the conference room set and marveling at the memory of Captain Kirk looking around at those gathered together of different races, species and specialties and saying to them, "I want options."

---

[1] Leonard Nimoy provides one of the most articulate versions of this view explaining that *Star Trek* "was always a very *humanistic* show; one that celebrated the potential strengths of mankind, of our civilization, with great respect for all kinds of life, and a great hope that there be communication between civilizations and cultures." (Quoted in Greenwald, Jeff. *Future Perfect: How Star Trek Conquered Planet Earth*. New York: Penguin Books, 1998, p. 111.)

Something about that seemed encouragingly democratic, meritocractic, American. That conference room was where decisions were made, and destinies were shaped—where all that mattered was if you had the brains and imagination to sit with the best and the brightest, think through problems and create solutions. The position you earned counted. The wealth of your parents, the color of your skin, did not. That's a pretty powerful idea when you are seven years old, and I suspect I've carried the image of that briefing room with me into committee meetings, board rooms and conference tables throughout my adult life.

But the picture of that idealized briefing room was not the whole picture of *Star Trek*. This complex series had its share of contradictions: yes, the show featured a groundbreaking mix of ethnicities and nationalities and featured many guest stars of color in nonstereotypical parts, even playing authority roles;[2] yet the recurring actors of color were kept in subordinate parts (as the TV satire *In Living Color* would brilliantly lampoon twenty years later). Yes, the show featured aliens who while initially feared as monsters, were eventually understood as beings who were just trying to defend their homes, protect their children or survive as a species; however, the Federation and Starfleet were largely "homo sapiens only" clubs.[3] Yes, the show featured TV's first interracial kiss, but that was hardly a breakthrough: Kirk and Uhura were forced into that kiss—it was desired by neither and resisted by both. And a Black woman forced to kiss a White man against her will ain't romance. It's rape. And a kind of rape with a disconcerting resonance in a country in which, for the majority of its history, Black women were subject to the sexual depredations of White slave holders.[4]

[2] Indeed African American actors were repeatedly cast as doctors, scientists, even commodores. This casting diversity seems to have been quite by design. While Gene Roddenberry had to fight for the inclusion of the alien Mr. Spock, an August 17, 1965 letter from NBC executive Mort Werner to Gene Roddenberry explained that NBC's non-discrimination policy included encouraging the casting of racial minorities in order to reflect accurately U.S. population demographics and that "mindful of our vast audience and the extent to which television influences taste and attitudes, we are not only determined but anxious that members of minority groups be treated in a manner consistent with their roles in our society." (Letter reprinted in Solow, Herbert F. and Justman, Robert. *Inside Star Trek: The* Real *Story*. New York: Pocket Books, 1996, pp.76–77.)

[3] As a Klingon would pointedly observe in *Star Trek VI: The Undiscovered Country*, in an admirable instance of those who made *Star Trek* actually challenging the legend themselves.

[4] What's actually striking about that much-hyped scene is not the obviously faked kiss (you never really see their mouths touch), but the surprising level of emotional intimacy in the dialogue leading up to the kiss. And *that* was not forced.

But *Star Trek*'s most interesting contradiction may be its central one: the Prime Directive. A close look reveals that the Prime Directive—that the Federation should not interfere with the social development of other planets, nor indicate to developing planets that there are other worlds or more advanced civilizations—was not a directive at all, in the sense of a binding standard. While we are told that a Starfleet captain's "most solemn oath is that he will give his life, even his entire crew, rather than violate the Prime Directive," in the course of the series, the Prime Directive was often debated, occasionally derided, but rarely obeyed. The Prime Directive was not a directive as much as it was the *Prime Question*: how much power should a superpower use when dealing with other peoples? Put another way: to intervene or not to intervene, that is the Prime Question. That very question, the central tension driving the stories of *Star Trek*, was at the heart of American politics and popular culture at the time.[5]

Following World War II, the United States of America emerged transformed into a global, nuclear superpower with military might, political influence and material affluence at levels it had never before achieved. This transformation necessitated a difficult internal debate: how much power should we use? In what situations? Subject to what limitations? The U.S.'s new superpower status made this debate a matter of importance. The war in Vietnam made this debate a matter of life and death.

Star Trek, like much pop culture, was both entertainment and a thought experiment: a means of debating society's pressing questions, symbolically putting into play various possible answers and challenging those answers' assumptions. The series embodied the post-World War II dilemma of a young, strong U.S. eager to exert influence but wary of the consequences of interference. *Star Trek*'s Prime Question is a prime example of popular culture addressing, debating and helping give meaning to a people's political and social conflicts.

While *Star Trek* began filming one year, almost to the day, after President John Kennedy's death, it was very much a show of the Ken-

[5] An overview of American intervention throughout the twentieth century may be found in *New York Times* reporter Stephen Kinzer's book *Overthrow: America's Century of Regime Change From Hawaii to Iraq*. New York: Times Books, 2006.

nedy Era. This was signaled by the opening narration, which placed the show in "Space, the final frontier" and linked Kirk to Kennedy through the reverential invocation of the frontier image. For centuries, of course, the United States' myths of the frontier had evoked images of heroism and sacrifice—and racial violence—on behalf of an expanding nation fulfilling its "manifest destiny" to conquer, prosper and "civilize." But the "frontier" concept had recently been given a renewed relevance as a way to conceptualize the American experience when, much as Franklin Roosevelt had declared a "New Deal," Kennedy promised the U.S. a "New Frontier" in the '60s. Kennedy adopted the "New Frontier" as a defining theme of his campaign and, later, his administration. *Star Trek*'s interstellar Federation was the ultimate fulfillment, both of Kennedy's "New Frontier" slogan and of the call Kennedy issued to the nations of the world in his inaugural address: "Together let us explore the stars, conquer the deserts, eradicate disease, tap the ocean depths and encourage the arts and commerce."

But Starfleet's Captain James Kirk, and by extension the Federation, also embodied Kennedy the Cold Warrior who, in that same speech, warned that the young superpower would "pay any price, bear any burden, meet any hardship, support any friend, oppose any foe, to assure the survival and the success of liberty." Kirk's mix of tolerance at home and hawkishness abroad—racially inclusive, willing to hold out the olive branch, yet ready to battle foreign competitors—made the show, generally speaking, a good reflection of mainstream Kennedy-style liberalism rather than an expression of the '60s counter-culture. (Although the vegetarian, pacifist-leaning, alien Mr. Spock offered a sympathetic identification figure for the more left-wing audience members, it was *Kirk* who combat veteran and former police officer Gene Roddenberry put in command. Counter-culture values were thus allowed a place on the *Enterprise*, but not a controlling one.)

That the show was addressing itself to fundamental divisions in the culture was evident in its main characters. As James Kirk, William Shatner was the handsome, bold Midwestern captain who recalled John Kennedy, the handsome, bold Northeastern president—the two leaders even shared the same first and last initials. *Star Trek* allowed the audience to both enjoy a fantasy of Kennedy's continued presence, if only in metaphor, and imagine the projection of Kennedy's heroic style "boldly going" into a bountiful interstellar future. On Earth Kennedy had pointed us toward the moon; on television Kirk led us to the stars. Shatner has done such a good job of spoofing himself in recent years that it is easy to forget that he was a very charismatic performer who, with some notable exceptions (and *you* try pulling off "E pleb neesta"), was remarkably effective as Kirk.

Alongside Kirk was the irascible humanism DeForest Kelley brought to Dr. McCoy, a Southern gentleman whose "playful" race baiting of the alien first officer was, oddly, never a barrier to a profound respect (and, even more oddly, never really objected to by Spock until the series' penultimate episode). At a time when some in the audience were inclined to distrust anyone over thirty, McCoy dared to suggest decency surviving into the late *forties*.

And then there was Leonard Nimoy's Vulcan, Mr. Spock: brilliant, reliable, free of animus, both White and, by virtue of his Vulcan heritage, non-White and so dignified he could have given Sidney Poitier a run for his money. More than a device for plot exposition or cultural critique, and he was both at times, the alien-human hybrid often embodied the most human struggles of the series. (It was largely through Spock, for instance, that *Star Trek* dealt with questions of racial identity and assimilation, and growing up as a multiracial kid, I especially identified with him because he was the only mixed-race character I knew of in pop culture. This resonance gave Spock a relevance that set him apart from almost any other TV character of that era.) All of this came together in Nimoy's quietly compelling performance. If you are lucky you will see several great Hamlets in your lifetime, but you will be hard pressed to find an actor better attuned to the rhythms, tone and spirit of a character.

More than the talents of the performers, the symbolic cultural makeup of the central triad—Northern, Midwestern and Southern, younger and older, White and non-White—was also significant: in a time of domestic disunity, the trio tackled vexing problems with skill and comradery, offering a symbolic bridging of political, regional, generational, racial and cultural differences.

Since *Star Trek* was created by artists living in a newly emerged superpower that was locked in competition with another superpower, it may not come as a surprise that one of the first problems Kirk and crew confronted was the threat superpowers pose. This problem was established early in the first season in "Charlie X" (1-2) when a teenage orphan with psychokinetic powers took over the *Enterprise*. In the next episode broadcast (actually the series' second pilot, "Where No Man Has Gone Before") Kirk's best friend, Gary Mitchell, gained similar powers, turned against Kirk and threatened the ship.[6] A number of episodes in the first season—"The Menagerie, Parts I and II" (1-11, 1-12), "The Squire of Gothos" (1-17), "Space Seed" (1-22)—as well as some in the later seasons—"Catspaw" (2-7), "Plato's Stepchildren" (3-10)—essentially addressed the same problem: the danger a superbeing poses to the rest of the community.

By exploring how a superbeing jeopardizes the *Enterprise* and its crew, the show took up in microcosm the macro concern of the series: the relationship of a superpower to other peoples and the danger a superpower poses to weaker nations. Throughout the first season, problems are introduced ("superior ability breeds superior ambition") and rules of engagement are posited ("above all a god needs compassion"). Repeatedly *Star Trek* argues that, left unrestrained, superbeings will bring misery and destruction to those around them. It's fair to say that the danger of super-powerful extraterrestrials was not the real concern of *Star Trek*'s producers. It is rather more likely that the caution being expressed was more about the power of our Cold War rivals. Or our own.

Charlie, Gary, Kahn, Trelane, the Talosians and similar characters cannot be integrated into a society of "lessers": they will always use their superior abilities, and superior ambition will always be a danger. As with powerful people, so too powerful planets, or Earthly nations, as the twentieth century's superpowers, master races and world empires had amply demonstrated. As a solution the show favored multi-lateralism: in a United Federation of Planets, mutual cooperation would be the norm, the power of each planet would be a buffer to the power of others and the Prime Directive would restrain the whole. Similarly the power of the (NATO-style) Starfleet would

---

[6] My thanks to Alan Sanborn and Bill Goodwin for pointing out the similarity between "Charlie X" and "Where No Man Has Gone Before."

counter the power of the (Soviet-inspired) Klingons and the (Chinese-esque) Romulans. Cold War geopolitics, complete with spheres of influence, balance of power and mutually assured destruction, were neatly replicated and served as a stage upon which the *Star Trek* creative team could debate the issues of the day.

After repeatedly raising, as a general matter, the problem of the superpower, *Star Trek* moved more specifically into the Cold War and Vietnam concerns that would fuel much of the series. "The Return of the Archons" (1-21), written by Boris Sobelman based on a story by Roddenberry, was one of the first examples of Kirk as Cold Warrior and set the tone for many later episodes. In "Archons," Kirk, as he would often in the series, acted in the name of freedom and progress, destroying a computer that had controlled a regimented collective where the will of the individual was subordinated to the will of "the Body."

In order to differentiate the Federation from its rivals, the episode helped establish a series of key oppositions which echoed the categories in which contemporary struggles against Fascism and Communism had been conceived: state control versus freedom, stagnation versus progress, collective action versus individual autonomy, aggression versus self-defense. Freedom and individual choice became a recurring justification throughout the series as Kirk and crew made a habit of confronting collectives in the name of progress.

A number of first-season *Star Trek* stories, such as "A Taste of Armageddon" (1-23) and "This Side of Paradise" (1-24), followed the pattern laid out in "Return of The Archons" by reproducing premises and themes of U.S. foreign policy and presenting metaphorical victories over Communist or totalitarian regimes. These were followed by second- and third-season episodes like "The Apple" (2-5), "For The World Is Hollow and I Have Touched the Sky" (3-8), and, yes, even "Spock's Brain" (3-1). In these episodes the *Enterprise* typically found a backward people living in a regulated or communal society (often controlled by a computer), determined that their collectivist lifestyle had made them stagnant, overcame native resistance, destroyed the source of control and promised the inhabitants Federation aid in adjusting to their new freedom and achieving progress. (These communal alien cultures in the original *Star Trek* were the first of many Communist analogues in *Trek* lore, and prefigured the more elaborate Soviet metaphor of "The Borg" collective introduced in *Star Trek: The Next Generation.*)

When, in "Return of the Archons," Spock raised the Prime Directive's noninterference mandate, Kirk offered the prime exception: the Prime Directive applies only "to a living, growing culture" and so did not apply in this case. In fact, so regularly was that rationale invoked that it would seem the Federation's *real* Prime Directive was an interventionist imperative that the *Enterprise*/Federation *must* interfere when a culture is deemed to be not "living and growing" up to the Federation's standards.[7]

The intervention question was explored later that season by writer and series producer Gene Coon in "Errand of Mercy" (1-26). Coon's voice was critical to the series and he was often one of *Star Trek*'s most compelling writers. While series creator Roddenberry historically has received credit for *Star Trek*'s merits, in recent years Coon increasingly has been acknowledged as *Star Trek*'s unsung hero.[8] Unlike in Roddenberry's story for "Archons," the interventionist agenda did not play out as neatly in Coon's "Errand of Mercy." Here Coon introduced the Klingons, the Federation's main antagonists, and began to take seriously the complexities of the Vietnam War, raising questions about the standard way U.S. counter-insurgency policy was conceived and presented to the American public.

Seeking "to deny" the planet Organia to the Klingons and to win Organia's allegiance to the Federation, Kirk offered Organia medical, educational, technical and military assistance—the trademark nation-building and counter-insurgency tools the U.S. used "to deny" developing nations to the Communists. The pacifist Organians refused to take sides in the Federation-Klingon dispute. When a Klingon oc-

---

[7] This was not only the real Prime Directive of the series, but also corresponded to the mythic worldview guiding U.S. policy makers during the Cold War. Cultural historian Richard Slotkin notes that "the Frontier Myth was particularly important during the formative period of counter-insurgency doctrine. The myth taught us that historical progress is achieved only through the advance of White European races/cultures into and against the terrain of 'primitive' non White 'natives' who are inherently lacking in the capacity to generate 'progress.'" (Slotkin, Richard. *Gunfighter Nation: The Myth of the Frontier in 20th Century America.* New York: Atheneum. 1992, p. 446. See also pp. 494–511.)

[8] Solow and Justman go so far as to say that when Coon joined the production he became "*Star Trek*'s savior and Justman's new 'hero.'" (Solow and Justman, *Inside Star Trek*, p. 205.)

cupation force landed, Kirk launched a guerrilla operation against the Klingons, hoping to inspire the Organians to fight the invading forces, just as the stated goal of the U.S. was to transform the South Vietnamese into a fighting force which would resist the Communist North.

Because Kirk's mission in "Errand of Mercy" mirrored both the official line regarding our involvement in Vietnam and the way that line was reflected in popular genres, most notably Westerns, which had served as Vietnam allegories, the early audiences for this episode may very well have expected, or even hoped, that Kirk would succeed in turning the Organians into a partisan resistance, in keeping with the political script we were supposed to be following in Southeast Asia.

However, when warfare broke out between Kirk and the Klingons, the episode took an unexpected turn: the Organians revealed they were an ancient and powerful race, rendered the weapons of both sides useless and prevented them from fighting. Those the *Enterprise* sought to save, saved the *Enterprise* instead. It was as if the South Vietnamese had forced disarmament throughout Vietnam, engineered peace between the Warsaw Pact and NATO and ended the Cold War. The episode replicated the early stages of the Vietnam conflict, but then fantasized extracting us from the Cold War altogether. Not surprisingly, the normally interventionist Kirk was furious at the Organians' intervention.[9]

Even as "Errand of Mercy" parroted the language of the Cold War struggle, it undermined the clear categories that the Federation—and by implication the U.S.—used to assess the political culture of other peoples. Spock initially concluded that Organia was another culture failing to "live and grow," which made it a prime target for the Federation's paternalistic intervention. But the Organians turned out to be highly advanced, which called into question the Federation's ability to assess other cultures accurately and implicitly linked the Federation's dilemma to the situation in Vietnam where the failure to understand the indigenous political culture similarly led the U.S. to disastrous errors. The Federation continued to make similar

---

[9] The Organians' actions were ironically the inverse of Kirk's from "A Taste of Armageddon" only a few episodes earlier—the Organians sought to end a war by forcing the combatants to abandon their weapons; Kirk had sought to end a war by forcing the combatants to use real weapons.

kinds of mistakes as the series' second season repeatedly confronted the issue of intervention by a superior power.

Star Trek's second season was the series' most sustained engagement with debates about Vietnam and the implications of U.S. intervention. While this was of particular interest to Roddenberry and Coon, they were not alone in crafting episodes which addressed directly, or were influenced implicitly, by the war. Series story editor, D. C. Fontana, was the writer of "Friday's Child" (2-11), an episode produced early in the second season, in which the Federation again competed with the Klingons for the allegiance of a developing planet. And again, the Federation's failure to understand the indigenous political culture jeopardized the mission and embroiled them in a civil war. While the natives initially admired the Klingons' militarism, it became the symbol of the Klingons' untrustworthy nature and the Federation eventually won an ally. Like "Errand of Mercy," this episode recreated the early stage of the Vietnam conflict but transformed it into a recuperative fantasy in which the Federation achieved in outer space the success that had eluded the Americans in Vietnam.

Perhaps nowhere in *Star Trek* did the debate over Vietnam reverberate more than in "The Apple," written by Coon and Max Ehrlich, from Ehrlich's story. "The Apple," in which Kirk found a primitive collective whose needs were provided by a god/machine they worshipped called "Vaal," largely conformed to the "intervention to prevent stagnation" pattern established in the first season. However, new to "The Apple" was a debate between Spock and McCoy on the merits of interfering with the natives.

In "The Apple," as in a number of episodes, the alien Spock urged restraint, citing the Prime Directive's noninterference clause and arguing against intervention. Here Spock delivered the series' most explicit critique of the ideology of paternalistic intervention, arguing, "You insist on applying human standards to nonhuman cultures. I remind you that humans are only a tiny minority in this galaxy." Substitute "American" for "human" and the point being made is quite clear. McCoy argued for "certain absolutes... [including] the right to a free and unchained environment...which permit[s] growth." Spock countered that "another is the right to choose a system which seems to work for them. These people are healthy and they are happy. Whatever you chose to call it, this system works.... This may not be an ideal society but it is a viable one." This opposition of intervention versus self-determination succinctly echoed much of the debate over the U.S. "police action" that was raging at the time.

Similarly, Kirk's response repeated the assumptions underlying U.S. policy. He sided with McCoy, concluding, "These people aren't living, they are existing. They don't create, they don't produce, they don't even think. They should have the opportunity of choice. We owe it to them to interfere." As Kirk spoke, the series' theme music swelled in the background, indicating that he was expressing the "official" ethos of the show. The music was an endorsement underscoring the point that Kirk was not just in command, more importantly, he was in the right.

While "The Apple" seems ultimately to endorse the interventionist position, the episode, perhaps unwittingly, highlights a dilemma in the policy of nation-building and counter-insurgency. Kirk's actions contradicted the premises upon which he based them. Kirk insisted on interfering because the people "should have the opportunity of choice" but he actually denied the natives the choice of either being freed or serving Vaal. By destroying Vaal, against the wishes of the planet's inhabitants, Kirk limited their freedom of choice to a single option which *he* chose. Just as American policy makers would have not accepted an autonomous South Vietnam democratically electing a communist government, and maneuvered to prevent just such an election, Kirk did not allow the natives the freedom to choose Vaal.

This was an implicit, and often fatal, contradiction of U.S. counter-insurgency and nation-building: a democratic choice to choose an anti-democratic, or even just anti-American, way could not be tolerated. Making the "wrong" decision demonstrates an inability to make a right decision, thus calling into question the capacity to handle the self-determination that was the stated goal of the intervention policy. This bias was inconsistent with spreading democracy. The fact that Kirk was not authorized by the Federation to contravene the Prime Directive here highlighted the fundamentally unaccountable and undemocratic nature of his unilateral actions. "The Apple" left this paradox unaddressed and certainly unresolved.

Almost as if in deliberate answer to Coon and Ehrlichs' questioning of superpower intervention in "The Apple," Roddenberry was heavily involved in the writing of two episodes, both of which implicitly challenged the viability of the Federation's Prime Directive and one of which explicitly endorsed the U.S. involvement in Vietnam. In "Bread and Circuses" (2-25), credited to Roddenberry and Coon from a story by John Kneubuhl, the *Enterprise* came across a planet which paralleled ancient Rome, complete with slaves forced to fight in gladiator clashes. While Kirk could overthrow the empire, or at least aid the nascent resistance movement, Kirk uncharacteristically followed the Prime Directive and decided not to interfere.

The episode vividly demonstrates the bind in which the noninterference limitation traps the Federation. When Kirk began to suggest that he could bring down one hundred officers with phasers, the planet's gloating leader cut him off. "You could probably defeat the combined armies of our entire empire—and violate your oath regarding noninterference with other societies. I believe you all swear you'd die before you violate that directive, am I right?" Delighting in the Federation's self-imposed helplessness he taunted Kirk, "Why even bother to send your men down? Your vessel could lay waste to the entire surface of the world, oh, but there's that Prime Directive in the way again, can't interfere."

Thus the Prime Directive renders the Federation effectively impotent—even when confronted by a weaker power. The Federation here is little more than a "paper tiger," a label which the U.S. desperately wanted—and took desperate actions—to avoid in the '60s. The episode implicitly says that the Prime Directive is weakness; here noninterference resulted in unchallenged brutality.

While the episode essentially posed the options for the Federation as either acceptance of tyranny or armed intervention, Kirk and crew never wrestled with the implications of their refusal to get involved. Ever the intervener in other episodes, ironically Kirk here called for a commendation for Mr. Scott for resisting the temptation to intervene. The crew happily departed, unconcerned that they had left the enslaving dictatorship in place. Thus the episode presented the Prime Directive as impractical, even absurd. The episode even went so far as to imply that human action is unnecessary because divine intervention cometh in the morning.

Furthermore, "Bread and Circuses" is hard to square with episodes like "Return of the Archons" and "The Apple": why is it acceptable to force unwanted aid upon those who (apparently willingly) serve a machine, but unacceptable to offer (presumably welcomed) aid to those forced to serve slave masters? This was perhaps the first—and arguably the only—time in the series that the Prime Directive was really followed, and the results were entirely unsatisfying. This is not accidental. In fact, the underlying conviction of much of *Star Trek* was that the Prime Directive, while perhaps laudable, *is* unsatisfactory.[10]

Roddenberry made a similar point in "A Private Little War" (2-19). In this episode Roddenberry had the *Enterprise* visit a formerly Edenic pre-industrial planet rent by civil war. Urged to intervene using the advanced weaponry of the Federation, Kirk initially refused, honoring the Prime Directive and summarizing its virtues by explaining, "We are wise enough to know that we are not wise enough to interfere in the way...of another world." Kirk later discovered that the Klingons were arming one side in the war and decided he must intervene to restore the status quo that the Klingons had altered. McCoy objected to fueling the bloodshed, giving Roddenberry the chance, through Kirk, to lay bare the Cold War/Vietnam concerns at the heart of the series:

> KIRK: Bones, do you remember the twentieth-century brush wars on the Asian continent, two giant powers much like the Klingons and ourselves. Neither side felt that they could pull out?
>
> MCCOY: Yes, I remember. It went on bloody year after bloody year!
>
> KIRK: What would you have suggested? That one side arm its friends with an overpowering weapon?...No, the only solution is what happened back then. Balance of power.
>
> MCCOY: And if the Klingons give their side even more?

---

[10] The fact that the script is credited both to Roddenberry and Coon is intriguing since their stories tended to express contrary views of intervention and force. Kirk's reluctance to use violence, characteristic of Coon's writing, coupled with the skeptical view of restraint and noninterference, characteristic of Rodenberry's stories, made the episode *feel* as if Gene Coon's Kirk had been placed in a Gene Roddenberry story.

KIRK: Then we arm our side with exactly that much more. A balance of power. The trickiest, most difficult, dirtiest game of them all, but the only one that preserves both sides.[11]

Kirk's plan was to limit the engagement to arms and advisors, much like the early years of U.S. involvement in Vietnam. The episode thus represented the roots of the Vietnam conflict as noble and necessary, albeit regrettable. But Kirk's assertion that what was done during the Vietnam War was the "only solution" went farther; it was explicit support not only for where U.S. involvement had started, but for where it had gone. Having established the beginnings as honorable, the episode endorsed the subsequent extensions of the policy by insisting on the need for escalation. But while the episode seems intended as an endorsement of U.S. policy in Vietnam, it also dramatized the dilemma of that policy: Kirk acknowledged no limiting principle, no stopping point and, significantly, no strategy for success, only a strategy for stalemate. Ironically, this episode defending the U.S. position in Vietnam aired on February 2, 1968, just three days after the beginning of the Tet Offensive, popularly seen as a turning point that eroded American support for the war.[12]

After Kirk ordered weapons for the planet's inhabitants, the *Enterprise* departed—but the normally triumphal or playful music that closed the episodes was replaced by a somber dirge-like piece, as if to emphasize the tragic necessity of what the audience had just seen

---

[11] The absence of Spock from this debate is peculiar. Normally we might expect him to take up the non-intervention perspective advocated here by McCoy. Sidelined by an injury, the alien Mr. Spock's exclusion from the discussion clarified the debate into an internal conversation between Americans (the Midwestern Kirk and the Southern McCoy), mirroring the debates the American audience would have been engaged in at the time the episode first aired.

In one of the episode's scenes, suffering from delirium, Spock asked Chapel to hit him, reasoning that fighting the pain would help him regain consciousness. When she was reluctant to hit him with full force, Doctor M'Benga, a Black physician, came in, saw what was happening and violently slapped Spock repeatedly until the pain helped revive him. While the scene seemed oddly disconnected to the story, it literalized the ideological point of the episode—the necessity and saving power of violence. The point was made through the beating of the pacifist, non-White Spock, who himself recognized the need for redemptive violence and requested the violence on his own behalf.

[12] *Star Trek* co-producer Robert Justman recalls that, strangely, the network production executive assigned to the series "never seemed to realize that the story was supposed to be an allegory about the growing 'police action' in Vietnam. In fact, no one at NBC made the connection and took us to task. But the audience did; we got letters. Lots of them." (Solow and Justman, *Inside Star Trek*, p. 356.)

and, by implication, the necessity of what it would see later that night on the evening news.

With the exception of the end music there was little recognition of the hazards posed by Kirk's actions in "A Private Little War." But a pair of episodes produced later in the season explored that issue, though less directly. If "Bread and Circuses" highlighted the Prime Directive's implausibility, and "A Private Little War" stressed the necessity of violating it, "A Piece of the Action" (2-17) and "Patterns of Force" (2-21) argued for the Prime Directive's wisdom. More than just an excuse to dress Kirk and Spock up in funny-looking (for them) clothing, repositioning *Star Trek*'s characters in the gangster and World War II genres was an attempt to use those genres' iconography to give an historical resonance and weight to the episodes' arguments.

In "A Piece of the Action," written by Coon and David P. Harmon, from Harmon's story, the *Enterprise* discovered that the people of *Sigma Iotia II* had learned about 1920's Chicago mobs from *The Horizon,* a Federation ship which had visited the planet prior to the Prime Directive's promulgation. Subsequently, the imitative Iotians had based their whole society on the example of the prohibition-era gangsters. The *Enterprise* found tommy-gun toting mobsters ruling the planet through brutality and violence. Faced with the deadly results of the "contamination" by the Federation, Kirk decided "this mess is our responsibility" and that he had to "straighten it out."

Kirk and his party were fired upon and taken hostage by rival gang leaders, both of whom wanted Federation backing so they could defeat their enemies and seize control. Kirk refused to back either gang boss but, nonetheless, as he tried to undo the damage caused by the Horizon, Kirk became increasingly embroiled in the complicated internal politics of the planet. Eventually, through a show of *Enterprise* firepower, Kirk convinced all the bosses to agree to a unified government under Federation tutelage, despite Spock's concern over the wisdom of leaving the planet under the control of criminals.

While the sets, costumes and weaponry of the gangster picture give "A Piece of the Action" a distinct look, the story is not unlike a number of other *Star Trek* episodes in which, mirroring the U.S. situation in Vietnam, the Federation was asked to intervene in an internal struggle on a developing planet. The gangsters tried to force

Kirk to do exactly what the U.S. had done in Vietnam—supply weapons, "advisors and troops"—thus implicitly comparing U.S. policy to gangsterism (the use of the term "advisor" would have been a code word easily recognized by audiences in the context of Vietnam policy). Unlike the U.S., however, Kirk refused to intervene in the civil war. Kirk's predicament of trying to find trustworthy indigenous leaders among gangs of criminals also recalled that of the U.S. government, which, even in the case of victory, would have been faced with leaving South Vietnam in the hands of a South Vietnamese government hobbled by persistent corruption and a lack of popular support (even after a number of U.S.-backed coups were designed to install "acceptable" leadership).

In some ways, "A Piece of the Action" provided a resolution fantasy for war-weary Americans: the Federation ends a civil war and imposes a Federation-approved peace with little violence. Thus the episode would seem both to recreate and sanitize the U.S. presence in Vietnam. Yet the script did not let the Federation—or the audience—off that easily. The episode also warned that intervention might spin out of control and create crises even worse than the original problem the intervention was supposed to cure. At the episode's conclusion, McCoy revealed that he accidentally left his communicator behind, the components of which held the key to all the Federation's technology, thus raising the possibility that the violent Iotians might replicate the Federation's advanced weaponry, become a rival power and present a new "mess" to "straighten out."

If either the *Horizon*'s initial contamination or the *Enterprise*'s corrective intervention is seen as a metaphor for U.S. involvement in Vietnam, the episode raised the possibility that the end result of our policy might be a quagmire, a continuing spiral in which later interventions, designed to correct earlier missteps, create new problems requiring further interventions. The use of the gangster film motif to make the point about good intentions gone wrong was significant, as gangster pictures were often social-problem stories dealing with the unintended consequences of prohibition.

Writer John Meredyth Lucas echoed the theme of intervention gone wrong with his script for "Patterns of Force." Here the *Enterprise* discovered that Federation historian John Gill, sent to planet Ekos as a cultural observer, had violated the prime directive and helped create a society modeled on Nazi Germany with himself as fuehrer. Kirk decided that he had to correct the damage done by Gill's interference. Questioned by Kirk, the incapacitated Gill explained that he found Ekos fragmented, had only meant to replicate the "efficiency" of fascist Germany, and that it was his deputy Melekon who had drugged Gill, taken the reins of power and embarked on genocidal warfare against the planet Zeon and those Zeons living on Ekos. In the end Gil repented, saying, "I was wrong, the noninterference directive was the only way."

As in "A Piece of the Action," in "Patterns of Force" we again have a cautionary tale: an observer becomes an intervener and sets into motion a disastrous chain of events dramatizing the unforseen lethal consequences that can flow from even well-intentioned interference. Taken together "A Piece of the Action" and "Patterns of Force" extended the non-intervention critique made in "The Apple" and rebutted the pro-intervention position of "A Private Little War." This pair of episodes went beyond a philosophical defense of the Prime Directive in the abstract to argue that violating the noninterference directive results in a planet of gangsters or nazis. Interference in the internal affairs or civil wars of others—precisely what the U.S. was then doing in Vietnam—runs the risk of turning our charges into the most violent and antisocial version of ourselves.

"Patterns of Force" also suggested that the danger to the interveners is as great as to the intervenees: the roots of the Ekosian-Zeon conflict went back to when the peaceful Zeons initially intervened to civilize the violent Ekosians. And, as if to underscore once again the undesirability of intervention, it was the Ekosians, not Kirk, who defeated Melakon, and further help from the Federation was not wanted. The Ekosians told Kirk simply, "Thank you, but go now, we must do the rest."

While noninterference was ably defended in these two episodes, Roddenberry had the last word for the season. The final episode produced, and the final one aired, in the second season was "Assignment: Earth" (2-26), again from a story credited to Roddenberry, in which the *only* thing that saved Earth from annihilation *was* the intervention of an alien species who, apparently, "knew better" than to limit itself with a noninterference directive.

While *Star Trek*'s engagement with Vietnam-related issues had peaked in its second season, the show did not totally abandon the issue in its third year. Two episodes—"Spectre of the Gun" (3-6),which challenged America's past, and "Day of the Dove" (3-7), which questioned America's present—vividly registered the impact of late '60s political turmoil and reflected the country's faltering faith in itself.

Star Trek's third season premiered in the fall of 1968, a particularly difficult year in a particularly difficult era. In the preceding months, the viewing audience had suffered a severe series of traumas: in January and February, the Tet Offensive shook the country's faith that the steadily escalating Vietnam War was winnable; in April, the assassination of Dr. Martin Luther King Jr., and the attendant race riots, shook the faith in the nation's ability to resolve, peacefully, its legacy of racial oppression; during the summer and fall of '68, the assassination of presidential candidate Robert Kennedy, police brutality and rioting at the Chicago Democratic convention, and the disturbingly popular presidential campaign of segregationist George Wallace shook the faith in the nation's ability to sustain a sane democratic system. Events like these severely damaged the nation's sense of itself as a just nation capable of rational functioning and left many wondering if America was somehow morally polluted, genetically or culturally predisposed to peculiar levels of violence. In some ways, you might say that 1968 was the year "the Sixties" died.

All of this led to a cultural, cognitive dissonance, an unsettling awakening: the traditional ways the country had of understanding itself, the stories the nation told itself about itself, the myths that gave meaning and a sense of purpose to the national experience, were revealed as no longer—if they ever had been—truthful and reliable. For generations a prime source of the country's public myths had been stories of the old frontier West, passed down through popular media like dime novels, movies and television. The television audience, and the television producing community, had been thoroughly steeped in Western myths. Westerns made up a significant portion of prime-time TV shows in the '60s. In fact, Gene Roddenberry, Gene Coon and story editor D. C. Fontana all had experience in TV Westerns (Roddenberry had even pitched *Star Trek* as "*Wagon Train* to the stars.") The potent myths and symbols provided by Westerns— virtuous settlers and savage Indians, depraved outlaws and straight-shootin' sheriffs—were more than popular clichés, though they certainly were that. Westerns had given much of the viewing audience a set of moral coordinates with which to understand America's place in the world, profoundly impacted our politics and been central to America's understanding of its role in Vietnam.

To many, the American soldier in Vietnam was the latest incarnation of the Cowboy fighting the Indians. Policy makers and soldiers, for instance, had repeatedly used comparisons to Western archetypes to conceptualize the Vietnam War to themselves, and to rationalize it to the public, combat operations were named after popular Western figures like Davy Crockett and Sam Houston and "regiments of the air cavalry traced their lineage directly to the cavalry of the Plains Indian wars."[13] As a result Western symbolism had been an important means for the American public to "understand and control their unprecedented and dismaying experiences in Vietnam... but under the stress of application to Vietnam the saving simplicities of Western-movie symbolism broke down, revealing internal contradictions and ambivalences that made them problematic as a guide" to responding to the crisis.[14]

As the nation's inherited myths began to break down under scrutiny, the resulting loss of confidence impacted the popular culture. In the early 1970s critic Pauline Kael noted that impact when she observed that "the Vietnam War has been barely mentioned on the screen but it has been overwhelmingly present in the movies of the past decade.... In action pictures there was no longer a right side to identify with and nobody you really felt good cheering for. The lack of principles was the same on both sides; only the styles were different, and it was a matter of preferring the less gross and despicable characters to the total monsters."[15]

---

[13] See Slotkin, Richard. *Gunfighter Nation*, p. 524. Also pp. 494–498, 525. This association was enhanced by Western star John Wayne's starring in *The Green Berets* (with *Trek* actor George Takei), the only Vietnam combat film made during the Vietnam War. See Slotkin's discussion of the film in *Gunfighter Nation*, pp. 520–533.

[14] Slotkin, Richard. *Gunfighter Nation*. pp. 546–547.

[15] Pauline Kael, "Commencement Address, Smith College," May 27, 1973. (Cited in: Greene, Eric. *Planet of the Apes as American Myth: Race, Politics and Popular Culture*. Middletown: Wesleyan University Press, 1998. p. 8.)

That crisis of public myth was confronted by Gene Coon's major contribution to *Star Trek*'s third season, a complex tale called "Spectre of the Gun" (3-6). Using the pseudonym "Lee Cronin," Coon questioned the Western myths upon which so much U.S. culture and politics had relied.

In "Spectre of the Gun," the first episode filmed for the final season, after the *Enterprise* violated the space of the Melkotians, Kirk, Spock, McCoy, Scotty and Chekov found themselves in a replica of Tombstone, Arizona, on the day of the legendary gunfight at the O.K. Corral. The townspeople insisted that the Starfleet officers were the Clanton gang, which was defeated in the famous fight by Wyatt Earp, Earp's brothers and Doc Holliday. Thinking Chekov was Clanton gang member William Claiborne, Morgan Earp shot him down. Since, as Spock, noted, "History cannot be changed," the rest of the group was doomed to replay the gunfight and die.

Spock and McCoy attempted to create a gas grenade that would knock out the Earps and Holliday and prevent the fatal shoot out. When tested, however, the surefire gas failed to work. From this Spock deduced that natural laws did not work there and that the Melkotians had trapped them in an artificial environment where belief was more important than reality. He argued that they key to surviving the gunfight at the O.K. Corral was to remember that the guns and the bullets were unreal and therefore could not cause harm. When the belief in its reality was broken, the spell of the fantasy was broken and the Earps' bullets passed through Kirk and the others. Kirk violently confronted Earp, but stopped himself from killing him. The *Enterprise* crew, including a revived Chekov, was returned to the ship, and the Melkotians, impressed by Kirk's refusal to kill, invited the Federation to establish diplomatic relations.

At the same moment that the cognitive dissonance caused by Vietnam was undermining the country's belief in its inherited mythologies, "Spectre of the Gun" depicted Kirk and company realizing the falsity of those myths, ceasing to believe in them—thus disarming them of their power—saving themselves by ceasing to be controlled by the belief that the myths were true. The episode was built on a series of inversions of expectations—both the characters' expectations and the audience's—which provided the means for the crewmembers to extract themselves from the myth.

The first inversion was that *Star Trek*'s heroes were cast by the Melkotians as the villains, while the Earps, whom the audience would have expected to be noble based on received accounts of the O.K. Corral, were entirely unsympathetic. This inversion of expectations regarding good and bad, similar to the blurring of the line between hero and villain Pauline Kael noted, created the uncomfortable feeling of seeing the normally heroic Wyatt Earp as hostile and antagonistic. It encouraged the audience to question the truth of what they were experiencing in the episode and of what they had come to expect from myths of the West.[16]

The second inversion was that Chekov died, even though the actual William Claiborne survived the O.K. Corral. Kirk interpreted the death to mean that events "don't have to happen the way [they] happened, we can change it." Thus Chekov's death suggested both that myth might fail as a record of the past and, more importantly, that myth's *predictive* power as a guide to the present or future might be faulty. This is the essential step to escaping a mythological view of life in which we are endlessly doomed to replay past patterns and archetypes, in which we are constantly reenacting the O.K. Corral, or the Alamo, or Custer's last stand—in which a war in Vietnam is conceived as replaying a war against Apaches.

The third key inversion was the failure of the tranquilizer gas. Spock noted, "We are faced with a staggering contradiction, the tranquilizer . . . should have been effective. Physical reality is consistent with universal law, where the laws do not operate, there is no reality. All of this is unreal . . . once we are convinced of the reality of a given situation we abide by its rules," meaning that we internalize the biases and moral imperatives of our inherited myths. We surrender

---

[16] The audience's expectations of the heroic Earps might best be encapsulated by the lyrics to the theme song of the 1955–61 TV series *The Life and Legend of Wyatt Earp*: "I'll tell you a story, a real true life story, a tale of the Western frontier. The West, it was lawless, but one man was flawless, and his is the story you'll hear. Wyatt Earp, Wyatt Earp, brave, courageous and bold. Long live his fame and long live his glory and long may his story be told. . . . He wasn't partial to being a marshal but fate went and dealt him his hand. While outlaws were lootin' and killin' and shootin' he knew that he must take a stand. He cleaned up the country, the Old Wild West country, he made law and order prevail. And none can deny it, the legend of Wyatt forever will live on the trail."

to myths and invest them with their power through our belief. As Spock explained, "Chekov is dead because he believed that the bullets would kill him." Earlier, the death-dealing bullets were assumed to be the one real thing in a situation which seemed unreal. By the episode's end, Spock saw the bullets as mere "shadows, illusions, nothing but ghosts of reality."

The episode's visual presentation underscored this point: the set was a bunch of false building facades which looked obviously fake. Dozens of Western movies and TV shows were in production in Hollywood at the time the episode was filmed. It should have been easy and relatively economical to borrow one of those existing sets and provide a more authentic-looking environment. But it was precisely the *inauthenticity* of the situation that the episode stressed. Kirk believed that the Melkotians had read his thoughts and placed the crew in the old West because Kirk's ancestors had settled the American frontier. "The violence of your own heritage is to be the pattern of our execution," said Spock. But what the Melkotians produced looked like a fake set on a sound stage, rather than a real Western town, because Kirk's knowledge of the West was drawn from mythology, not history. Kirk and his crew couldn't seem to tell the difference: so enthralled were they by the mythology that, like the inhabitants of the artificial "Tombstone," none of them remarked on the fact that they were not in an actual town.[17]

In this play-set version of the West, the coherence of the myth was breaking down: heroes turned out to be bad guys, villains seemed like victims, events didn't happen the way we'd been told they happened, scientific laws didn't apply. The worldview that we'd inherited was distorted, misleading, unhelpful. The experiences and realizations of the characters paralleled the crisis of myth and *belief* that much of the audience was enduring when the show aired.

It is from here that the final inversion was possible. Spock rea-

[17] "Why does this *Star Trek* episode look like a *Lost in Space* episode?" I, unhappily, wondered when I first saw "Spectre of the Gun" in the early '80s. Solow and Justman maintain that the use of the stylized, minimalist set was a budgetary decision made to save the expense of building new sets. But there should have been a number of sets on the Paramount lot or nearby studios that could have been used. If it was simply a matter of cost, this was an occasion where cost-cutting actually enhanced the thematic content. The whole episode is about confronting artificiality; an artificial environment makes that point more effectively than a more realistic set.

soned that "if the tranquilizer does not function, which is clearly impossible, then a radical alteration of our thought patterns must be in order." What Spock urged was a change of perception, a recognition of the falseness of the myth, of its inability to accurately account for the past and predict the future—just as the death of Chekov could not have been predicted within the false framework that the Melkotians had set up, just as the failure of the tranquilizer violated the laws of nature, just as the bewildering bloodshed, loss and horror of the Vietnam War failed to follow the traditional "cowboys and Indians" script through which the U.S. had mythologized its history. Once the crew stopped believing that the enemy's bullets were real, the bullets had no power.

The separation of fantasy from reality is the radical change in thought patterns which Spock counseled. It was the final key to turning away from mythological determinism and toward a mature understanding of the role that human choice, contingency and historical specificity have in shaping human affairs. What dooms us is not history passed down as a genetic legacy, as Spock initially assumed, but a mythology about that history and an ideology about ourselves that is uncritically embraced. Kirk's overcoming the urge to take revenge and kill Wyatt Earp represented his victory over the myth, his extraction from the deterministic logic of mythic repetition and the rejection of the narrow choice of kill or be killed.

Even the title "Spectre of the Gun" speaks to being haunted by that which is not really there.[18] Coon here argued that it was not our history, but rather our beliefs, that trapped and condemned us, and that if the belief does not fit the facts, survival requires changing the belief. It's rarely easy to admit a mistake. Yet the failure to do this, to revisit and honestly reassess the assumptions of U.S. myth and politics, was leading to mass destruction in Vietnam and a demoralization, both of the troops and the home front.

The demoralization of the home front was the focus of another key final-season episode, "The Day of the Dove," written by Jerome Bixby.

[18] The original title was "The Last Gunfight" which again suggests an end to the Western mythology. The theme of the end of the West, or more precisely the end of the *Western*, was fairly frequent in contemporaneous Western films, like *The Wild Bunch* (1969) and *Butch Cassidy and the Sundance Kid* (1969), that focused on characters who had reached their limits just as the genre seemed to have reached the limits of its ideological usefulness.

In his second season episode "Mirror, Mirror" (2-4), Bixby touched upon the sense of domestic unease by creating an evil *Enterprise* in an alternate universe. The irony was that the evil *Enterprise*—where power was transferred through assassination, where the authorities used surveillance and abuse to control the population and force was used against lesser powers—more accurately reflected the U.S. at the time than the utopian *Enterprise* the series showcased every week. Consider Slotkin's point that "the hope of counter-insurgency had always been that some day Vietnamese politics would begin to mirror [the] American model. Instead our engagement in Vietnam had carried us to the other side of the looking-glass and had made our politics seem a mirror-image of Saigon's coups, conspiracies, riots and assassinations."[19]

In "Day of the Dove" Bixby again painted a dark picture of the *Enterprise* which reflected the country's troubled environment. Lured by a faked distress call, Kirk was confronted by a group of Klingons who had also been falsely lured to the area. Chekov was particularly enraged at the Klingons for killing his brother, but Kirk later learned that Chekov was an only child. Kirk imprisoned the Klingons on board the *Enterprise* and soon discovered that they and the *Enterprise* crew were all victims of a mysterious alien entity which provoked and gained strength from their mutual hatred. The alien took control of the ship, provided both the *Enterprise* and Klingon crews weapons and kept them alive so they could continue fighting endlessly, allowing the alien to feed off of the hostility they generated.

Having been lured into battle through imagined distress calls, phantom provocations and an artificial blood vendetta to avenge a brother who never existed (all of which recalled the Tonkin Gulf incident and other falsified or exaggerated reports used to bolster U.S. policy in Vietnam), both crews committed atrocities and suffered wounds to their honor, which further fueled the fight.

The hostility against the Klingons was turned inward as well: when an agitated Scotty called the mixed-species Spock "a freak," Kirk stopped them from coming to blows and, in a fit of rage, contemptuously called Spock a "half-human." Controlling his anger, Kirk asked, "Why are we behaving like a group of savages?" Then,

---

[19] Slotkin, Richard. *Gunfighter Nation*, p. 579.

realizing the influence of the alien, Kirk put it together: "Two forces aboard this ship, each of them equally armed. Has a war been staged for us complete with weapons and ideology and patriotic drum beating? Even... even race hatred?" Kirk's words here, while directed at the conflict on the ship, echoed the questions of much of the audience regarding the war in Vietnam.[20] Spock's observation that "Apparently, it is by design that we fight. We seem to be pawns," would also have echoed the conclusions of many in the audience (and note the large numbers of episodes throughout the series in which the *Enterprise* crew was manipulated or forced into a fight).[21]

Hurtling through space, out of control, marred by violence, racial hostility, mistrust and an inability to restore rationality, the *Enterprise* was transformed from a symbol of an integrated America, progressive and hopeful, into a symbol of a debased America shamed by violence abroad and scarred by racial bigotry at home—a vision of what we should be replaced by a picture of what we had become. Kirk and Spock eventually convinced the Klingons to cease hostilities or be forever trapped on "a doomed ship... filled with eternal blood lust, eternal warfare."[22]

"Spectre of the Gun" and "Day of the Dove" were two of the thematic high points in a season which, while it featured some entertaining episodes, lacked the thematic coherence and technical competence that had enriched the first two years. In addition to losing D. C. Fontana, Gene Roddenberry and Gene Coon both had left their full-time positions with *Star Trek* by the time the third season was under way. Without the give and take between *Star Trek*'s two

---

[20] Kirk's statement that, "It goes on and on, the good old game of war. Pawn against pawn, stopping the bad guys. While somewhere, something sits back and laughs and starts it all over again," recalled the terms in which some condemned contemporary American military policy. Compare Kirk's statement to Bob Dylan's 1963 song "Masters of War": "You fasten the triggers, for the others to fire. Then you sit back and watch, when the death count gets higher. You hide in your mansion as young people's blood flows out of their bodies and is buried in the mud."

Similarly, Kirk's critique in "Mirror, Mirror" of the waste of "lives, potential, resources, time" and his assessment of the alternate universe empire as "illogical because it cannot endure" also seemed to address contemporary times.

[21] These included "Arena" (1-18), "The Squire of Gothos" (1-17), "The Menagerie, Parts I and II" (1-11, 1-12), "Amok Time" (2-1), "Gamesters of Triskellion" (2-16), "Spectre of the Gun" (3-6) and "The Savage Curtain" (3-22).

[22] Ironically, by arming the Federation and Klingon crew equally, thus ensuring a balance of power which "preserves both sides" and allows the fighting to continue, the alien's actions resemble Kirk's in "A Private Little War."

Genes, the series lost much of the dramatic and ideological tension that was woven throughout the second season.

But that tension was not totally absent. One Roddenberry contribution toward the end of the series again felt like an address to *Trek*'s other Gene. Written by Roddenberry and Arthur Heinemann, from Roddenberry's story, "The Savage Curtain" (3-22) was one of the final episodes filmed. Here, as in "Spectre of the Gun," an alien species kidnapped members of the crew and forced them to fight to the death against historical figures. But there were significant differences: here the good guys were good and the bad guys were bad, just as we would expect. Furthermore, Roddenberry allowed Kirk an extremely limited range of responses, having Kirk conclude that "We play their game. Fight, or lose the ship." Whereas "Spectre" showed our heroes going along with the charade until they could think their way out, "Savage" found them unable to imagine a response that could extricate them from the deadly logic of kill or be killed.

Roddenberry's version of Kirk here was consistent with his Kirk in "A Private Little War," who saw no solution but escalation. And yet this Kirk was a stark departure from the more resourceful and courageous Kirk who, in Gene Coon's hands, found a way *not* to kill the Gorn in "Arena" (1-18), the Horta in "The Devil in the Dark" and Earp in "Spectre of the Gun," who declared in "A Taste of Armageddon" that "We can admit that we're killers, but we won't kill—today." It was Coon's Kirk who so often ingeniously managed to "trick his way out of death"—who, fifteen years later, would so famously reject the "no-win scenario" and change the conditions of the test. By contrast, the Kirk in "The Savage Curtain" passively accepted the rules that had been made for him. When told he must kill or be killed, he killed. Put bluntly, Gene Roddenberry's Kirk lacked the moral imagination of Gene Coon's Kirk.

This struggle between Gene Roddenberry's Kirk and Gene Coon's Kirk—Kirk as hawk and Kirk as dove—between the Kirks who faced off against each other in "The Enemy Within" (1-5), not only enlivened the television drama, it also encapsulated much of the debate about U.S. domestic and foreign policy in the divided '60s. That struggle stayed relevant in the '70s as we continued to debate those issues in the aftermath of the war and *Star Trek* became a hit in syndication. The Prime Directive and the political tensions it addressed were largely absent from the 1973–75 *Star Trek* animated series and entirely missing from the 1980's *Star Trek* feature films, where the Prime Directive is *never* mentioned. Perhaps this absence manifested the weariness of the post-Vietnam era. Maybe, chastened by our experience in Vietnam, for a time we were content to presume that the answer to the Prime Question—to intervene or not to intervene—was "no" and to let the question rest. That is, until a re-asserted foreign policy in the Ronald Reagan era was aggressive enough to provoke the question again in *Star Trek: The Next Generation.*

Yet this struggle between the two Kirks, this conversation between the two Genes, would culminate over twenty years after the series' conclusion in the final film featuring the original characters. Although Coon passed away in the early '70s and Roddenberry lost control of *Star Trek* in the early '80s, *Star Trek VI: The Undiscovered Country* is largely about the struggle between Roddenberry's Cold Warrior Kirk, who maintains a posture of "don't trust them, let them die," and Coon's peacemaker Kirk, who sees that while "change can be very difficult," a leap of faith may be necessary to achieve peace.[23] In fact, *Star Trek VI* is perhaps not really so much a good *Star Trek* film—its wannabe Sherlock Holmes whodunit feels far too derivative and too far removed from the science fiction milieu and its political allegorizing is a bit too obvious—as much as it is a good film *about Star Trek* (just as films like *The Wild Bunch, Butch Cassidy and the Sundance Kid* and *Unforgiven* (1992) were Westerns about the Western), about the need to push past the limitations of the original series' Cold War ideology as the country moved out of the Cold War period, to acknowledge the truth of *Star Trek*'s history without abandoning the best of *Star Trek*'s legend.

Even as the original characters were retired, *Star Trek*'s successor series have returned to some of the questions explored by the original series and mirrored some of the political changes of their times: the Federation-friendly Worf appeared on the *Enterprise-D* bridge

[23] To a degree *Star Trek VI* is essentially *The Enemy Within: The Motion Picture*. And, really, what *Star Trek* fan didn't get a kick out of seeing James Kirk fight himself—again. The struggle of dual, and dueling, Kirks, after all, as demonstrated by "The Enemy Within," "What Are Little Girls Made Of?" (1-7), "Whom Gods Destroy" (3-14) and "Turnabout Intruder" (3-24), was one of *Star Trek*'s signature, and most apt, motifs.

shortly after the Western-friendly Gorbachev appeared on the world stage; the Borg Collective began to disintegrate just as the Soviet Union was dismantling; and, while *Star Trek* is still not above titillation in tight costumes, the women's movement was belatedly accommodated as Major Kira, Captain Janeway and Subcommander T'Pol replaced the mini-skirted yeomen of the original series. But, its aesthetic strengths or weaknesses aside, the relatively short run of *Star Trek: Enterprise* demonstrated that, despite its third season, post-9/11 arc about a surprise attack followed by a mission of retaliation and preemption, the producers and caretakers of *Star Trek* have yet to accommodate fully those political and cultural changes and adjust the Star Trek format to stay relevant, the way that, for instance, the producers of the re-created *Battlestar Galactica* have.

The U.S. is no longer a superpower facing another superpower, but a superpower with multiple rivals and challenges on a new field of threats and opportunities, contending with the real limits of military might, economic strength, cultural capital and moral suasion. And yet *Star Trek*'s Prime Question—how much force should a superpower use, under what situations, subject to what limitations—is, for the moment, still *the* Prime Question. More so than at any time since the Vietnam War, the Prime Question drives the debate over American policy and America's future.

It is ironic that, at the precise moment that the Prime Question is more relevant than it has been at any time in the past thirty years, *Star Trek*—which has served as such a popular vehicle for debating the Prime Question during much of that time—has passed from the stage, and is no longer an arena for TV and filmmakers to engage in that debate. *Star Trek* may in time return to the Prime Question, but before it can, Paramount must address the Immediate Question: what would a relevant *Star Trek* look like in the twenty-first century? How would it reconfigure the questions and shape of Roddenberry's original series? What would it say about our views toward science? Power? The military? The government? The future? Would it be a utopian projection of the future or a dystopian refraction of the present? Would it be both? Neither? We may have to wait a while for a satisfactory answer to the Immediate Question.

"*Star Trek* Lives" was a rallying cry for fans in the '70s. But more than that, it was an article of faith that, eventually, was rewarded. For now, it seems that *Star Trek*, as a film or television vehicle, is dead. But to paraphrase Mr. Spock—it's been dead before. If viable answers can be found to the Immediate Question then perhaps *Star Trek*, like Spock, will be reborn. And live long and prosper.

After writing a book hailed as "groundbreaking," the critically acclaimed *Planet of the Apes as American Myth: Race, Politics and Popular Culture*, Eric Greene received a JD from Stanford Law School where he served as vice president of the Black Law Students Association and was a founder of the West Coast Conference on Progressive Lawyering. A graduate of the religious studies department at Wesleyan University, Greene's professional hats have included actor, writer and civil rights activist. Greene lives in Los Angeles where he is on the staff of the American Civil Liberties Union of Southern California and on the board of the Progressive Jewish Alliance.

Michael A. Burstein

WE FIND THE ONE QUITE ADEQUATE: RELIGIOUS ATTITUDES IN STAR TREK

Captain Kirk said something fascinating at the end of "Who Mourns for Adonais?" (2-2). Looking at the Greek god Apollo, he declared, "Mankind has no need for gods. We find the one quite adequate." It's almost as if the scriptwriter had wanted to portray a secular twenty-third century, but a nervous network suit had insisted that the second sentence be tacked on. The result, however unintentionally, is wonderfully evocative of *Star Trek*'s very ambiguous relationship to religion, as Michael A. Burstein, winner of the John W. Campbell Award and frequent Hugo Award finalist, explains.

IN THE THIRD SEASON of *Star Trek*, the episode "Is There in Truth No Beauty?" (3-5) introduced the Vulcan concept of Infinite Diversity in Infinite Combinations, abbreviated as IDIC. IDIC was their philosophy of respecting the differences of others.

If *Star Trek* stood for anything, it stood for that concept, the idea that people (and aliens) existed with different customs, cultures and beliefs, and that this diversity needed to be respected. IDIC was an expression of the governing philosophy behind the show: humanity had survived the turmoil of the 1960s and had gone to the stars as a united planet.

The crew of the ship reflected the diversity of the future. The members of the senior staff included all races and backgrounds: Uhura, an African woman, was a senior officer, and starting in the second season, Pavel Chekov, a Russian, joined the crew. To the American audience of the time, a Russian was probably much more alien than a Vulcan.

But it seems that one aspect of our culture that did not travel with us was religion. In fact, the attitude of the original *Star Trek* series toward religion was less one of respect for diversity and more one of disdain.

There are four places we can look to determine the religious attitudes found in *Star Trek*: the religious behavior of the crew, the religious behavior of other Federation humans, the religious behavior of aliens, and the godlike beings found roaming about the Star Trek universe.

I. RELIGIOUS BEHAVIOR AMONG THE CREW AND MEMBERS OF STARFLEET

Trying to find an episode that shows the religious views of the crew is like trying to find a sterile tribble. The lack of portrayal of religion on the *Enterprise* is perhaps only evidence for indifference toward religion, not necessarily evidence of a bias against religion, but it's a good place to begin. And in the Star Trek universe, there were a few events portrayed in which religion normally popped up in American society, but where it was noticeably absent in *Star Trek*.

The episode "Balance of Terror" (1-14), for example, opened with a wedding. Now, who was performing the wedding? Was it the starship chaplain? No, in fact, it was Captain Kirk. He made a quick reference to the wedding being performed "in accordance with our laws and our many beliefs," but there was nothing in what we saw to indicate that the marriage had a religious component. The chapel had candles, but no religious icons were present on the walls.

The chapel appeared only once more, in "The Tholian Web" (3-9). In the episode, a lost Kirk was presumed dead, and a short memorial service was held for him in the chapel. Again, there was no chaplain; Spock ran the service. And again, there was no mention of God or religion, just a vague comment from Spock to the crew that "Each of you must evaluate the loss in the privacy of your own thoughts."

Surely, the death of the captain would rate a ship's chaplain leading his memorial service. The only conclusion we can draw is that the *Enterprise* had not a single chaplain on board to serve the needs of the 430 crewmembers. No wonder we never saw a single, regular, religious service.

Where else do we see religion make an appearance, however small, in American society? In the courtroom. As much as the United States proclaims the separation of church and state, when giving testimony in court people often take an oath to tell the truth on the Bible or some other holy book. Even if that practice has waned today, it was still prevalent in the 1960s.

And yet, in the few episodes in which we see courtroom proceedings—"The Menagerie, Parts I and II" (1-11, 1-12) and "Court Martial" (1-20)—the people taking the stand as witnesses never even went so far as to affirm that their testimony was truthful, let alone take an oath that mentioned God.

The fact that even a tiny mention of God was omitted from these episodes indicates a society that had "moved beyond" religion, or at the very least assumed that religious belief was not enough to ensure moral behavior.

Finally, looking beyond Christianity, there were other indications that Starfleet Command eschewed religion. Religious male Jews, for example, wear *kippot*, or small skullcaps, on their heads at all times. Muslim women often wear a head scarf for reasons of modesty. And in the United States, at least, the right to wear clothing of a religious nature along with a uniform has generally been upheld by the courts. So the fact that we never saw a single person on the *Enterprise* wearing some sort of religious garb tells us either that everyone on the ship was a Christian or that religion did not seem to matter anymore in the twenty-third century.

Of course, most other American TV shows in the 1960s would not have shown religious Jews or Muslims either. But most also wouldn't have put Russians and Africans on the bridge of a ship as officers.

II. Religious Behavior Among Other Humans

So the crew of the *Enterprise* was irreligious; that didn't necessarily mean that the average Federation citizen rejected religion. Surely, on its five-year mission, the *Enterprise* crew would have encountered some sort of religious group.

Sure they did. Once.

"The Way to Eden" (3-20) portrayed quasi-religious behavior at its absolute worst. A group of young Federation citizens and an ambassador's son had fallen under the influence of Dr. Sevrin, a research engineer who had started a movement that embraced the primitive. They sought the planet Eden (get it?) with a religious fervor that bordered on the fanatical. Sevrin and his followers were portrayed as futuristic hippies, wearing odd clothes, singing songs and insulting the establishment as represented by Kirk and the crew.

And when they reached Eden, what did they find? The vegetation of the planet was filled with poisonous acid, deadly to human beings. The metaphor was blatant, especially when they discovered that one of the followers had eaten an apple and died. The kid's name? Adam.

Sevrin himself refused to leave Eden; he too bit into a piece of fruit and died. It would appear that the Star Trek universe equates religion with self-destructive behavior.

The metaphor of Eden showed up in one other episode involving Federation citizens, "This Side of Paradise" (1-24). A few years before the episode took place, a man named Elias Sandoval established an agricultural colony on the planet Omicron Ceti III. However, the planet was exposed to deadly berthold rays, and the *Enterprise* crew expected that everyone there had died.

To their surprise the colony was alive and thriving, a pastoral planet. They eschewed mechanical devices, opting instead for a simpler life that was almost Amish in its portrayal of Ludditism. But all was not what it seemed. The colonists had been taken over by spores, which thrived on the berthold rays. In return, the spores gave the colonists complete health and peace of mind. No one lacked for anything; all the colonists, and soon the entire crew, were blissfully happy. Under the influence of the spores, Spock referred to the colony as a "true Eden."

Kirk was able to restore everyone to normal with the discovery that violent emotions killed the spores. And as the episode ended, Sandoval condemned the society that the spores helped him build. When he finally shook off the spores, he said, "We've done nothing here. No accomplishments, no progress. Three years wasted." And in the final scene, McCoy noted that this was "the second time man's been thrown out of paradise," to which Kirk responded, "This time we walked out on our own.... Maybe we weren't meant for paradise."

The implication was that there was no room for a religious colony in the Federation, not even a self-sufficient one.

Okay, so humans of the twenty-third century seemed to have dispatched with religion. Why does that imply an antireligious message in *Star Trek*? Is there any other evidence for this view?

The answer is yes, because not every human we met on the show was from the twenty-third century. *Star Trek* played around with time travel, allowing the crew to interact with humans in the past. In "The City on the Edge of Forever" (1-28), Kirk and Spock chased after a delusional McCoy, who had gone back to 1930s New York City at the height of the Depression. Kirk and Spock took refuge in the Twenty-First Street Mission, run by Edith Keeler, who considered it her calling to help her fellow human being.

If anyone was going to present a religious view of the world, surely it would have been a twentieth-century woman running a mission during the Depression.

But listen to her "sermon" delivered during lunch, the price the indigent had to pay for the free food:

> Now, let's start by getting one thing straight. I'm not a do-gooder. If you're a bum, if you can't break off with the booze or whatever it is that makes you a bad risk, then get out. Now, I don't pretend to tell you how to find happiness and love when every day is just a struggle to survive, but I do insist that you do survive because the days and the years ahead are worth living for. One day soon, man is going to be able to harness incredible energies, maybe even the atom. Energies that could ultimately hurl us to other worlds in... in some sort of spaceship. And the men that reach out into space will be able to find ways to feed the hungry millions of the world and to cure their diseases. They will be able to find a way to give each man hope and a common future, and those are the days worth living for.

In the real Depression-era New York City, a woman running a mission would be sure to invoke God in her sermon. This is one place and time where religious talk would be expected, and it was instead blatantly omitted. Keeler's words were not those of a woman running a mission. They were the words of a Golden Age science fiction fan reading his pulps and trying to explain to the rest of the world why science fiction is not junk, but the literature of ideas.

III. RELIGIOUS BEHAVIOR AMONG THE ALIENS

There is a plot that became a cliché among the fans. Kirk and company come to a planet and encounter a humanoid alien race that worships some sort of godlike being. The society has stagnated, and perhaps they perform some sort of ritual sacrifice that is barbaric by our standards. Kirk discovers that the "god" being worshipped is actually some sort of computer. Then, using human illogic, Kirk convinces the computer to blow itself up and saves the day.

In reality, there were only a handful of episodes in which something like this happened. The two closest were "The Return of the Archons" (1-21) and "The Apple" (2-5). In the first one, a man named Landru programmed a computer to keep his people safe; it did so by absorbing them into "the body," so that their individuality was subsumed into the collective consciousness. As a result, Landru ruled over a stagnant society, in which free will was nonexistent. Kirk noted that the real Landru was able to program the machine "with all his knowledge but couldn't give it his wisdom, his compassion, his understanding, his soul." It would seem that organized religion doesn't lift the soul, but squashes it instead.

And in the second one, "The Apple," the Eden metaphor once more reared its head. The crew visited a paradisiacal planet, Gamma Trianguli VI. They met a native named Akuta, who explained to the crew that his people worshiped a being called Vaal (close in name to Baal, one of the idols mentioned in the Bible) who "causes the rains to fall and the sun to shine." When Akuta took the crew to Vaal, Kirk discovered that Vaal was an idol that looked like a giant reptilian head with a glowing red mouth, an access point to a power source below the surface.

Vaal's worshippers lived for one purpose—to bring fuel to Vaal, an intelligent machine that needed to "eat" to keep functioning. McCoy was repulsed by their society, but Spock took the opposing view:

McCoy: There are certain absolutes, Mr. Spock, and one of them is the right of humanoids to a free and unchained environment, the right to have conditions which permit growth.

Spock: Another is their right to choose a system which seems to work for them.

McCoy condemned the society as one that had stagnated for 10,000 years, but Spock noted that the people were healthy and happy, and that their system worked. McCoy replied, "It might work for you, Mr. Spock, but it doesn't work for me. Humanoids living so they can service a hunk of tin?"

But this paradise was disrupted by the presence of the crew, even without Kirk's interfence. Two of the natives observed Chekov and Yeoman Martha Landon kissing. They imitated the kiss, which angered Vaal. Vaal ordered the worshippers to kill the crew. Instead, the crew killed Vaal by preventing the humanoids from feeding it, thus freeing the society from the burdens of worship. Kirk told them, "You'll learn to build for yourselves, think for yourselves, work for yourselves. And what you create is yours. That's what we call freedom."

The episode ended by making the Eden metaphor explicit. Spock brought up the biblical story of Genesis and said that "in a manner of speaking, we have given the people of Vaal the apple—the knowledge of good and evil, if you will—as a result of which, they too have been driven out of paradise." The episode ended with the joke that Spock looked like Satan.

What are we to make of this? The episode's implication is obvious—religion stifles freedom. The people of Vaal might have been happy, but Kirk and McCoy presented the "correct" view, that such happiness was meaningless. It is curious that Spock, the rationalist, presented the opposing argument; perhaps the joke at the end of the episode, in which his appearance was equated to that of Satan's, was meant to cast further doubt on his statements.

Another episode with an alien religious culture was "For the World Is Hollow and I Have Touched the Sky" (3-8). A society of humanoids lived inside the asteroid world Yonada, but they thought they lived on a planet's surface. Their asteroid spacecraft was on a

In "Charlie X," a teenager named Charlie Evans was rescued by a cargo vessel and passed along to the *Enterprise*. The crew soon discovered that he had the power to will almost anything. As a baby, Charlie was the sole survivor of a transport crash on the planet Thasus, and the Thasians, who were highly evolved energy beings, gave Charlie these powers so he could survive. But combined with his natural teenage impulses and insecurities, as well as his lack of socialization, his powers were dangerous to the people around him. Charlie ended up taking control of the ship.

Mitchell and Evans could both be forgiven for one thing. They might have had the powers of a god, but they still had the emotional weaknesses of a human being. As Kirk pointed out, they were gods driven by human frailty. Perhaps a being that had natural omnipotence would also have the moral fortitude to match.

But you wouldn't necessarily know it from *Star Trek*.

In "The Squire of Gothos" (1-17), for example, the crew encountered Trelane, who appeared human but had power over space and matter. And he was anything but moral. As Spock put it, Trelane was "intellect without discipline... power without constructive purpose." Trelane used his powers to play games with and torment the crew. Kirk referred to Trelane as a "god of war" and "a small boy, and a very naughty one at that."

In almost every episode with powerful beings—"Arena" (1-18), "Catspaw" (2-7), "Plato's Stepchildren" (3-10), "The Savage Curtain" (3-22) and "And the Children Shall Lead" (3-4), just to name a few—the beings toyed with the *Enterprise* crew and had to be defeated. Very few of these beings claimed to be gods, but one did.

In "Who Mourns for Adonais?" (2-2), the Greek god Apollo stopped the *Enterprise* dead in space and ordered members of the crew to beam down to his planet. They discovered that the ancient Greek gods were all-powerful aliens who once visited Earth, and whom human beings once worshipped. When Apollo told the crew that they could now worship him as a god again, Kirk replied, "Mankind has no need for gods. We find the one quite adequate." Of course, as we've already seen, it would appear from their behavior that the *Enterprise* crew found atheism quite adequate for their own spiritual and religious needs.

The lesson we learn here is that absolute power appears to corrupt absolutely. A being who achieves mastery over space, time and matter is led to play maliciously with lower forms of intelligence. Only the Organians from "Errand of Mercy" (1-26) appear to have some sort of moral sense when they step in to prevent a war—and some would argue that by taking away humanity's free will and right to choose good or evil for ourselves, the Organians are just as corrupt as anyone else.

Star Trek presented a future in which religion was at best irrelevant, and at worst a force for stagnation and oppression; a future in which aliens needed to be freed from their incorrect religious beliefs; and a universe filled with godlike beings whose natures were capricious or malevolent.

So where did this view come from?

Star Trek was not created in a vacuum. There are three sources for the show's attitudes toward religion.

The first was the field of science fiction itself, of which *Star Trek* was obviously a part. A disdain for religion wasn't peculiar to *Star Trek*. Its view of religion was part of a grand tradition in science fiction, going back to the days of H.G. Wells' *Things to Come*, where science and rationality win out against an irrational, religious view of the world. Science fiction promoted science as the new religion. Science was the only truth that existed, and the only truth that humanity needed.

The second source of this attitude was Gene Roddenberry, the creator of *Star Trek*. It should be no surprise that the show would reflect his own views on the world. Roddenberry, whose family came from the South, was exposed to the Baptist religion at a young age but rejected it. His view of religion can be summed up by his comments in an interview from the March/April 1991 issue of *The Humanist*, in which he described his epiphany during a sermon on the Communion ceremony:

> I was listening to the sermon and I remember complete astonishment because what they were talking about were things that were just crazy. . . . For some time I puzzled over this and puzzled over why they

> were saying these things, because the connection between what they were saying and reality was very tenuous. . .I guess from that time it was clear to me that religion was largely nonsense, and was largely magical, superstitious things.[1]

Given his reaction to the sermon, it's no wonder that Roddenberry's vision of the future presented a human race that had "grown up" beyond the needs of religion.

Finally, Roddenberry's *Star Trek* presented an antireligious view of the future simply because it was a reflection of its time. America in the 1960s was a society undergoing great turmoil. People were questioning all sorts of authority, including religious authority.

One good indicator of religious attitudes in the 1960s comes from *The Gallup Poll: Public Opinion 1935-1971*. Every few years the poll asked, "At the present time, do you think religion as a whole is increasing its influence on American life, or losing its influence?"

In February, 1962, 31% of the people responding said that religion was losing influence. That number climbed to 45% in February, 1965. By March, 1967, at which point *Star Trek* had been on the air for most of its first season, 57% of people responding said that religion was losing influence. By April, 1968, that number had increased to 67%, and in May, 1969, it had climbed again to 70%. From that perspective, one can say that the show tapped into the general zeitgeist, just as it did with so many other cultural touchstones of the time.

It is unfortunate that Roddenberry's view of the future did not have room for religion. But his view, sadly, was based on the flawed premise that religion is a way for people to abjure responsibility for their actions and to hand over control of their lives to others. Given that premise, it's no wonder that *Star Trek* presented religion as bad, and promoted self-responsibility as the antidote. But by doing so, *Star Trek* betrayed its own basic principles: a commitment to diversity and the belief that, in the end, all of us can get along, no matter who we are or what we believe.

---

[1] Cited in Alexander, David. *Star Trek Creator: The Authorized Biography of Gene Roddenberry*. New York: Roc Books, 1994.

Religion is a vital part of the human experience, and one that will not be as easily left behind in the future as Roddenberry hoped. Religion, like all human endeavors, has both its good and bad influences on our society, and like it or not, it will accompany us on our journey to the stars.

Michael A. Burstein, winner of the 1997 Campbell Award for Best New Writer, has earned ten Hugo nominations and two Nebula nominations for his short fiction, which appears mostly in *Analog*. Burstein lives with his wife Nomi in the town of Brookline, Massachusetts, where he is an elected Town Meeting Member and Library Trustee. When not writing, he has worked as a science teacher and textbook editor. He has two degrees in physics and attended the Clarion Workshop. More information on Burstein and his work can be found on his Web page, http://www.mabfan.com.

Lyle Zynda

WHO AM I? PERSONAL IDENTITY IN THE ORIGINAL STAR TREK

The British TV series *Spitting Image* used puppets of celebrities to biting satiric effect. In one memorable episode, a floppy-eared avatar of Leonard Nimoy was seen walking around a Hollywood party proclaiming: "Mr. Spock, Lieutenant Commander Spock, Commander Spock, Science Officer Spock, First Officer Spock, Captain Spock, Ambassador Spock—just a few of the many roles that I, Leonard Nimoy, have made famous!" Are they all in fact the same person? And, for that matter, are Nimoy and Spock different entities? The actor wrote a book in 1975 called *I Am Not Spock*, but seemed to change his mind by 1995 when he authored *I Am Spock*. It's no wonder he's confused; issues of personal identity are very tricky things indeed, as philosophy professor Lyle Zynda explains.

IN "WHAT ARE LITTLE GIRLS MADE OF?" (1-7) the *Enterprise* visited the planet Exo III and found Dr. Roger Korby, who had not been heard from in five years. As it happens, Korby was once engaged to Nurse Christine Chapel, who was overjoyed to have found him. As the episode unfolded we learned that years earlier, with his body dying, Korby's memories, knowledge and personality—his "soul," he suggested—had been transferred into an android body. This became known when Korby's android hand was damaged during a fight, revealing circuits under his artificial skin. Responding to Nurse Chapel's apparent dismay at the sight, Korby said imploringly, "It's still me, Christine—Roger—I'm in here." However, Chapel and

Kirk both rejected this identification. After "Korby," in despair, dematerialized himself (and a female android assistant) with a phaser, Spock arrived on the scene and asked, "Where is Dr. Korby?" Kirk replied, "Dr. Korby was never here." But could the android have actually *been* Dr. Korby?

The issue just raised is discussed under the rubric *personal identity* in philosophy. In *An Essay Concerning Human Understanding* (1690),[1] John Locke defends a theory of personal identity that would allow transfers such as the one Korby underwent to be transfers of a *person*. Locke argues that the continued existence of a person does not essentially involve the continuance of any *entity* or *object*, such as a body, brain or non-physical soul. Instead, a kind of *pattern* is transmitted—in particular, the patterns that encode *memories*—and this *process* (the transmission of memories) is what constitutes the continuance of a person. In short, according to Locke, a person is simply a series of psychological stages in which later stages remember what happened to the earlier ones. Now, since patterns are abstract in nature, memories can be transferred—e.g., between two bodies, from a physical body to a non-physical soul after death or even between two souls. Thus, Locke's theory implies that a single person could exist in different bodies (or souls) at different stages in its existence. Moreover, a single body (or soul) could be (or "contain," to use a common metaphor) several people over time.

In what follows, I will discuss Locke's theory in more detail, along with several alternatives to it, and apply these to the episode just described and several others from the original *Star Trek*. As we will see, the episodes' various writers implicitly assume quite different theories of personal identity. Along the way, we will also discuss whether *Star Trek*'s transporter is truly a method of *transportation* (which requires that the person who materializes at the end is the same person who was "beamed" at the start) or an instrument of *death-and-duplication*.

DEFINING THE CONCEPT OF PERSONAL IDENTITY

Before we begin, it is essential to clarify our terms. What is meant by "personal identity"? Let us begin by specifying a common sense

[1] See Book II, Chapter xxvii, "Of Identity and Diversity."

of "identity" that will *not* concern us. Sometimes the term "personal identity" is used to refer to how you as an individual *categorize* yourself. In other words, this sense of "identity" refers to the *kind* of person you think you are—in particular, you regard yourself as *belonging* to various social groups, and, to varying degrees, you regard the lifestyles, values and worldviews they espouse as your *own*, or as *part* of you or your history. Let us call this complex set of identifications your *social identity*.

This essay is not concerned with social identity, but with what in philosophy is called *quantitative* identity. It is easiest to approach the issue (as Locke did) by first considering the identity of *objects*. Think, for example, of a pair of shoes you own. It would be natural for you to say something like, "That is the pair of shoes I bought to go to my best friend's wedding last year." Even though the shoes may have changed considerably—once shiny and new, they may now be worn and unfit for wearing—the verb "is" and definite article "the" indicate they are *one and the same* pair of shoes.[2] Similarly, if you as a child planted an oak sapling on your front lawn and returned to your childhood home decades later to see a tall, proud oak tree towering over the house, you might say, "That is the tree I planted as a child." Even though the tree is *qualitatively* very different from the sapling it once was, it is *one and the same object* as the sapling. Simply put, it *is* the sapling, at a later point in its existence, now fully grown.

The term "identical" is closely related to "same" and also has qualitative and quantitative senses. Identical twins are two people, not one, though they share many of the same qualities (e.g., their visual appearance), making it hard to tell them apart. They are "identical" in the *qualitative* sense—they are (more or less) *exactly similar*. By contrast, Cassius Clay and Muhammad Ali are identical in the *quantitative* sense—"they" are *one and the same person*, under different names, at different points in *his* life.

Now, "personal identity" as it is used here refers to this *quantita-*

[2] "One and the same" is admittedly redundant—why not just say "the same"? It is useful at first to use the wordier phase because "the same" is ambiguous. When you say, "That is the same pair of shoes I bought to go to my best friend's wedding," you could mean either that it is one and the same pair (a *quantitative* claim), or that it is the same *kind* of shoe, *exactly similar* to the pair you bought for the wedding (a *qualitative* claim).

tive identity of persons—Cassius Clay and Muhammad Ali have it, Mary-Kate and Ashley Olsen don't. Similarly, the William Shatner who is the current spokesperson for Priceline.com is (quantitatively) the same William Shatner who played Captain Kirk on *Star Trek*. What *makes* this so?

In everyday life, we identify people both by their bodies (how they appear) and by their behavior, verbal and otherwise, which we take to reveal their inner psychology (i.e., their memories, knowledge, personality traits, etc.). Fortunately, these two criteria for determining identity always (or nearly always) coincide. Even when we meet old friends and completely fail to recognize them because their appearance is drastically different, we implicitly assume that their physical body, though different in appearance, is (quantitatively) the same body they had when we knew them earlier.

In science fiction, however—and in our imaginations generally—such assumptions can be overturned. For example, Korby the android had (nearly) all the personality traits and memories that Korby had while he was a living human being. He considered himself Korby and "not a computer." Indeed, he proposed to Kirk that all humans should undergo the same procedure, making them immortal physically (android "hosts" can be replaced when they wear out) and improvable psychologically (e.g., aggression can be reduced by suitable reprogramming). In doing this, he thought, the *essence* (identity) of each person would be preserved.

Kirk and Chapel didn't regard the android as Korby, though it was unclear in the episode exactly why. There are several possible explanations: (a) the android was non-biological, (b) the android's body was distinct from Korby's original body or (c) Korby did not behave 100% like the old Korby—e.g., he seemed to value biological life less and was willing to sacrifice lives to achieve his grandiose goals. Chapel said, "Everything you've done has proved it isn't you"—meaning *the Roger Korby I knew would never do that*. However, this is not a particularly compelling argument unless you assume that flesh-and-blood people cannot fundamentally change. Social psychologists warn us against this assumption, calling it the "fundamental attribution error"—namely, the assumption that people have permanent traits essential to them (their "character") rather than situationally determined characteristics. A flesh-and-blood person may be kind in one set of circumstances and later (with a change in circumstances) become indifferent to others' lives or well-being. Perhaps this was what happened to Korby; after all, given his astounding discoveries and long isolation, one can imagine the same changes having occurred to him without any transfer to another body, android or otherwise. So, (c) by itself cannot be a sufficient explanation.

Perhaps more relevant is that Korby seemed to *malfunction* slightly after his android body was discovered (he babbled irrelevant words), and an android copy made of Kirk was defective, too. During the creation of the android Kirk, the real Kirk uttered a racial slur against Spock, which was implanted as a reflex in the duplicate (even though the real Kirk would never have referred to Spock as a "half-breed"). This gave the duplicate away to Spock. However, a true psychological duplicate would have inherited Kirk's motivations for the ruse and his attitudes toward Spock; hence, he would not have been prone to behave uncharacteristically by complaining to Spock about his "half-breed interference." That he was so prone showed the duplication to be imperfect. Moreover, unlike Kirk, android-Kirk was at Korby's command. He ultimately had no will of his own.

However, Korby did not pretend the duplicate Kirk *was* Kirk; the process had to be continued, he said, for the *duplication* to become a *transfer*. With a true transfer, *everything* essential to the person would have been in the android's body and would (presumably) no longer have remained in the original biological body.[3] Korby supposedly underwent whatever such a transfer requires, yet the verdict of the episode was summed up in Kirk's words: "Dr. Korby was never here." Why is that?

THEORIES OF PERSONAL IDENTITY

To help address this question, we will consider briefly several theories of personal identity. Each provides an account of what *constitutes* a person.

A primary distinction is whether personal identity requires (1) that some *object* persist through time (e.g., a physical body or non-

[3] Korby said, "By continuing the process, I could have transferred *you*, your very consciousness, into that android. Your soul, if you wish. All of you."

physical soul, conceived of as an object[4]) or (2) that some *pattern* or *process* persist through time (e.g., our experiences *causing* our later memories of them in certain ways, with our memories *resembling* the earlier experiences). Let us call (1) the *object theory* and (2) the *pattern/process theory*. As my example of the latter might suggest, typical proponents of pattern/process theories concentrate on *psychological* patterns and processes—memories, knowledge, personality traits, etc. I will thus refer to this below as the *psychological pattern view*.

There are several types of object theories. One division is whether continuation of (1a) a *physical body* or (1b) a *non-physical soul* is required for personal identity. Furthermore, among those who hold view (1a), some regard *the body as a whole* to be necessary (call this *the bodily view*), whereas others single out only *part* of the body, typically the *brain*, as essential (call this *the brain view*). Theorists of the latter sort would regard a brain transplant to be a *person* transplant, and would allow that a disembodied "brain in a vat" could be *you*.[5]

APPLYING THE THEORIES

To explore how these theories apply, let us start with an episode that illuminates the difference between the bodily and brain views. In "Spock's Brain" (3-1), the *Enterprise* encountered a strange ship. A female alien named Kara beamed aboard the *Enterprise* and stole Spock's brain. She then returned to an underground colony on her planet (Sigma Draconis VII) and connected Spock's brain to the computer that maintained the colony. His brain became the "Controller," i.e., the computer's control center. McCoy placed Spock's body on life-support, but the crew had only twenty-four hours to find and replace the brain before life-support failed.

In this episode, it was unclear exactly who "Spock" was. When

[4] One example of a *non*-object view of the soul would be Aristotle's view (espoused in *De Anima*, "On the Soul") that the soul is the "form" of the body, i.e., the pattern or organization of matter that makes a living, material body what it is. A "soul," in this sense, is no more an object separate from the body than the shape of a statue is something separate from it. Also, in his view a person is not a soul, but a combination of body and soul (matter and form). By contrast, Descartes (*Meditations on First Philosophy*) thought of the soul as a *thing*, the essence of which was pure consciousness, and identified the soul/mind with the person. (There are far too many different concepts of the soul to recount here. For further information, the reader may consult the various entries on the soul in the *Encyclopedia of Religion*, pp. 8530–8571.)

[5] Of course, the brain must be functioning properly.

Kirk discovered that Spock's brain could talk to them through their communicators, he called it "Spock" and treated it as Spock.[6] However, McCoy stated that if the brain was not replaced in twenty-four hours, "Spock will die." The others accepted his description of the situation. Now, if Spock's brain was Spock (as the brain view implies), Spock would not die. In fact, according to Kara, he (i.e., his brain) would live 10,000 years as the "Controller." Only his brainless body would die. On the other hand, if Spock's body as a whole was Spock (as the bodily view implies), then when Spock's brainless body died, *Spock* would die—the situation as Kirk and the others believed it to be.[7] Thus, "Spock's Brain" seems to assume the *bodily* view of personal identity.

Let us return to Roger Korby. The verdict of "What Are Little Girls Made Of?" was that android-Korby was not Korby. Each of the theories we have described can provide some justification for thinking this, although the psychological pattern view (2) leans against it. Certainly, the physical body view (1a) would have that verdict. Korby's body was dead—and no part of it arguably essential to his personhood (e.g., his brain) remained alive—therefore, Korby no longer existed.

By contrast, it is difficult to say exactly what the non-physical soul view (1b) would imply. It is certainly *consistent* with this view to say that transferring psychological *patterns* (memories, knowledge, personality traits, etc.) would not transfer any non-physical *object*, and, since Korby's non-physical "soul" wasn't transferred to the android body, the android was not him. However, this requires that similarity of psychological patterns (the continuance of Korby's memories, knowledge, personality traits, etc. in the android) not even provide *evidence* for sameness of soul. If we allow this, the question arises: how do we know that *our* souls remain the same from moment to moment? For as Hume pointed out,[8] even when we introspect the contents of our own minds, all we are aware of are our constantly changing psychological patterns (memories, sensations, feelings, thoughts, etc.).

---

[6] Kirk said to the brain, "We came to put you back."

[7] In response to Kirk's charge of murder, Kara said indignantly, "The Controller [i.e., Spock's brain] will live for 10,000 years." Kirk replied, "But *Spock* will be dead. His body is dying this minute."

[8] See *A Treatise of Human Nature*, Book 1.4.6 and Appendix.

With others, the case is worse, since we only observe their external behavior. The only way out of this difficulty is simply to assert without proof that each "stream" of consciousness (in our subjective case) or coherent behavioral pattern (in others) corresponds to a single "soul." In any case, it is also *consistent* with view (1b) to say that souls *can* be transferred along with psychological patterns. So, android-Korby *could* have been Korby. Who knows?[9] In sum, without some supplementary thesis about how and to where souls can be transferred, view (1b) implies *nothing* about whether android-Korby was Korby. This is, of course, not very satisfactory. (Things will get worse for view (1b) shortly, when we consider the transporter.)

The psychological pattern view (2) would seem to offer support for the verdict that the android was Korby, since the android had Korby's memories, knowledge, personality traits, etc.—at least, *most* of them. Perhaps (as Chapel and Kirk believed) the psychological differences between android-Korby and human-Korby were too great.[10] Alternatively, perhaps the transfer was simply of the "wrong" sort. To consider a quite different case, if Korby's psychological profile (memories, knowledge, personality traits, etc., as represented in his brain) were recorded in a *book*, bit by bit, and then reproduced hundreds of years later in an android's electronic brain, many people would regard this android as only a psychological *duplicate* of Korby.[11] The android would "remember" everything Korby did, and these "memories" would seem real to him, but they would be *false* memories of things that did not happen to *him*. One explanation for this is that the normal method whereby one's experiences leave "traces" in the brain, which are stored there (uniquely) and then recalled later through a certain biological brain process (today only partially understood), has been replaced by some other process, which seems not to preserve personal identity. This of course raises the question of exactly which ways of preserving and transferring the information in memories *would* preserve personal identity.

[9] Perhaps it could be said that souls can "inhabit" biological human bodies but not android ones. However, it is mysterious, to say the least, why a non-physical entity would have an affinity for some physical objects and not others. Why *couldn't* a non-physical soul inhabit an android body?

[10] Recall Chapel's comment, "Everything you've done has proved it isn't you."

[11] The basic intuition behind this verdict of duplication is if it can be done once, it can be done several times.

To explore these issues further, let us turn to another episode from the first season of *Star Trek*—"The Enemy Within" (1-5). In this episode, a transporter malfunction occurred that created duplicates of everything transferred through it. Interestingly, however, these were not exact duplicates; as Scotty said, they were "opposites." A dog-like alien animal was "split" into a gentle dog and a vicious dog. Similarly, Kirk was "split" into a gentle Kirk and a vicious Kirk. The gentle Kirk lacked "strength of will"; the vicious Kirk was strong-willed but abusive, self-indulgent and destructive. He stole brandy from the sickbay, sexually assaulted his yeoman, Janice Rand, and attacked many others. He was also not fully in rational control of his emotions (e.g., fear), though he could make plans, sometimes cunningly. This Evil Kirk was initially identified as an "impostor," though it was stated later that both Kirks were different sides, or "parts," of Kirk. They were eventually rejoined by re-transportation.

This is a different case than we have hitherto considered. What do the various theories imply about it? First, on the physical body view (1a), *at most* one of the two could be Kirk, since there were two Kirk-bodies. Since they were physically distinct, Good Kirk ≠ Evil Kirk. It then follows that they could not both be Kirk, since Kirk = Good Kirk, Kirk = Evil Kirk and Good Kirk ≠ Evil Kirk is a contradiction (just like a = b, a = c and b ≠ c). The non-physical soul view (1b) concurs with this verdict, insofar as having a non-physical soul is connected with consciousness—each Kirk was a separate consciousness, as separate as any two humans are. Which was Kirk, then? One option is that Good Kirk was Kirk, since he came through the transporter first. The second body created (Evil Kirk) would then be the "duplicate." The psychological pattern theory might support the idea that Good Kirk was "really" Kirk, since it resembled him more closely, psychologically speaking. (Consider the crewmembers' reactions: Good Kirk was regarded as rightfully sitting in the captain's chair, while Evil Kirk was restrained.) However, the episode itself clearly suggested that *neither* was fully Kirk.

An interesting thing about this episode is that it brings out the problematic nature of the transporter, as far as personal identity is concerned. Is using the transporter truly *transportation*, or *death-and-duplication*? There are two things to consider in answering this question: (a) how the transporter is supposed to work, and (b) which theory of personal identity is correct. With regard to (a), does the transporter transfer *matter*—e.g., by converting it to energy and back again—or does it merely send *information about a material pattern* (e.g., the arrangement of atoms in a body), which is used to construct an exact duplicate? In "The Enemy Within," Good Kirk and Evil Kirk had separate bodies—the extra matter must have come from somewhere. It is highly unlikely that the primary mode of operation of the transporter can be changed by a mere malfunction. Thus, this episode suggests that the transporter works not by "sending" matter, but information.[12]

If the transporter sends matter, the physical body view (1a) seems to be the most natural way to make sense of it as a true "transporter."[13] The non-physical soul view (1b) faces too many unanswered questions. Why does the same body always have to have the same soul? How (and why) would a non-physical soul "catch a ride" on a matter-energy beam? On the other hand, if the transporter sends information, then on all but the psychological pattern view (2), *Star Trek*'s transporter is not a "transporter" at all. If the body that results is not the original, but a duplicate, the physical body view (1a) implies it is not the same person. If the body is duplicated but a non-physical soul is the person (1b), how would one know the soul was beamed into the duplicate body? However, according to the psychological pattern view, as long as the memories, knowledge and personality traits are reproduced at the other end, we seem to be on safe ground in claiming that the transporter really *transports*, since *there is no difference between sending information fully describing a pattern and sending the pattern itself.*

Nonetheless, "The Enemy Within" raises a difficulty. Most of the time the transporter does not produce duplicates. The problem with information is that it *can* always be duplicated. Does the mere pos-

---

[12] In other episodes, the opposite is suggested. I will not discuss this issue further, since my focus is on the *philosophy* of the transporter. Physicist Lawrence Krauss provides an excellent discussion of the *physics* of the transporter in Chapter 5 ("Atoms or Bits") of *The Physics of Star Trek*. In his view, "probably no single piece of science fiction technology aboard the *Enterprise* is so utterly implausible."

[13] That said, it is not obvious that converting a body's matter to energy and back again (in the same configuration) would necessarily produce (quantitatively) the same body. Would *melting* a body, recovering the atoms and then recombining them do this? Why is the transporter any different?

sibility that a duplicate *might* be made (even when it is not) undermine its status as a true transporter? Philosopher Robert Nozick[14] has argued that the mere possibility of duplication does not matter. On his view, called the "closest continuer" view, the being closest to the original *is* the original, even if there are some qualitative differences—so long as the resemblance is close enough in the respects that matter. In the normal case, there is only one "closest continuer." Thus, if only one being produced by the transporter closely resembles Kirk (both physically and psychologically), it *is* Kirk. In cases such as "The Enemy Within," where two "Kirks" were produced, the one that most resembled Kirk (assuming some minimal threshold of resemblance) would *be* Kirk. Thus, arguably, in Nozick's view Good Kirk *was* Kirk (with only his "strength of will" impaired).

"Body Switching" and Multiple Personalities

In "Turnabout Intruder" (3-24), Dr. Janice Lester (an old lover of Kirk's) forcibly traded bodies with Kirk, using a machine she found on a planet. This transfer of each person's "life-entity" (as Spock put it) was presented visually by ghostly figures resembling each person's body (Lester and Kirk) switching between the two bodies. Janice Lester's memories, personality and knowledge—in our terms, her various psychological patterns—were then present in Kirk's body, and vice versa. Lester was motivated by hatred of Kirk; he (a man) could become a starship commander, whereas she (a woman) could not. Her obsessive hatred had left her psychologically unstable. This gave her away to Spock and other crewmembers, such as McCoy, who noticed her "emotional instability" and "erratic mental attitudes," even though when McCoy forced her (in Kirk's body) to undergo a physical and psychological examination, she passed. Spock mind-melded with Lester's body and was convinced Kirk was "in" it. The dominant metaphor in the episode is clearly of the body as a "container" for a "life-entity," which seems to be conceived of as a kind of *object* separate from the body—*perhaps* non-physical, though how it could have been transferred by a machine then would be puzzling. Moreover, it seemed to have a kind of *affinity* for its body, since the transfer

[14] See his *Philosophical Explanations*, Chapter 1.

"broke" during a fight (seemingly of its own accord) as the episode reached its climax—Kirk's "life-entity" returned to his body, Lester's to hers. Thus, though what clearly separated and helped the crew to identify Kirk and Lester were their *psychological* characteristics, the episode assumed an object view, as evinced by the term "life-entity."

An equally puzzling episode about body switching is "Return to Tomorrow" (2-20). In this episode, three beings that existed as "pure energy" were found in a hitherto unexplored region of the galaxy. The being first encountered, Sargon, was able to manipulate the *Enterprise* mechanically and was aware of what was in everyone's mind. The ship's instruments could read the "energy" that composed him (though he wasn't identified as a life form). Since this "energy" was physically detectable, it would seemingly have to have been physical; it was even "stored" in globular "receptacles." (Consistent with this, Spock referred to it as "pure energy... matter without form.") He and the other two survivors, Thalassa (Sargon's wife) and Henoch (a former enemy), asked to take over three human bodies (Kirk's, Spock's and Dr. Ann Mulhall's) to build androids into which each would transfer its consciousness. While their bodies were inhabited by the aliens, the crewmembers' three consciousnesses were stored in the globular receptacles (apparently humans are the *same kind* of "energy," only "weaker"). Unknown to Sargon, however, Henoch planned not to "return" Spock's body (androids, he said, are "without feeling") and almost convinced Thalassa to do the same with Mulhall's body. Henoch was thwarted when Sargon, "inhabiting" the *Enterprise*, convinced Henoch that Spock's body was dying. Henoch fled the body, and, as his "energy" supposedly had to be housed in some physical container (a human or android body, a ship or a globular "receptacle"), he went out of existence. Meanwhile, Spock's consciousness was "stored" side-by-side with Nurse Chapel's (in her body) until it could be put back "into" Spock's body.

Notably, throughout "Return to Tomorrow" it was assumed that once Sargon, Thalassa and Henoch transferred their consciousness (i.e., themselves) into androids, that was who the androids would *be*. Unlike "What are Little Girls Made Of?", there was no suggestion that an android body was an impossible "receptacle" for a conscious being. The people involved (both alien and human) had to be "stored" and could be transferred as *bundles of energy* between the various "receptacles." Thus, this episode also leaned toward some sort of *object* view.[15] However, it is an object view distinct from both (1a) and (1b). Each person was identified with "energy," which could be picked up by physical instruments and had other physical effects. Moreover, this "energy" required physical storage, which meant that it was also affected by physical things.[16] Now, although some might think of "energy" as non-material, physicists certainly do not—anything having physical effects must possess physical energy[17] (defined as the ability to do work), and there is no essential distinction between physical energy and mass (recall $E=mc^2$). Thus, the aliens (and we) were supposed to be neither our bodies nor a non-physical soul, but "pure energy... matter without form." This is an interesting concept of a person, though it is foreign to science as we know it, which says the only "energy" our brains need to produce consciousness is that obtained biologically through food!

Conclusion

In this essay, we have explored various theories of personal identity and what they imply about several episodes of the original *Star Trek*. "Spock's Brain" seems to assume a bodily view, and the ubiquitous transporter, if it transfers matter, seems to make the most sense as such when explained using that view. On the other hand, the transporter (if it transfers information) seems to make the most sense as such using the psychological pattern view. Other episodes, such as "Turnabout Intruder" and "Return to Tomorrow," strongly suggest an object view where a person is an object (not necessarily *non-physical*) separate from the body. Thus, there is no one theory at work across the episodes; instead, the series does a great job of illustrating the wide variety of philosophical opinions out there on personal identity. Indeed, it is this sort of richness that explains why the original *Star Trek* has endured and why it will continue to be enjoyed for generations to come.

---

[15] Bundles of energy, e.g., photons, are "objects" in the required sense.

[16] This resembles how Kirk and Lester's "life-entities" were switched by machine.

[17] The alternative is that physical energy appears out of nowhere, violating a fundamental law of physics (conservation of energy).

REFERENCES

Aristotle, *De Anima*. Books II, III. Trans. D.W. Hamlyn London. Oxford University Press, 1968.

Descartes, René. *Meditations on First Philosophy*. Trans. Donald Cress. Indianapolis: Hackett, 1979.

Hume, David. *A Treatise of Human Nature*. Ed. Ernest Mossner. London: Penguin, 1969.

Jones, Lindsay (ed.). *Encyclopedia of Religion*. Farmington Hills, MI: Thomson Gale, 2005.

Krauss, Lawrence. *The Physics of Star Trek*. New York: HarperPerennial, 1996.

Locke, John. *An Essay Concerning Human Understanding*. Ed. J. Yolton. London: Dent, 1961.

Nozick, Robert. *Philosophical Explanations*. Cambridge: Harvard University Press, 1981.

Lyle Zynda received his Ph.D. in philosophy from Princeton University in 1995. After spending a year teaching at Caltech, he took up his current position in the philosophy department at Indiana University South Bend (IUSB), where he is now associate professor. Dr. Zynda specializes in philosophy of science, philosophy of mind, cognitive science, epistemology, metaphysics and logic. He has published articles in internationally renowned journals such as *Synthese, Philosophy of Science* and *Philosophical Studies*. He also periodically teaches a course at IUSB called "Philosophy, Science and Science Fiction."

Don DeBrandt

WHAT HAVE YOU DONE WITH SPOCK'S BRAIN?!?

One of the knocks against the last version of *Star Trek*, the ill-fated *Enterprise*, was that the Vulcans portrayed in that series seemed irrational, emotional and quite unlike the cool cucumbers we so fondly remembered from *The Original Series*. But it *has* been forty years since we first met Spock, and maybe fans' memories aren't quite as good as we'd like to think (after all, Spock smiled quite openly not just in the series pilot, "The Cage," but also as Uhura was teasing him in "Charlie X"—was he really all that restrained?). Don DeBrandt, the hip Canadian SF writer who wrote the biting novels *Steel Driver* and *Timberjak*, looks at what goes on inside Vulcan heads.

> Logic is a little tweeting bird, chirping in a meadow. Logic is a wreath of pretty flowers—which smell *bad*.
>
> —Mr. Spock, "I, Mudd" (2-8)

VULCANS ARE AN IRRATIONAL RACE.

They can't help it. Neo-Beatles haircuts, Frodo ears and Joan Crawford eyebrows aside, this is a culture that holds that emotion should be rigidly held in check while pure, cold logic should be embraced—embraced in a stiff, overly formal hug, like two homophobic brothers-in-law saying goodbye for the first time, but embraced all the same.

This is a philosophy with admirable but unattainable goals. In many ways, feelings represent chaos itself: mercurial and unpredictable, the depth, intensity and complexity of emotions can manifest in an uncountable number of permutations and change from second to second. Anyone who's run into his ex-spouse on the arm of the celebrity he's been stalking while at a Baptist wedding reception for his adopted, transsexual half-sister and his best friend understands what I'm talking about... especially if you're drunk enough, and can remember anything after the first punch was thrown.

Come. Let us *reason* together.

Mr. Spock, the best-known example of his species, is only half-Vulcan, which is probably why he demonstrates a sense of humor—an extremely sarcastic, deadpan sense of humor, but a sense of humor nonetheless. And it could be worse: what if it expressed itself in practical jokes, instead? (This was, in fact, the premise of a sketch once performed by the now-defunct Legend of Bonefish comedy troupe from Vancouver, B.C. You haven't seen a Vulcan until you've seen one, with all due solemnity, slap a "STUN ME" sign on Kirk's back.)

And speaking of practical jokes, I'm convinced Spock's name is the result of a prolonged argument between his parents, the Vulcan Sarek and the human Amanda:

SAREK: Perhaps we could name him Sarin.

AMANDA: That's a nerve gas.

SAREK: Saran?

AMANDA: That's plastic wrap.

SAREK: Saram?

AMANDA: Okay, now you're just changing one letter at a time. Let me add that I'm also not crazy about Sarab, Sarac, Sarad, Saraf or Sarag, all right?

SAREK: Saraj?

AMANDA: Oh, for—I knew I should have married that guy from Andoria. Sure, he looked like a Smurf with a couple of anteaters growing out of his skull, but at least I could talk to him without wanting to rip my own brain out.

SAREK: That would be highly inadvisable, not to mention difficult.

AMANDA: Sigh. If only you weren't so good in the sack.

SAREK: I look forward to pleasuring you again in six point eight nine years.

AMANDA: WHAT?

Which is how the first Vulcan/human hybrid came to be named after a famous Terran baby doctor—partly out of a sense of irony, partly out of sheer spite. I mean, sex every seven years? Sarek's lucky she didn't call their son Sporadik.

The whole *pon farr* thing demonstrates just how faulty the Vulcan system is. It isn't like some Vulcan committee sat down and decided "Sex every seven years—yeah, that sounds about right. It'll give us a lot more time to work on that new Q-tip technology." No, the reason they have sex every seven years is because if they wait any longer, their brains explode. They go crazy, and all their emotions—you know, the ones they claim they don't have?—run rampant.

It's not that Vulcans don't possess emotions, it's that they rigorously suppress them, so much so that they're living in a state of denial. Denial is when you refuse to accept the facts—in other words, the exact opposite of logic. Their whole system is based on a lie... which is too bad, because it might still have worked, if they'd just been honest about it:

SAAVIK: Good morning, Mr. Spock.

SPOCK: Good morning, Lieutenant. I see you've chosen to wear that distressingly tight uniform today.

SAAVIK: Yes. Although you're old enough to be my father, you are still a male with a fully functioning reproductive system. I believe that emphasizing certain aspects of my physique will cause you discomfort, which is payback for the poor performance evaluation you gave me yesterday.

SPOCK: Indeed. A wise choice—completely within protocol, yet with detectable and satisfying results. I am currently feeling desire, guilt, frustration and just a touch of envy.

SAAVIK: Excellent. I look forward to tormenting you for the rest of the day.

Okay, maybe that wouldn't work so great. . . .

The basic flaw in the Vulcan system, though, isn't with emotion—it's with *logic*. Logic itself is deeply flawed, and any system that holds it up as some sort of ultimate answer is inherently unreliable.

Logic is supposed to work like this: Fact A plus Fact B equals Fact

C. Essentially, you gather information, analyze it and come to a conclusion. Nice, neat, simple.

And *wrong*.

The problem is that the universe doesn't work in tidy little increments. Between Fact A and Fact B are a gajillion little sub-facts, all of which may or may not have a bearing on Fact C, and many of which are subject to change in the time it takes to add A to B.

This, however, does not make the problem unsolvable, just very complex. What makes it unsolvable is that many of those sub-facts are not only unknown, but unknowable; they change too rapidly or in undetectable ways. To put it simply, you can't know everything, and without all the data you can't come up with an accurate answer.

Human beings solved this problem neatly with a little invention called assumption:

GRAG: Urr! Jag go in cave, not come out.
GRUNK: Screams come out.
GRAG: Screams sound like Jag.
GRUNK: Maybe bear in cave?
GRAG: Maybe bear eat Jag.
GRUNK: Hmm. Good theory, no proof. Grag should go in cave and verify supposition.
GRAG: Grunk funny. Grag laugh so hard he drop club on Grunk's foot.

Assumptions in logic work like the frog DNA in *Jurassic Park*; they fill in the gaps where data is missing, letting us form an unbroken chain of reasoning (or a dinosaur, I guess). Either way, those froggy bits are not reliable. Whether producing transsexual T. rexes or a dispute among cavemen, assumptions are essentially subjective in nature. They are based not on evidence but on supposition, and what fuels that supposition is not rationality but faith.

I mean faith in the small "f" sense here, the actual emotion as opposed to the religious concept. Perhaps a better word would be *conviction*—again, in an emotional as opposed to prison-record definition. Convictions are the set of beliefs we hold that we don't question, the ones that let us function on a day-to-day basis. Things like:

gravity will continue to work, the food we eat isn't poisonous, cars will stop for a red light. None of these things—even gravity—is guaranteed; they're simply things that have always worked a particular way, and we assume that they always will. It's necessary for us to hold these beliefs, because we couldn't function otherwise—you can't question every event in your life.

DUDE: Hey, how's it going?
OTHER DUDE: How's *what* going? Where's it going *to*, and where's it coming *from*? What *is* it, *why* do you want to know and who the hell *are* you, anyway?
DUDE: Just put the bong down, man.

Logic is a system of connecting facts. Facts are supposedly stable—something is true, or it isn't. Facts are the particles of logic, if you will, the solid matter that reason is built of. Assumptions are the connecting fabric between them, much less solid and therefore more flexible. They can change, make new connections, alter our very way of thinking.

And unlike facts, they're not based on objective reality. They're subjective, and closer to a wave than a particle—a wave composed of emotion. Call it faith, call it belief, call it conviction—without the bonding of emotion to hold it together, the structure of rationality falls apart.

DUDE: Okay, so if I drop this penny, it'll fall and hit the ground.
OTHER DUDE: You don't *know* that, you only *believe* it. You only know that every other time you've done it, that's what's happened.
DUDE: Why should this time be any different?
OTHER DUDE: Beats me. But just because I don't know doesn't prove a thing—no matter what I think of, I can't possibly be aware of every possibility. Besides, I'm only a fictional representation of a hypothetical argument.
DUDE: Give me that bong.

So logic itself is intrinsically bound up in an irrational process, that of belief. The phrase "leap of faith" is entirely accurate; faith is what allows us to bound from fact to fact, drawing a line of reasoning behind. Feeling is what drives us, with logic in its wake; we are rationalizing beings, not rational ones.

So how did the Vulcans get it so wrong? Well, I'm guessing they had a pretty good reason—an emotional one, of course. They used to be an extremely volatile, warlike race, until something sufficiently culture-altering happened to shake them up.

They met the Klingons.

I mean, nothing will get an alcoholic to an AA meeting quicker than meeting a down-and-out drunk and realizing just how much they have in common. One good look at a culture based on institutionalized mayhem and the Vulcans probably saw the writing on the wall. Being an extremely volatile race, they overreacted, and the emotional equivalent of Prohibition began. (Kinda makes me wonder if, back in the day, there were emotional bootleggers: "*Psst!* Hey, you! Wanna score some primo angst? Guaranteed pure, got it from a mindmelder poet who just broke up with his girlfriend. . . .")

So they went from one extreme to another, which is the real problem. Spock, being a human/Vulcan hybrid, probably had the best chance of showing his people the error of their ways, by integrating logic and emotion—but he went the other way, trying to be some kind of *Über*-Vulcan instead. It took years of friendship with Kirk and Bones before he finally admitted that emotion was, after all, a pretty good thing.

Of course, almost every time Spock let his emotions off their leashes it went badly. In "All Our Yesterdays" (3-23), he traveled back in time, which had the effect of bringing his primitive feelings to the fore; he fell in love, but lost the girl. In "This Side of Paradise" (1-24), an alien spore let him fall in love—with much the same result. In "Amok Time" (2-1), he went through the Vulcan mating cycle, fell in love (well, not really in love—more like psychotic romantic obsession) and wound up almost killing his best friend. No wonder that when a highly contagious disease suppressed the inhibitions of the *Enterprise*'s crew, Spock reacted by bursting into uncontrollable sobs. Poor guy—if I was that unhappy, I'd probably want to suppress my emotions, too.

Vulcan logic is often called a philosophy, but in fact it is modeled after an entirely different system. Suppression of the sex drive, denial of self-evident facts, ritual greetings and periods of solitary meditation . . . sounds like a religion to me. Just look at all the all the ceremonial trappings surrounding the *pon farr* ritual. These are a people so steeped in tradition they'll let a murder take place rather than change. This kind of bloody-minded adherence to a particular set of beliefs crops up again and again in religions, which are essentially an organized set of assumptions driven by faith . . . just like logic.

Okay, so if logic and religion are both actually based on faith, then what about objective truth? Isn't there anything solid and reliable that we can actually point to and say, "This is real, this is verifiable, this is definitely not going to change or vanish or do something unpredictable"?

Beats me. (See "Other Dude" for a more detailed explanation.)

The logic the Vulcans prize so highly is based, more than anything, on wishful thinking. If they behave a certain way, if they insist that the universe follows certain rules, then it *will* follow those rules. They aren't *being* logical—they're trying to *impose* logic on a chaotic world, while denying that chaos affects them. In a sense, this is what every religious and political system tries to do—actually, it's a pretty good definition of civilization itself.

But just because we *want* things to make sense doesn't mean they will. The reason none of these systems ever work quite the way they're supposed to is the denial factor—the idea that if we just ignore certain facts they'll cease to affect us, like Wile E. Coyote running off the edge of a cliff but not falling until he looks down. While this may seem willfully stupid, it's amazing how many human societies function on exactly this level. If enough people all agree to stick their heads in the sand at the same time, they can get away with fooling themselves for a long, long while. People endorse and follow all sorts of creeds, regardless of that creed's flaws, not because the creed is accurate but because it reflects the world the way they wish it was. The part of the brain that produces emotion evolved before the part that thinks—feeling came before thought, and still does.

This dominance of emotion over reason was cleverly portrayed in the episode "This Side of Paradise," where the entire crew was seduced by an alien spore into—well, being happy, essentially. That's it. The spores didn't want to eat their brains, or make them conquer the universe, or anything at all. They just wanted a nice warm frontal lobe to live in—in return for which they produced perfect health and happiness. Sort of like intergalactic Prozac with immortality thrown in.

So how did Kirk react to seeing his best friend finally happy and in love?

"All right, you mutinous, computerized, disloyal half-breed—we'll see about you deserting my ship!"

See, *nobody would do what Kirk said anymore.* This really hacked him off...so much so that he didn't *care* that everyone else was perfectly happy. *He* wasn't, and he was the *captain*, dammit.

"What makes you think you're a man?" he snapped at Spock. "You're an overgrown jackrabbit, an elf with an overactive thyroid."

Remember, this was Kirk talking—not some mirror-universe version, not some evil transporter double. He was supposedly saying these things to make Spock angry, because Kirk had figured out anger killed the spores...but why kill the spores in the first place? Why not just let everyone be *happy*?

"What can you expect from a simpering, devil-eared freak, whose father was a computer and whose mother was an encyclopedia?...a carcass full of memory banks who should be squatting on a *mushroom* instead of passing himself off as a man. You belong in a circus, Spock, not on a starship—right next to the dog-faced boy!"

Boy, Kirk was really on a roll, wasn't he? It should be noted that he never apologized to Spock afterward, either; as far as Kirk was concerned, he hadn't done anything wrong. Destroying what might have been his First Officer's only chance for happiness and love didn't really matter...because once Spock was back to his "old self," everything would be all right. Kirk told himself that—and *believed* it—despite the fact that *he knew full well Spock possessed emotions.*

After all, the "cure" wouldn't have worked without them. Kirk couldn't handle the actual truth, which was that his merciless brutalizing of his best friend would condemn Spock back to the emotionally crippled hell that was his normal existence.

This is why people embrace philosophies that are foolish or contradictory or cruel. They're told the version of the truth they want to hear. In Kirk's case, his notion of duty told him that his crew would be better off serving under him on a Federation starship than living in some idyllic utopia and, true or not, it was what he wanted to believe. Just as Spock never held it against him afterward—because Spock wanted to believe that Kirk was his friend.

Friendship is probably the best example there is of a relationship based on selective belief. The same flaws that we hate in others we forgive in our friends—because we expect them to do the same for us. No one is perfect, and those who hold their friends to rigorous standards have few of them. Vulcans, with their keen intellects, might be expected to have exacting standards indeed... but who did Spock choose as his friend and confidant? James Tiberius Kirk, almost as well known for his womanizing as his cavalier disregard of Starfleet regulations. Logical?

Right.

Spock chose Kirk for the same reason Potsie and Ralph hung around Fonzie—because he was *cool*. When you come right down to it, Vulcans are the geeks of the universe—they're really smart, they get things done, but they can't get a date on a Saturday night. Because all those hot Starfleet babes don't care about how many places you can calculate pi to; they want someone with a fast ship, who solves his problems with a flying dropkick or a phaser set on stun. Sure, the Vulcan nerve pinch is neat, but it's not as dramatic as knocking someone out by hitting them on the back of the neck with both hands clasped together in a single giant fist (a maneuver now taught to all first-year students at Starfleet Academy in the course "Hand-to-Hand 101: How to Kirk Someone Effectively.") Hanging out with Kirk was always unpredictable, but as a general rule beautiful women and adventure abounded.

It might not have been the most logical choice, but it was one guaranteed to produce results that were interesting—*fascinating*, even. Blame it on Spock's irrational side....

The Vulcan one.

Don DeBrandt has been accused of authoring *The Quicksilver Screen*, *Steeldriver*, *Timberjak, V.I.* and the *Angel* novel *Shakedown*, as well as writing two books under the pseudonym Donn Cortez: *The Closer*, a thriller, and *The Man Burns Tonight*, a mystery set at Burning Man. He does not deny these charges. His two current novels are *CSI: Miami–Cult Following* and *CSI: Miami–Riptide*.

Lawrence Watt-Evans

LOST SECRETS OF PRE-WAR HUMAN TECHNOLOGY: SEAT BELTS, CIRCUIT BREAKERS AND MEMORY ALLOCATION

When it came time for Paramount to make the fifth *Star Trek* TV series, the studio was faced with a quandary. *Enterprise* was to be set a century or more before *The Original Series*, meaning the technology had to look more primitive than anything we'd seen aboard Kirk's ship, and yet it also had to appeal to a more sophisticated TV audience, one used to a lot of high-tech razzle-dazzle. But, in fact, as Hugo winner Lawrence Watt-Evans points out in this witty report, a lot of the technology aboard our favorite 1966 starship was out of pace with the times even then.

From: Third Xenopsychologist Gleep
Transmission Analysis Department
Imperial Strategic Defense Directorate

To: First Determiner Quarg
Response Implementation Department
Imperial Strategic Defense Directorate

Re: Discrepancies in human video transmissions

Quarg:

As you know, I did not request this assignment. I had believed it, frankly, to be beneath my talents, and hoped for something in Retrieval & Interrogation. I now see that I was wrong, and that the analysis of these video transmissions may hold the key to understanding human psychology and devising an appropriate response to their expansion into the galaxy. I hereby offer a nuanced apology of the thirty-first category, indicating acknowledgment of an understandable error in interpretation of ambiguous data.

I further proffer self-congratulation of the thirteenth category, indicating belief in a breakthrough in understanding that few could have achieved.

Second Xenopsychologist Zitch has already told you our conclusions regarding why we have so many more transmissions from the humans' twentieth century than we do from any subsequent centuries; I have nothing substantive to add, but feel I should mention that while Zitch has clearly identified for you the major elements in the change, I would place more emphasis on cultural exhaustion and less on the transition to shielded transmission technology during and after the wars. I am prepared to defend this, should you feel it worthy of further discussion.

As for my own assignment, determining how human civilization managed to lose several simple technologies while preserving many far more complex ones, I am pleased to say that I can now safely dismiss Nulb's "random war damage" hypothesis as unfounded, and offer my own conclusions in its stead.

To review, we had noticed that at some point between the many prewar transmissions from twentieth- and twenty-first-century Earth, and the handful of current twenty-third-century transmissions from the human-led Federation, many basic devices have fallen into disuse, apparently forgotten. An early guess that the discrepancy might be sampling error due to our very limited access to twenty-third-century material, all of it from a single series of narratives, was given full consideration but eventually dismissed; while *Star Trek* does not provide a very varied view of life in the Federation, the idea that such technology as seat belts and safety harnesses might have survived elsewhere in human civilization, yet not have been installed on the bridge of humanity's finest starship, is simply ridiculous. No, if human beings still made seat belts, the USS *Enterprise* would have had them. The existing records show crew members being flung from their seats by various impacts on several occasions, and the resources to install improvised seat belts were clearly available; we must conclude that either seat belts were unknown, or there were reasons *not* to install them that outweighed the obvious benefits.

Likewise, the idea that seat belts had been utterly forgotten was hard to credit. Yes, human civilization had been crippled by war, but human history had not been forgotten—even the half-Vulcan, Mr. Spock, knew enough of human history to recognize analogues of ancient Rome and Nazi Germany, and Captain Kirk could quote pre-war documents, such as the preamble to the Constitution of the United States, word-for-word without prompting. Judging by other transmissions, seat belts were ubiquitous for half a century prior to the war; could the concept really have been lost?

Let us leave that question open for a moment while we look at some of the other apparently lost technology.

Circuit breakers, as we know from many horror movies and situation comedies, were devices that would turn off electric currents during power surges, to prevent overloads and subsequent damage. Older transmissions show a more primitive version called "fuses" that required replacement, rather than just resetting, when triggered, but which served the same purpose. The *Enterprise* clearly was not equipped with either sort of device, as instrument consoles regularly overloaded, exploded, spat sparks or burst into flame when the ship was under attack and power surges occurred.

Memory allocation is a technique in computer designs that prevents badly composed instructions from causing complete systems failure by devoting a computer's entire memory to an impossible task. A properly designed computer system will protect its basic functions by refusing to allocate memory beyond a certain limit to any one task, and any reasonably sophisticated system will use multitasking to carry on other operations even while hopelessly struggling with an impossible job in one area. Federation computers, however—and oddly, the computers of certain other civilizations the *Enterprise* encounters—cannot do this, even when they are otherwise so advanced as to appear nearly sentient. They can be rendered completely impotent by such simple tasks as calculating the exact value of an irrational number, or resolving straightforward binary paradoxes. In some cases the computers clearly lack not just circuit breakers or fuses, but any sort of internal cooling or regulation whatsoever, and will overheat and destroy themselves when overtaxed.

There is no evidence that most pre-war computers were so poorly designed—well, apart from those operated by megalomaniacs bent on world conquest, which did seem to have a tendency to explode spectacularly when the megalomaniac's plans were disrupted, but that appears to have been due to deliberate booby-traps rather than faulty design. Computers used by ordinary citizens of the final decade or two of the twentieth century appear to have had reasonably sensible operating systems that used memory allocation properly.

In yet another example of seemingly inexplicable backwardness, medical prosthetics in the Federation appear to be relatively primitive compared to their pre-war peak; the motorized wheelchair and life-support system used by Captain Christopher Pike, with its rudimentary flashing-light communications system, appears noticeably inferior to devices seen on pre-war medical dramas. This, despite Dr. McCoy's description of twentieth-century medicine as crude and barbaric.

The horrible scarring on Captain Pike's face also seems inconsistent with the cosmetic surgery available on pre-war make-over shows, but we must acknowledge that refusing skin repair may have been a deliberate choice on his part, rather than an indication that such surgery was unavailable.

There were other Federation technologies that were noticeably *different* from its pre-war equivalents, such as the communicator's limited functionality compared to a reasonably advanced cellphone, but that does not indicate anything was actually *lost*. The communicators may have been designed to emphasize ruggedness and efficient use of its power supply, at the cost of frivolous extras.

Still, even allowing for any reasonable differences in emphasis it's plain that, despite possessing warp drive, transporters, replicators, phasers and innumerable other advances on the technology of the twentieth or early twenty-first century, the Federation had lost several basic safety devices and some medical technology. How could this happen?

Let us consider for a moment another field of technology in which the Federation was, if no worse than pre-war humanity, not noticeably advanced. I refer to biotechnology and genetic engineering. Yes, the Federation could produce high-yielding grains such as quadrotriticale, but they did little or no experimentation with the human genome. Why? Because such research was banned, absolutely forbidden. It's not that they didn't know it was possible; it was that they wouldn't allow it. Why? Because the Eugenics Wars, in which genetically engineered superhumans led by Khan Noonian Singh attempted to conquer Earth, devastated vast areas and slaughtered millions. This led—understandably, to anyone who has studied humans—to widespread distrust of genetic engineering.

And not long after the wars, humanity discovered warp drive and began encountering other civilizations.

And this is where I found my insight, which I believe rather remarkable, as my category thirteen self-congratulation indicates. Human beings launched themselves out into the galaxy and confronted dozens of alien civilizations, many of them far more technologically sophisticated than their own, immediately after defeating a budding culture of artificial beings more genetically advanced than themselves. They emphatically did not want to repeat that experience, but realistically, they surely knew they might find themselves in conflict with some of these older, more advanced cultures. They needed to find some way to build themselves up quickly, before this potential threat became real.

They did not want to rely too heavily on technological assistance; they knew that could fail them.

They did not trust artificial intelligences; their culture had a long tradition of stories about robots and computers rebelling against their creators.

They could not improve themselves through genetic manipulation; the Eugenics Wars had shown them how easily that could go wrong.

That left the humans of the immediate post-war period no option but to somehow accelerate the natural evolution of the species, adapting it to survive in the harsh rough-and-tumble of interstellar existence. They had, in the two centuries prior to the wars, come to a reasonable understanding of natural selection as the chief mechanism of evolution, and they saw what had to be done—they had to increase selection pressure on their own species, and force themselves to become tougher, stronger, smarter, faster, more fit—*without* using any artificial methods, but simply by allowing their own species to be culled by their environment.

Surely, this is not something a sane and healthy culture could ever do—but humans were *not* a sane and healthy culture at that point. They had just come through the massive trauma of a world-wrecking war, followed almost immediately by contact with various alien species; they were in shock—a species-wide state of post-traumatic stress. So they did something that seems almost incredible when we look at the risk-averse pre-war culture—they outlawed safety equipment and applied the same suppression methods to the entire field of safety engineering that they had applied to genetic engineering.

It's the only sensible explanation.

The result is the USS *Enterprise* we see—no seat belts, no circuit breakers, no fail safes, no redundant systems, no emergency heat, no emergency oxygen, no backups, no spacesuit lockers on every deck, no backup transporter. The obvious possibility of using the transporter for medical purposes or to replace lost members of the crew from the recording in the signal buffer is never considered. Initial contacts and surface exploration are regularly carried out by unprotected crew members rather than by robots or tele-operated probes—in fact, the senior officers, the most valuable members of the crew, are frequently and pointlessly risked in landing parties. Safety has not just been compromised, it's been actively avoided.

But the crew has been taught to fight hand-to-hand, has been trained to jerry-rig the most sophisticated equipment should it be damaged, has memorized everything from political documents to the exact proportions for making effective gunpowder.

Why? Because these people are being tested. Only the fittest are to survive—only those who can save themselves from any threat without the aid of prepared safety equipment.

I believe that this, the core of my work, is inarguable. Somewhat more speculative is my hypothesis that red shirts are used to indicate those crew members not considered prime breeding stock and who may therefore be risked freely in dangerous situations.

And speaking of breeding stock, it is clear that Captain Kirk sees it as his duty to do his best to spread his genes throughout the galaxy. He never misses an opportunity to make the acquaintance of an attractive female of his own species, or any species sufficiently similar. In this, he is simply doing his part as an example of the best the human race has to offer.

Consider also the Federation's Prime Directive: noninterference. This is obviously a defensive measure, designed to avoid bringing humanity's existence to the attention of any species that might become a potential threat and to avoid giving any such species technology that might later be turned against the Federation.

Consider also that although this is a multi-species alliance, we see a ship crewed by hundreds of humans and one Vulcan half-breed. Obviously, the other species in the Federation do not share the human obsession with forcing natural selection, and prefer not to serve on these human-built deathtraps. Spock's presence is not as readily explained, but perhaps he is testing the viability of human/Vulcan hybrids—should he survive and flourish, then further interspecies pairings would be encouraged. A berth in a Vulcan vessel, which presumably *would* have seat belts and circuit breakers, would be insufficiently challenging.

But one might ask—if humanity is sufficiently convinced of the inevitability of all-out interstellar war that they have suppressed the very concept of safety engineering, then why are they part of a grand alliance at all, and not cowering in xenophobic terror in their own little empire?

Because they are not stupid. Their alliance is less vulnerable than a humans-only empire would be. Common sense dictates that any species that can be brought into peaceful cooperation, should be. The old proverb, shared by many species, that the best way to destroy an enemy is to make him a friend, is the very basis of the Federation and human attempts at making every contact as peaceful as possible. By cooperating with the Vulcans, Andorians and others, they hope to remove any possible threat those species might pose. It's not some utopian dream of peaceful cooperation that has prompted the Federation, but the perceived need for defense—the Federation serves the same purpose as a street gang.

That may seem unkind, but observe that while the Federation speaks of equality and justice, what we actually *see* of it is often harsh and unfair—brutal prison colonies using agonizing brainwashing techniques, mining colonies on unbelievably inhospitable planets and so on. These are presumably designed to weed out the unfit as surely as does service in Starfleet.

And while preaching equality, the Federation does not allow human females to serve as starship captains. Is this because females of sufficient merit for the post are too valuable as breeding stock back on Earth? We see women serving on starships, true, but these are women who have not yet proven themselves, often wearing the red attire of the genetically expendable; women who distinguish themselves sufficiently to a degree that, in a male, would warrant a command position are presumably shipped back to Earth to begin procreating.

But then why *preach* equality and justice? Surely any reasonably intelligent human must recognize the stark facts of the evolutionary struggle.

But no, they preach equality and community because the point of the exercise is to strengthen humanity enough that it can survive confrontations with hostile civilizations, and that means that the entire species must be united and cooperative, ready to stand together against any external foe. Presumably human beings who have successfully reproduced *do* live lives of comfort, in a just and fair society.

But those who have not yet produced offspring are deliberately put at risk, and subjected to the harshest possible conditions.

Thus we see that the *Enterprise*'s five-year mission is a survival test for its crew, a part of humanity's drive to improve its gene pool without the use of genetic engineering—but then note that in the chronicles of that mission we see another species that probably uses even *less* safety equipment than humans.

I refer, of course, to the Klingons.

It's immediately obvious why Kirk hates the Klingons; these are exactly the sort of beings that humans expect to fight eventually in a genocidal war—that they have been preparing to fight since first contact.

And for their part, the Klingons see the Federation as a threat. The two are natural enemies because they are so very alike in many ways, competing for the same evolutionary niche. They have, in fact, resorted to many of the same methods of toughening up their respective species to meet the challenge of a hostile galaxy. Both have foregone basic safety equipment, and send their young males out on long, potentially suicidal voyages of exploration.

The Klingons, however, have chosen a warrior society, where they compete against one another as well as against the environment—an option the humans deliberately avoided—and one reason for the intensity of the conflict between the two groups may well be the fear on each side that the other's method may be more effective as a survival strategy. Neither species was willing to risk all-out war until certain of a clear advantage; a narrow victory would have been fatal, as other powers (such as the Romulans) would surely have descended like vultures upon the weakened survivor. Only a quick, decisive victory would have been worth having—thus the all-out war never happened, and in the end the Klingon warrior culture proved less fit, causing the accidental destruction of their homeworld's moon and bringing down the Empire as a serious power.

Notice that we have received a glimpse of an alternate reality in which humanity chose the internal-competition route, with promotion by assassination, and that that culture does not appear to be as successful as the cooperation-based version.

Let us not be deceived by the pretense of gentleness in the Federation; the Klingons mistook that pretense for weakness and wound up as little more than vassals to the humans. As Captain Kirk says when putting an end to the war between Eminiar and Vendikar, humans acknowledge that they are killers—they simply choose when, where and how the killing will be done. These humans are people who deliberately send their young adults out into space without safety equipment and with reckless rules of engagement, in full expectation that loss of life will be heavy, but that those who return alive to breed will be the strong, the fit, the crafty—people who can survive being flung from a chair, who are not fazed by sparking, flaming instrument panels, who can talk a balky computer into suicide, who can walk unafraid and unprotected onto the open surface of an alien planet and come home unscathed.

Determiner Quarg, I hope you will see that my conclusions are required by the evidence—the elimination of safety equipment can only be a deliberate choice, and it must surely be motivated by a determination to accelerate natural selection.

I am but a xenopsychologist; it is up to you to determine how to deal with humans now that I have given you my best understanding of their motivations.

I would advise you, though, not to anger them.

Lawrence Watt-Evans is the author of some three dozen novels and over a hundred short stories, mostly in the fields of fantasy, science fiction and horror. He won the Hugo award for short story in 1988 for "Why I Left Harry's All-Night Hamburgers," served as president of the Horror Writers Association from 1994 to 1996, treasurer of SFWA from 2003 to 2004 and lives in Maryland. He has two kids in college and shares his home with Chanel, the obligatory writer's cat.

Robert A. Metzger

EXAGGERATE WITH EXTREME PREJUDICE

It's often said that the heart and soul of the *Enterprise* were embodied in the big three: Kirk, Spock and McCoy. But maybe we're overlooking someone equally important—and if we tell you that Robert A. Metzger writes for geek magazine *Wired* and is the author of two of the hardest hard-SF novels of recent years, *CUSP* and the Nebula nominee *Picoverse*, perhaps you can guess who he might suggest as the real driving force aboard NCC-1701...no bloody A, B, C or D!

WHO IS THE MOST CRITICALLY important member of the *Star Trek* crew?

While the answer should be obvious, you'd be amazed at just how many people come up with the wrong answer, many naming Kirk or Spock without giving the question any real thought. To really answer this question, it needs to be personalized a bit—you have to put your own skin on the line.

Let me rephrase.

Imagine you are a member of a Federation negotiating team being sent to Rigel XII to hammer out the details of a dilithium trade pact with the local miners. You are not the head of the team, but a technical advisor, knowledgeable in dilithium crystal defects and able to point the way to the mines with the very best crystals. The mission is high priority, so the *Enterprise* has been shanghaied by the Powers-That-Be to transport you and the rest of the team to Rigel XII, the ship's high-warp capabilities making it the only vessel in the quadrant capable of getting you there in time. The question should now be put to you—if only a *single* member of the core Enterprise team could accompany you on what should be a boring transport mission, just who would you most want to see along for the ride?

Now it's personal.

Would you pick Captain Kirk? It should take less than a moment's reflection to realize that he would be the *last* member of the crew you'd want along. All you want to do is get to Rigel XII, but if Captain Kirk is seated on the bridge you know the prospect of arriving on time is slim to none. Without a doubt, a distress call will be received, an anomalous burst of radiation will be detected, an unknown entity will be beamed into the ship or the entire crew (including you) will be transformed into cubes when the ship is taken over by a group of aliens from another galaxy looking for a ride home.

There is no question that Captain Kirk exhibits a wide range of talents, but none more powerful than his ability to attract trouble. With a bit of luck, Kirk won't be with you on the Rigel XII run but instead away on some secret mission in search of cloaking devices on the wrong side of the Romulan Neutral Zone.

So how about Spock?

This might seem to be the *logical* choice. Spock understands what it is to complete a mission, to focus all of his immense mental powers on the problem at hand and get the job done. Unfortunately there is one major problem when it comes to trusting Spock with your well-being. Just beneath Spock's cool, logical exterior boils a maelstrom of writhing emotions—and anything can release them.

Spock's emotions can be unleashed after exposure to spores, traveling back in time, viewing certain alien races or even as a result of his own biochemistry—God help you if he's sitting in the captain's chair when *pon farr* strikes and he goes into heat. No, Spock's potential emotional outbursts simply make him too unstable.

Dr. Leonard McCoy? Be serious. If you need your brain reintegrated with your nervous system, a plague serum synthesized from moss and mud or a rather grumpy individual to stand around the bridge and needle the crew with sarcastic barbs, then McCoy is your man. But to sit in the captain's chair? To expect him to be able to make a decision as to whether to fire a photon torpedo or to shift power to the fore or aft shielding is just asking for disaster. As McCoy would no doubt tell you—for God's sake, he's a doctor, not a cab driver.

So whom do we have left?

The individual you should have picked at the get-go, the only member of *Enterprise*'s senior staff that I would ever trust, is none other than Chief Engineer Montgomery Scott. Think about it. This is the man who is responsible for the warp drives, the deflector shields, the transporters, the computers and the replicators; he practically sleeps in the Jeffries tube. If the waste system aboard the *Enterprise* becomes quantum entangled with the storage vats of a Vulcan sludge transport carrying *le-matya* scat, and every toilet aboard the *Enterprise* starts spewing the noxious cat waste, whom are you going to call? Montgomery Scott will be to your quarters with a hyperdimensional wrench in hand before Kirk can finish signing logs for Yeoman Rand, before Spock can stop crying as he dredges up his childhood memory of the tragic death of his *le-matya* and before McCoy can tell you that he's "a doctor, not a plumber."

Scotty is the go-to guy.

And this is because he's an engineer. Engineers have two very remarkable abilities—they can make things work, and they know how to lie to those in command. The first attribute is obviously a good thing. If I'm going to be transported up from some mudball of a planet during an ion storm, I want Scotty at the controls of the transporter. He can play the graphic equalizer control board of that machine like Bach banging at a piano keyboard; he has the *feel* for machinery.

But what about his ability to lie?

Perhaps lie is too strong a word. How about exaggerate with extreme prejudice?

I've been an engineer for better than twenty years. While it's true that I've never actually been on a starship, attempted to alter the matter/antimatter mix of a warp drive while under power or tweaked shield harmonics so that an away crew can be beamed up from Tycho IV while the *Enterprise* is still able to deflect incoming photon torpedoes, I've performed the one task that *every* engineer faces, whether mass producing wing nuts or calibrating tricorders.

Engineers make projections.

From personal experience, this is how it goes. A section head makes a visit to the lab, where I stand before a big, hulking sprawl of stainless steel and vacuum pumps. My job is to use that machine to grow synthetic crystals of various semiconductor materials, one atomic layer at a time, onto a substrate—a process called epitaxial growth. In the vernacular of my job, the final products that come out of my machine are called "wafers." This is the first step in a several hundred step process that will eventually spit out a high-frequency integrated circuit destined to fly in a satellite due to be launched in thirty-six months. The name of the division, of the company and of the satellite will remain unnamed in order to protect the innocent (me). The viability of this $300 million satellite depends solely on the performance of this critical high-frequency chip, which in turn depends on my ability to place a whole spectrum of atoms in just the correct atomic locations as I grow the epitaxial layer.

Management has a strategy—they always do.

The more wafers I can produce, the more integrated circuits will be generated at the end of the production line, which in turn will increase the odds of fabricating one that meets the obscenely impossible operating specifications that some office-bound design geek in a distant division has specified. Management's strategy centers around the premise that the more wafers I can produce, the greater the odds of finding the golden integrated circuit.

Being a good engineer, having worked on numerous programs in the past and not having gotten fired for missing production quotas, I know what has to be done. I have honed the ability to exaggerate with extreme prejudice to razor perfection.

The section head asks me how many wafers my machine can produce a week. This is an extremely complex question, requiring me to consider hundreds of machine and physics parameters, yield statistics, raw material inventories, technician hours and program budgets. But I don't actually have to run those numbers, because I know *my* machine; I have an empathic connection with it in the same way that Scotty knows *his* warp engines.

If I stroke my machine and whisper affectionately to it, making sure that no one else puts their clumsy hands on it, I can squeeze out forty wafers a week.

Of course I don't tell this to the section head.

I spend several minutes telling my section head the gruesome details of how my machine can implode, melt, fry its electronics, blow its vacuum, become contaminated, crunch substrates, have its bearings seize and get its transfer arms warped if it is stressed in the least.

I then go to my notebook and appear to check a long list of figures before going to the computer and grimacing as I run my finger along some complex lines that have popped up on the screen. I scribble a few things on a piece of paper and then slowly walk back to the section head, being sure to maintain a properly furrowed brow.

I hand the paper to the section head.

"What's this?" he asks.

I've handed him a list of $300,000 worth of gizmos that I want to strap onto my machine in order to improve its efficiency. Being a good engineer, I know that such money is never available during normal budget projection periods, but can often be *found* during a program crunch.

"This is the bare minimum of funds I will need in order to get the machine to the specs that will be needed to meet the program requirements," I say. This is my first exaggeration with extreme prejudice. My machine could grow the needed wafers that very day without any improvement. But my section head does not know this.

The section head's expression is that of someone who just took a bite from a two-week-old egg-salad sandwich. He scratches his head and tells me that he doubts upper management will be able to scrape up even $200,000, much less $300,000. I just shrug and remind him that this is a $300 million program.

He slowly nods.

Then I give him the *bad* news. *If nothing goes wrong,* I tell him (every engineer worth his socket set will preface a prediction with that clause), I can deliver three wafers a week.

He groans.

How did I arrive at that number?

It was not overly complex.

The other three programs I'm providing for will eat ten wafers a week, leaving me with thirty more I could potentially produce.

Knowing my machine, six wafers a week will be toasted somewhere along the process, meaning that I have twenty-four that should be production worthy.

And this is where the calculation becomes tricky.

There are three levels of management between me and the program office. So this is how it works. I tell my section head I can produce three wafers a week. He will tell the department head that if he puts the screws to me he can probably get me to generate five per week, at which point the department head will stomp about and tell him that is totally unacceptable—they will need six wafers a week. But to throw me a bone she will not only provide the capital budget I ask for, but increase it to $400,000. She then goes to the lab manager and informs him of the six wafers that can be generated, all at the cost of $750,000 in capital expense (the additional $350,000 going to operating expenses at the department level).

The lab director screams, a sound which represents the opening volley of negotiations. By the time the smoke clears, nine wafers a week have been promised and $1.2 million will be provided. The lab director drives over to the satellite division to inform the program manager of the wafer status. The program manager then pretends to have a heart attack on hearing the news, requiring the placing of a pill (actually a breath mint) under his tongue and the downing of a slug of cold water brought in by the secretary. Negotiations then proceed. It is finally agreed that ten wafers will be delivered a week and the program director will pitch in $1.5 million.

Hands are shaken.

Each level of management takes its cut of funding, and about a week later I am informed by my section head that, due to his utter brilliance as a negotiator, I will be receiving $600,000 in funding and will have to deliver ten wafers.

I tell him that will be impossible.

He reminds me that he has provided twice the additional funding that I asked. I remind him that the $300,000 was going to get him three wafers a week, so that $600,000 will at best get him only six wafers a week. After intense negotiations he gives me an additional $300,000, money that he will pull back from the funds that had been skimmed by him and the department head, if I deliver eleven wafers a week.

Deal done.

Now remember that I know I can deliver twenty-four wafers a week at no added expense. But being the extraordinary engineer that I am, I have to deliver less than half that number of wafers and get $900,000 for new gizmos to strap onto the machine.

Of course, I will actually deliver thirteen wafers a week and be deemed a hero.

Now I'm a good engineer, but Scotty is the best engineer in Starfleet. He knows exactly how the game is played and never forgets that those who sit in the cozy command center, having coffee brought to them by blond yeomen in miniskirts, are no different than the upper management found in any company. And just as I discovered, the only way to get noticed, to be a hero, to be deemed a great engineer, is to come through for upper management during the crisis.

But upper management needs to be cultivated—taught their lessons.

And Scotty knows just how to do it.

During the big battle, when the *Enterprise* is outnumbered by attacking Romulan or Klingon vessels and those in command are being bounced about from the left to the right and then from the right to the left, with several even falling out of their chairs, you know that Mr. Scott is going to call up to the bridge. Is he going to tell the captain that the shields are operating remarkably well and that the *Enterprise* can take the pounding for several more hours?

Of course not.

"Captain, the aft shields are failing. One more direct hit and we'll be blown to bits," Scotty will report.

At that moment, Captain Kirk is about to do something brilliant—either pull a tricky maneuver that will forever be referred to as the Kirk-gambit or spring a psychological trap to befuddle the enemy. But in order to pull off this piece of command magic, those shields will have to hold for at least another ten seconds.

"Reroute power to those aft shields, Mr. Scott," barks Captain Kirk. "Do whatever has to be done to keep those shields up!"

"Aye, Captain," Mr. Scott replies stoically.

And by God, those shields do hold, enabling Kirk and Spock to again save the *Enterprise*. But we all know who really saved the day—

Scotty and his ability to hold those shields together by sheer force of engineering will. Well, that and the fact he held back enough power in reserves to operate another entire starship.

Scotty knows just how to play every situation.

He's never informed the captain during a high-speed chase that he could probably squeeze another point-five out of the warp engines. No way. Those engines are always on the verge of buckling during the big chase. And would Scotty ever inform the captain at a critical moment that the dilithium crystals are in great shape, that more matter/antimatter could be poured through them and the energy created could be coupled into the tractor beam in order to deflect that rogue asteroid from crashing into a planet? Of course not. At the drop of a phaser Scotty will be happy to tell you that the dilithium crystals are about to shatter. Of course he's not about to mention anything about that drawer full of spare dilithium crystals he has hidden away in his desk, right behind all those bottles of Romulan brandy.

And then there is the Jeffries tube.

The *Enterprise* is big enough to haul a crew of over 400 people, but was designed in such a way that all critical engineering elements must pass through the walls of a tube that a person can barely squeeze into. Only an ingenious and brave engineer would dare attempt a journey into the Jeffries tube, especially as the *Enterprise* is being buffeted about by some evil alien power and the slightest misstep in the tube would get you fried.

Step back for a minute.

Just who do you think designed the Jeffries tube in the first place?

Engineers, of course. So why would they cram so many critical systems in such an inaccessible, dangerous place? You now know the reason why, and if you suspect that the Jeffries tube does little more than offer access to the ship's microwave oven network, you're right.

So it's obvious that Scotty knows just how to play the engineering game.

And nowhere is this more apparent than with the transporters.

The first thing to notice about the transporters is that no one actually explains how they work. This is a critical element in any engineering design. The fewer people who understand them, the less that is expected of them, and the less apt people are to complain when they break down—and of course, only the anointed few of Engineering are allowed to touch them. When something or someone important is going to be transported, it is always Scotty who is at the controls.

So just how do these transporters actually work?

Well, this is what the folks in Engineering claim: the transporter system scans its target, dematerializes it, holds it in a pattern buffer for a moment and then transmits a matter stream out of the buffer and into an annular confinement beam, where it is shot out from an emitter array located on the hull of the ship. Once the matter stream reaches its destination, the annular confinement beam reconstructs the target.

This is what Scotty will tell you.

Of course this explanation is a classic example of exaggeration with extreme prejudice. The crux of the exaggeration lies with the misnomer of referring to what is being transported about as the "matter" stream.

No one in their right mind would ever consider transporting "matter," especially not any engineer worthy of their red uniform. As with so many other things involving the *Enterprise*'s engineering requirements, it comes down to a problem of energy. If you scan and then break down a person into small bits of material (which may be molecules, atoms, neutrons, protons, electrons or even quarks), and then shoot this matter stream down to the surface of the planet, you have a huge energy requirement. The transport system has a range on the order of 40,000 kilometers, and it appears that the transmission of the matter stream across that distance is almost instantaneous—as a person is dematerializing on the *Enterprise*, they are also materializing on the planet's surface. Instantaneous transmission is impossible over a finite distance, unless warp principles are applied and the fabric of space-time is compressed in such a manner that the *Enterprise*-to-planet-surface distance is reduced to zero. We have no evidence of that, as the ship does not shift positions as transporting takes place. This means that the fastest a person can be transported is at the speed of light—the upper speed limit in non-warped space.

(Of course, when the warp engines are engaged and the geometry of space/time is altered, the *Enterprise* can go better than 1,000 times the speed of light, and in later *Trek* series transwarp technologies are investigated in which infinite speeds are attempted, allowing a ship to go anywhere in the universe in zero time. Though this technique is never fully demonstrated by the Federation, one would assume that there are species which can perform it, such as those from the Q-Continuum).

Because of special relativity effects, as an object approaches the speed of light, its mass increases. In fact, if an object moves at the speed of light its mass becomes infinite, and all the energy in the entire universe would be inadequate to budge it. So let's scale back and assume the matter stream is moving at half the speed of light (under those conditions, the relativistic effects on mass only increase it by twenty-five percent, which for this example can be ignored). Most of us are familiar with Einstein's equation relating the rest mass of an object (m) with the energy (E) represented by that mass through the equation $E=mc^2$, where c is the speed of light (and in this case is "squared," so its value is multiplied by itself). This represents the upper energy limit contained in a lump of any mass. However, when dealing with mass moving at less than the speed of light at a velocity, v, it possesses kinetic energy (E_k) which is expressed as $E_k=1/2mv^2$, a form very similar to that of Einstein's equation. If you are transporting a 100-kilogram person in a matter stream moving at half the speed of light, you plug in the numbers and discover that the energy required to do this is around $1x10^{17}$ joules (that would be a one followed by seventeen zeros!).

The joule is probably not an energy unit that you're used to dealing with. To put it in terms that show just what a tremendous amount of energy this represents, $1x10^{17}$ joules is equivalent to the energy liberated by a four-megaton nuclear hydrogen weapon, or about 200 times more than the energy generated by the atomic bomb dropped on Hiroshima. Put another way, it would be equivalent to the total energy conversion of twelve kilograms of antimatter when it comes in contact with matter. And this is to transport just one person.

Imagine what would happen if the annular confinement beam malfunctions and instead of delivering a person, releases a four-megaton explosion. No engineer would ever agree to operate such a dangerous system.

And fortunately for all concerned, the transport system cannot possibly function in this manner, despite what Scotty and the rest of the engineering folks would have you believe. All you have to do is recall what happened in episode five of the first season, "The Enemy Within." In this episode a transporter malfunction generated *two* Captain Kirks (along with two dog-like creatures). This is impossible if we are to believe that transporters utilize "matter" streams, since there would be no additional matter to create that second Kirk or dog creature.

So what does this imply?

The only obvious explanation is that matter is not actually transmitted during the transport. So what is it that gets stored in the pattern buffer and then gets transmitted through the annular confinement beam? Well, the very name used for the pattern buffer should give you a clue—"pattern." Rather than transmitting mass, what is transmitted is pattern, which is just another name for information, in this case referring to the information representing the object being transported.

Why would Scotty exaggerate the energy requirements for the transporter? Remember how engineers operate. Every time someone beams down or is beamed up, Engineering has convinced everyone in command that operation consumes twelve kilograms of antimatter. If that is not actually needed, then Scotty now has twelve *extra* kilograms of antimatter. He's obviously keeping two sets of books, knowing that the day will come when command believes that the antimatter tanks have just about been drained, and, of course, choose that moment to battle a horde of Klingon ships, telling Scotty that he'll just have to find fuel for the warp drives *somewhere*. Fortunately, he'll still have many thousands of kilograms of antimatter in his secret reserve tanks, just as any good engineer would.

While the hoarding of energy is probably the number one thing that engineers like to hide from upper management (equivalent to excess capacity in its many forms—in my case being the true number of wafers I could produce in a week), there is another item that comes in a close second, and that is computing power. Engineers always need newer, bigger and faster computers, with systems typically obsolete by the time they are installed. This would be especially true for use of the transporters.

Consider the fact that the typical human consists of 10^{28} atoms. As we've seen, the transporter does not actually transport matter, but it will need to transport the information that defines the object being transported, whether it is a pile of bulkhead plates or a Lieutenant Commander. This offers another opportunity for a quality engineer like Scotty to exaggerate just a bit. What he will tell you is that during the scanning process not only will each atom need to be precisely located in three dimensions, but that its energy states, bonding configurations, vibrational modes, nearest atomic neighbor interactions and a whole range of other quantum mechanical characteristics will need to be mapped.

And, of course, each atom will have to be mapped multiple times.

The big problem in measuring the quantum characteristics of a particle is that the act of measuring these properties will often change them (this is an artifact of the Heisenberg uncertainty principle). An example of this principle is that the product of the uncertainty in a particle's position and momentum (defined as the product of its mass and velocity) has a lower limit below which you can't make a determination. For example, the more accurately you define a particle's position, the less accurately you can determine its momentum. The engineers in the *Enterprise* will tell you that this limitation will require multiple measurements by different techniques in order to determine a relative probability for each of these quantum states, and all that data is crunched by what are called the Heisenberg compensators. By the time all this is accomplished, a single atom may well have 10,000 attributes assigned to it.

This means that a person is defined by 10^{32} bits.

The *Enterprise* engineers will gleefully rub their hands together when they consider this number, explaining that using state-of-the-art buffer storage technology—in which storage atoms (where each atom holds a data point) are stacked in a three-dimensional, quasi-gaseous state under extreme pressures, and where the atom-to-atom spacing is only ten angstroms (consider that a typical atom-to-atom distance in a solid is about three angstroms, where 10^8 angstroms is a distance of one centimeter)—means that the information to represent a person requires the storage volume of a cube roughly ten meters on a side (or thirty feet on a side).

Huge!

So Engineering always needs more storage space, and faster processors to move all those bits into the annular confinement beam. Now, of course, this is the story that the engineers tell command and budgeting personnel. Like everything else, it is just a "wee bit of an exaggeration," to paraphrase Scotty.

The truth is you don't need to map the quantum states of the atoms in a person's body in order to accurately map the person. For example, the computers on the *Enterprise* are more than sophisticated enough to understand the construction of a liver cell, knowing not only where each and every atom should go, but just where each and every one of those liver cells need to go in order to build a healthy liver.

This is an example of data compression in the extreme.

And if for some reason you have a few abnormal liver cells, they will be replaced by the standard liver cell when your transported body rematerializes—and so much the better for you, since any deviations in a liver cell are either incipient cancer cells or inefficiently operating cells. You can think of a transporter ride as a whole body tune-up.

But what about the brain, you may be asking.

What about the brain?

You have about $1x10^{11}$ neurons, and each of them sends out some $1x10^4$ dendrites to connect to other neurons (the connections are the synapses). This translates into $1x10^{15}$ connections in your head. A great deal of what you are is represented by how those neurons are connected in that tangled mess, the electrical resistance of the dendrites connecting them and the electric field gradients and specific ions in the synaptic clefts. Let's be very generous and suppose that each synapse will be given 100,000 associated data points in order to characterize how a particular synapse is working. You don't need to know where each atom in the synapse is, let alone the quantum states of those atoms. All you need to reproduce is a synapse that operates like the original synapse—100,000 data points should be more than enough to uniquely define the characteristics that describe the electrical and mechanical characteristics for a single synapse.

So your brain, the part of you that makes you who you are, could be described by $1x10^{20}$ bits. As for the rest of you, that liver and all the other associated parts, even if you needed a billion-billion-billion bits to describe it (which you won't by a long margin), this would only come to an additional $1x10^{18}$ bits. If you add those two numbers together, it means that you can be defined by $1.01x10^{20}$ bits. What that number shows you is that defining the body is trivial as compared to defining the brain, and that you can approximate the information requirements by considering only the brain—$1x10^{20}$ bits. Now, if we use the same storage buffer technology where each stored bit of information is encoded onto a single atom with a nearest neighbor spacing of ten angstroms, just how much memory space do we need?

It turns out to be a cube with each side measuring only *half a centimeter*.

But of course Scotty has convinced Kirk that he needs a storage buffer in which each side measures ten meters. The reality is that with a storage buffer ten meters on a side, in which each person's data requires only half a centimeter, Engineering could store eight billion people—more than the current population of Earth.

So information storage is no problem.

The last mystery we come to is that of where exactly the mass of a person goes when they are dematerialized, and where the mass comes from when they rematerialize. That, of course, is the real function of the Heisenberg compensators. When a person is being dematerialized, an atom-by-atom scan is performed. We already know that the more exactly we specify an atom's momentum, the less accurately we can determine its position—this is the core of the entire transport system. As each atom's momentum is determined more and more accurately, its position becomes less and less known, with the spooky nature of quantum mechanics allowing the atom to be in multiple locations at once. The Heisenberg compensators push this to such an extreme, measuring the momentum so perfectly that the location of each atom is spread out over a spherical volume with a radius of 40,000 kilometers (this is the same approach used to achieve transwarp drive, in which the wave-function of an object is spread across the entire universe, then collapsed to the desired destination).

All the transporter operator needs to do is to specify the desired location of these atoms, such as on a planet's surface, and the perfect measurement of each atom's momentum collapses, as the probabilistic nature of the atom is fixed on some point within that 40,000-kilometer sphere.

Transportation completed, the person is reassembled based on the 10^{20} bits in the storage buffer, no H-bomb level energy required and no massive storage volume needed. That's just how simple the transporter really is.

And for the case of those two Kirks, where did the extra mass come from?

As we've learned now, there is nothing really special about the mass used in constructing a person—the Heisenberg compensator just shifts the position of an atom (*any* atom) to the desired location and a person is fabricated. In the case of the second Kirk, the mass came from the waste storage vats beneath the transporter system. (Remember that one of Engineering's many tasks is waste management for the *Enterprise*.) At any given time there is more than enough unwanted mass in the bottom of the storage vats to create any number of extra captains.

But you still may be wondering why one of those Kirks was frightened and weak-willed while the other was a mean-spirited, yeoman-chasing tough guy. There was a transporter malfunction, of course, but not quite the one as detailed in "The Enemy Within."

Engineers love their toys and are always figuring out new ways to play with them. As we've learned, Engineering literally has energy to burn and sufficient storage space to store billions of people. It also has the basic template of every person on the *Enterprise* kept in the storage buffer. Don't shake your heads and tell me that information will degrade in the storage buffer so quickly that you can't keep a copy of a person viable for more than a few minutes (as was done to the Klingons in the seventh episode of season three, "Day of the Dove"). A person's pattern will remain viable for years, even *decades*. But Scotty never lets anyone in command know this, using the buffer's capacity only during a real emergency, such as in the *Next Generation* episode "Relics" (*ST:TNG*, 6-4), when Scotty crash-landed on a Dyson sphere. With no hope of rescue he placed himself in the storage buffer and was rematerialized *seventy-five years later*.

This is undoubtedly one of the many side projects *Enterprise* Engineering was working on. Others obviously included the manipulation of neuron and brain chemistry to alter the personality and abilities of a given person. If a romantic Kirk was needed to woo a female Romulan starship captain, one could be constructed by the transporter. If a brilliant tactician Kirk was needed to figure out how to defeat ten Klingon Birds-of-Prey, with nothing but the ballast blown from *Enterprise*'s waste system, then one of those could be constructed as well. Obviously Scotty's engineering had been experimenting with a whole range of Kirk replacements.

Why?

Because Kirk always insisted on being on that first landing party, the one where one out of five transportees would be killed within the first minute of hitting the planet's surface. The odds are one out of five, and despite the fact that Kirk must have beamed down over a hundred times, he was never killed.

Or so they'd like you to think.

No, Kirk was in fact killed on average during every fifth landing, just as Spock and McCoy were. What Engineering would then do was beam the survivors immediately back up, reconfigure synapses in order to remove the memories of the last few seconds in which a command person was killed and then send them back down to the planet along with a slightly altered version of Kirk—one less likely to get killed again in that situation.

It all makes such perfect sense.

It's what any good engineer would do. If you make sure you've got spare energy, spare shield reserves, spare buffer memory and spare warp performance, you'd naturally want to have at least a few spares of critical personnel.

Scotty is definitely *the* man—without him, Kirk, Spock and Bones would have all been killed well before the first season was half over, and the ship would have been destroyed either by a warp core breach, buckled shields or other-dimensional waste spewing from toilets.

If I'm ever offered that trip on the *Enterprise*, I'm staying close to Scotty.

Robert A. Metzger is a research scientist and a science fiction and science writer. His research focuses on the technique of molecular beam epitaxy, used to grow epitaxial films for high-speed electronics applications. His short fiction has appeared in most major SF magazines, including *Asimov's*, *Fantasy & Science Fiction* and *SF Age*, while his 2002 novel, *Picoverse,* was a Nebula finalist and his most recent novel, *CUSP*, was released by Ace in 2005. His science writing has appeared in *Wired* and *Analog*, and he is a contributing editor to the *Science Fiction Writers of America Bulletin*.

David DeGraff

TO BOLDLY TEACH WHAT NO ONE HAS TAUGHT BEFORE

James Doohan, who portrayed Scotty, used to say that nothing gave him greater joy than meeting scientists and engineers who had chosen their professions because they grew up watching *Star Trek*. Four decades on, *Star Trek* and other works of science fiction still fire the minds of the next generation of scientists and engineers, as Dr. David DeGraff, chair of the department of physics and astronomy at Alfred University, explains.

I DON'T KNOW WHO'S MORE to blame for my being an astronomer, Neil Armstrong or Gene Roddenberry. I remember wearing the astronaut's helmet I got for my sixth birthday as I watched Neil Armstrong step onto the lunar surface. A month later, my grandfather showed me the full moon through his binoculars. I told him I could see the flag sticking out of the side, and when he showed me the landmarks to look for to find the landing site, I was sure I was going to be an astronaut. Then came glasses three years later. I was devastated when I found out you can't be an astronaut if you need glasses. How could anything be better than being an astronaut? Six years later, I turned on the TV after school and there was this gray saucer with two big tubes on the back orbiting an orange, cloudy planet. I was hooked.

Now I'm a professional astronomer teaching physics and astronomy. Since *Star Trek* and science fiction in general played such a big role in my appreciation for the subject, I try to give my students the same feelings of awe and wonder I had watching *Star Trek*.

I discovered *Star Trek* in syndication, so even though this is the fortieth anniversary of the show, it's closer to my personal, thirtieth anniversary with it. It was a time when the U.S. had no space program. Apollo was over and the space shuttle was still years away from launch, but on my TV every day after school, men and women trekked through the galaxy, exploring strange new worlds. Every day there were more stars, more planets to investigate. The galaxy was a frontier with remote scientific outposts, scientists studying long-dead races on alien planets, cosmic mysteries to be solved. There were vastly superior aliens pretending to be gods, superior robots trying to take over people, controlling computers, alternate universes, even time travel. There was a whole universe to explore out there, a universe that could be explored with science. That's what I saw as a young teenager—not the Cold War parallels, so blatant from an adult point of view.

They visited real stars sometimes, stars I could look up in books at the library. Sometimes they weren't real stars, and that took a little longer to discover. Stars weren't just pretty things to see through binoculars or a telescope anymore. No, the stars were destinations. It no longer mattered that my eyesight would keep me from becoming an astronaut: the universe was opening before my eyes. I realized the thrill wasn't the ride up to space, or bouncing on the moon. The thrill was in the exploration, in pushing the frontiers, boldly going where no one had gone before. (And before you give me a hard time about the politically correct *Next Generation* version, there were plenty of women on Kirk's *Enterprise*.)

I remember looking with disappointment at a two-page spread on astronomy in our world atlas. Was that all there was to space? The solar system seemed so limited. The frontiers of science were expanding. There was so much more that I was beginning to learn about. It wasn't like school where I was learning things that everybody knew, old news. I knew there were new discoveries not in that atlas, or any other book. The twin *Viking* probes had landed on Mars. The results were disappointing, but I had a hard time taking my eyes off that *National Geographic* with the full-page color pictures from the dusty, red surface. *Voyagers 1* and *2* were on their way to the gas giants of the outer solar system, just like *Nomad* from "The Changeling" (2-3). A satellite called *Uhuru* had mapped the x-rays coming from space and discovered actual black holes, or at least possible black holes. And black holes really could be used to travel in time, just as in "Tomorrow Is Yesterday" (1-19). I needed to know more about these things.

Then one day in the astronomy section of my ninth grade earth science class, someone asked the teacher about black holes. If black holes don't emit light, then how can we see them? The teacher didn't know, so he called on me to explain. I knew we could only see the gas that fell toward the black hole and got hot enough to emit x-rays. We could see the gas before it reached the hole itself. But I didn't know why the gas got so hot, or why hot gas produced x-rays. If I wanted to know more astronomy, I had to learn more physics.

But as a physics major in college I was back to the old stuff. Old physics. Ideas people had figured out three hundred years ago. Even the course on "Modern Physics" was sixty, seventy, eighty years old. It wasn't as stale as "Modern Philosophy," which was older than any physics, but it was still the physics of my grandfather's generation. Where was the cool physics? Even in grad school at Chapel Hill the courses were still mostly old physics. Astronomy, though, was once again the frontier, and two events brought me back to my old love.

First, in Professor Bruce Carney's "Galactic Structure" course, Bruce frequently walked into class with handouts. "I just generated these with our new data. Let's see what it tells us." It wasn't exactly going where no one had gone before, but very few had seen these results. I was in sight of the final frontier.

The second event was being assigned to teach astronomy labs. I knew how to use a telescope, so they gave me three astronomy sections instead of physics labs. Saturn was out in the evening skies that first semester I taught. Out on the deck above the Moorehead Planetarium, groups of students pointed the tiny, three-inch Questar telescopes at Saturn. Exclamations of wonder popped around me like fireflies on a June evening. "Wow!" from behind me. "Cool!" to my left. "That's not real!" to my right. "That looks like a sticker!" from farther away. (I still hear that one fifteen years later, and I'm still not sure what it means.) Hearing the pure delight in their voices brought back strong memories of my first glimpse of the moon, the moon with the astronauts on it.

It seemed so selfish to keep the wonder to myself. By becoming a teacher, I could be a tour guide to wonder. In my classes, even the traditional ones, I could show how the basic concepts related to the weird ones and how concepts seemingly made up on the spot turned out later to have profound implications. "Secrets of the Universe," I called them.

I'm embarrassed to say that it took me a few years to realize that I could incorporate science fiction. I had already taught a separate "Science in Science Fiction" seminar for the honors program at Alfred University before it dawned on me that I could do the same thing in my astronomy class.

Science fiction can bring the galaxy to life, can inspire the same sense of wonder and awe that *Star Trek* gave me. Fresh science fiction can use ideas from the frontiers of science, or even from the other side of the frontiers, what Charles Sheffield called the "Borderlands of Science." This is where you find the wildest ideas. Ideas that just might be true, but are too far from any real experiment to be verified, too hypothetical to be called theories. And if it might be true, then it's ripe for a science fiction story.

In my classes I mostly use written science fiction, since it isn't hard to find short stories that take known science and use it to speculate about the cosmos. Science fiction makes the abstract concept a real matter of life and death, brings the distant objects closer and makes the future immediate. What does the ocean of Jupiter's moon, Europa, smell like? No textbook will tell you that, but Paul J. McAuley's 1998 novella *Sea Change, With Monsters* will. Jack McDevitt's *Deepsix* (2001) makes a distant event, a close passage of an interloping star through a quiet planetary system, into a looming disaster, and Poul Anderson's *Tau Zero* (1970) makes the end of the universe a pressing problem. Science fiction makes the universe come alive.

The fiction isn't something I just add onto the class. I integrate it into every assignment, trying to get my students to keep the science fictional state of mind. I want to make sure they understand the causes of the seasons, not just memorize a few facts about the solstices and equinoxes, so I shipwreck them on a new planet and give them data showing the times for sunrise, sunset and the altitude of the sun at noon for a 600-day period. The assignment is to figure out the tilt of the planet, the length of the year and when the seasons changed. In another assignment, the warp engines give out beyond even what Scotty could fix. They have to look at data for each of the planets and choose which one they could survive on while waiting for rescue. I don't always shipwreck them in places. Other assignments involve describing the night sky as seen by aliens with infrared or ultraviolet vision, or the sky as seen from a star high above the Milky Way or within a globular cluster. All these assignments are designed to make the students use their knowledge in a new setting to make a prediction about the universe. The science fictional aspects make the assignments more personal and more engaging than a traditional problem.

Sadly, though, *Star Trek* doesn't always exemplify the best science fiction has to offer. While *Star Trek* did bring the universe to life before my eyes, the actual science in the episodes is sometimes superficial and taken out of context. But even this "*Star Trek* science" can be useful—it can be used to teach critical thinking and show the creative side of science. What is wrong with this, and how could you fix it? A colleague of mine, in a Solid-State Physics exam, had a question that read, "Show that dilithium crystals are impossible. Use solid-state theory, not warp theory." I want to show *Star Trek* and science fiction in a positive light, so that's not the approach I generally use, but it is how I learned, and that process helped me become a more critical thinker.

Not that *Star Trek* was totally devoid of good science. On the one hand, when I started building model rockets, I thought the *Enterprise* was all wrong. Shouldn't it be streamlined? A few days later I saw a picture of an Apollo lunar lander mated to the command module, and realized that a ship that was a true space ship, not merely an atmospheric rocket, could be any shape it wanted to be. And the black star in "Tomorrow Is Yesterday" was fantastic. Just a year after the term "black hole" was coined for those ultra-dense objects that warped space and time, *Star Trek* was using them for time travel, traveling back to the 1960s to see how we averted annihilating ourselves in nuclear war. That was fantastic use of ideas from the borderlands of science.

On the other hand, in that very same episode, as the *Enterprise* warped from Earth to slingshot around the sun, we saw dozens of stars drift by. Oh dear. The scale of the galaxy is one of the main concepts I want my students to understand and incorporate into their worldview. The Milky Way is mostly empty. If we shrink the sun down to the size of a beach ball, the solar system easily fits within a small town. How far would the nearest star be? Not in the next town, not in the next county, not even in the next state, but thousands of miles distant. There wouldn't be star whipping by a spaceship, even if it could go warp seven. (An assignment could be, "If those are not stars, what are they?")

Some people say, "It's science *fiction*. You can't expect it to get everything right." Yes I can. Good science fiction does, and *Star Trek* at its best tried to set itself in the real universe. Before *Star Trek* came along, Asimov, Clarke and Heinlein were using real science as a starting point for gripping stories. At about the time *Star Trek* was on the air, Poul Anderson wrote the previously mentioned *Tau Zero*, one of the first science fiction books to use the relatively new Big Bang theory. An arcane, abstract subject of cosmology became, in Anderson's hands, a matter of life and death for the starship crew. The same is true in Robert J. Sawyer's *Starplex* (1996). Early in the novel, a green star shows up. When I first read about this green star, I was disappointed. You can't have a green star. A star's color is determined mostly by its temperature: cool stars, like Betelgeuse in Orion, emit most of their light in the infrared colors, so they have a reddish tint to them. Slightly warmer stars look orange, like Aldebaran in Taurus. Stars like the sun look yellow. The hottest stars, like Rigel, also in Orion, have a slightly bluish hue. Remembering the colors of the rainbow, ROY G BIV, you might expect stars cooler than Rigel but hotter than the sun to appear green, but in those stars all the visible colors have roughly the same intensity, making the star look white instead. So we just don't see stars as looking green. I was an instant Sawyer fan when, two paragraphs after the introduction of the green star, he had one of the characters say green stars can't exist. Sawyer's resolution to the mystery of this green star is a solution to one of the vexing problems facing cosmologists today. Science fiction *can* get it all right.

How much did *Star Trek* really teach me astronomy? I wouldn't have been so completely taken by the subject without *Star Trek*'s influence and the critical thinking it taught me. One way I learned was by looking up the named stars the *Enterprise* visited. While some of the star names were real, they were not the best stars the writers could have used. "This Side of Paradise" (1-24) sticks in my mind, thirty years later, as a particularly egregious example. The planet with the intoxicating spores that made even Spock emotional orbited the star Omicron Ceti. When I found Omicron Ceti in a star guide, I learned it was a variable star with a period of almost one year. In 331 days it changes from a star with roughly the same brightness of the sun to a beast one thousand times brighter. What kind of plants could survive a temperature increase like that? Well, maybe that's why the plants sprayed those spores, to make it through the bright times. But the writers didn't use this aspect of the star to make the planet hostile. They invented bogus berthold rays and had the *Enterprise* visit the colony to see how they were surviving these deadly rays, when they could have used the real properties of an unusual star to craft a much stronger story. Still, I learned from it.

Another example is "The Galileo Seven" (1-16), where Spock and McCoy and Scotty took a shuttle to study a nearby "quasar-like phenomenon." This was so important that the *Enterprise* had a standing order to study all such phenomena. So I was off to the books to learn about quasars. At the time, astronomers knew little about quasars, other than they had a huge redshift—that is, they are moving away from us very fast. If the redshift was similar to the redshift of galaxies, then these quasars were the most distant objects we knew about. They had to be billions of light-years from the Milky Way. There could be no such thing as a nearby quasar. But a quasar-like object, what would that be? The word "quasar" comes from "Quasi-Stellar Radio Source," one of the few times astronomers have resisted acronyms, and refers to objects that appear as ordinary stars in photographs, but coincide with powerful sources of static in the radio frequencies. So a quasar-like phenomenon could be a star that is putting out energy at radio frequencies. You don't have to be Spock to think that a phenomenon like that would be worth investigating. Only it had nothing to do with the rest of the episode; it was just a convenient excuse to get the crew stranded on a planet. The best science fiction would make the phenomenon somehow relevant to the events on the planet's surface. It was the first I had heard the term "quasar," though.

These were all real objects, things I could look up in books and learn more about. Some of the astronomical objects in *Star Trek* could be used as a jumping-off point for further studies, a space station from which to begin my interstellar journey. However, I never could find anything about the energy barrier at the edge of the galaxy in "Where No Man Has Gone Before" (1-3) and "By Any Other Name" (2-22). I looked for a long time before I decided the pink barrier was just a plot device. The critical question here becomes, "How do we *know* it's not there?" And actually, there is a reason something could be there. It could be a bow shock from the magnetic field of the galaxy plowing through some ambient intergalactic gas, like a wave in front of the bow of a boat. We see this where the magnetic field of the earth collides with the solar wind. *Voyager 1* is just now encountering the shock when the sun's magnetic field runs into the ultra-low density, interstellar gas. A similar mechanism is the source of the radio emission from quasars. So a barrier at the edge of the galaxy isn't as implausible as I first thought. I don't think I'll spend too much time looking for a radio signature of such a phenomenon, but there is a plausible mechanism to explain what the *Enterprise* encountered.

It's easy to find faults, but without *Star Trek*, I would never have become an astronomer. While some of the details of some of the episodes didn't hold up in the light of day, *Star Trek* made the universe a knowable place. Somehow, the idea that the universe, the galaxy, the cosmos, were things I could grasp, real places to be explored rather than mere abstractions, made me want to understand them as much as I could. Thanks to Gene Rodenberry, the infinite silence of empty space wasn't so infinite, so silent or so empty. I hope my students look back on my classes in the same way.

David DeGraff has been a space cadet since he was six years old, watching Neil Armstrong bounce across the lunar surface. No longer a cadet, Dr. DeGraff is now chair of the physics and astronomy department at Alfred University. In addition to the standard physics and astronomy classes, Dr. DeGraff also teaches "Life in the Universe," "Science in Science Fiction," "Living in Space" and "The Theory and Practice of Time Travel."

Adam Roberts

WHO KILLED THE SPACE RACE?

Robert A. Heinlein once famously quipped that only NASA—that is, only a government bureaucracy—could make something as exciting as space travel boring. Hundreds of SF writers, including Heinlein, predicted the first person would walk on the moon in the twentieth century—but no one predicted that the *last* person would do so just three years later. Why did the Space Race come to an end? Why aren't we out there exploring strange new worlds, seeking out new life and new civilizations? British SF writer and academic Adam Roberts scans for the answer.

I'M OLD ENOUGH (just) to remember the sheer excitement of the later Apollo missions. I remember the buzz that went round my school when *Viking* landed on Mars and those first gorgeous pictures of marmalade rocks and tangerine skies were beamed back. But nowadays the Space Race is ancient history. Pundits in the TV studios of the 1960s confidently predicted hotels on the moon by 2000 and interplanetary trade by 2020. Well, that hasn't happened. Re-watching Ron Howard's film *Apollo 13* recently, I was struck by a horrible thought: "Going to the moon," which was something generations of eager SF fans had *looked forward to,* was no longer something in mankind's future. Traveling to other planets is not something we do, and almost certainly won't be something our descendants will do. Instead it is something our *ancestors* did, like building pyramids or hand-gilding editions of the Bible. *Apollo 13* works brilliantly at evoking the *Saturn V* launch and the weightlessness of the astronauts; it works just as well at evoking the cultural milieu of the early 1970s, but we live in a new century now. Heroic space explorers will not walk on other worlds. The most we can hope for now is that a computer chip the size of a cornflake fitted to a thirty-kilo nuclear motor will have the glory of clapping its silicon eyes on the outer planets. It is simply *not the same.*

Now, it is true that we have the International Space Station to look forward to, but the truth is I'm finding it hard to get as excited as I should. Some part of my snide little mind is saying to me: "They are building a small research facility fifty miles away from where I live." That, when you come to think about it, is an awfully "so what?" sort of sentence. I live in London, U.K. Fifty miles away to the West there is the bland commuter town of Reading; to the south, Gatwick airport; to the north you might get to Ipswich. Reading-Gatwick-Ipswich: those are the places that chime in my mind when I think of the International Space Station. Any Brit will confirm that they're not places to set the heart pumping. On the other hand, the current U.S. president (I forget his name, although I think it has a "sh!" in it) has promised us a mission to Mars. That would certainly re-launch the Space Race, and would certainly get me excited if it weren't for one tiny problem: I don't believe him. Do you? I think he made that announcement to help himself win an election, not because he's really prepared to divert trillions of dollars into space exploration.

The truth is that the dream that fuelled the Space Race of the 1960s, the climate out of which *Star Trek* was created, has withered and died. I'm very far from being the only SF author to lament this state of affairs. Stephen Baxter, to drop one name, has a near-obsession with the glories of the old Space Race. His novel *Titan* even resurrects the last great *Saturn V* from its lying-in-state at Cape Canaveral, scrapes off the rust and sends it booming into space again. He applied for (and was turned down for) the space program. But I can't imagine there is an SF author or fan in the West who doesn't share Baxter's obsession to some degree. Personally, I'd happily sell my granny to reignite the dream—assuming I could find a senior-enough member of NASA prepared to take the old lovely in exchange for a place on the next shuttle launch.

The big question we have to answer is: what happened? Why did the Space Race, which we confidently thought was a boldly going Olympic Marathon, turn into a 100-meter sprint and then into a miniaturized slo-mo *Robot Wars*? Who is to blame?

Do you want to know the terrible truth? We are. SF authors and SF fans are. *Star Trek* is. It is the very success and popularity of science fiction itself that finished off the Space Race. There was once a space shuttle called *Enterprise* which spent most of its life sitting on the platform waiting for the clouds to thin out sufficiently to allow a launch, and a goodly portion of that time being wheeled back into its mega-garage because a light drizzle had started up. It looked like an overfed airplane, with Homer Simpson curves and stubby little chicken wings. It was crewed by a few decent, smiling professionals. It flew up a few miles, circled round and flew back down again. Then there was *another* spacecraft called *Enterprise*, crewed by an ethnically diverse mix of charismatic, sexy, passionately overacting humans. This *Enterprise* flew near-instantly to all the most exciting corners of the galaxy, got into edge-of-the-seat dramas, zoomed into and out of danger. It looked—madly, but somehow *rightly*—like a white Frisbee with spread-eagled legs, weirdly insect-like and techno; plausible and yet out-of-this-world. This last thing is, when you think about it, exactly what you want a spaceship to be.

Which would you rather watch? Be honest. SF is too good at what it does. Why should people bother with real space flight when fictional space flight is so much better in every way—more exciting, more engaging, more satisfying (and with a better view)? The idea of traveling to the stars *is* something that touches the souls of most human beings, but why should they invest emotionally and intellectually—and therefore financially—in actual space technology when they can get so much more from fictionalized space flight? It goes even further than this; SF has been so convincing that many people now assume we can zap from planet to planet, from star to star—hence the *X-Files*-ish culture that *just knows* Roswell is full of futuristic spaceships operated by the U.S. government. And what do these spaceships look like? Not like gone-to-seed 747s with withered wings, sitting on their tails, that's for sure. No—they look like the *Millennium Falcon*. Like the fighters from *Independence Day* (woo-hoo!). Like the armor-clad *Defiant* from *Deep Space Nine*.

If all the money invested in SF films over the last thirty years had been given to NASA, we'd have a moon base *and* a Mars base by now. But which would you rather have? A photo of a smiling, bland-faced, ex-USAF pilot standing in a flabby white suit on Mars? Or the two *Stars*, *Trek* and *Wars*, not to mention all the rest?

I have another memory of the real Space Race, one shared by millions. I remember exactly where I was when I heard that the *Challenger* had blown up during its launch. Something important is crystallized by the contradictory emotions experienced by those watching that terrible disaster. On the one hand, it was something appalling and tragic, something that moved many people to tears as it happened. But on another level, the live TV pictures bumped people from one mode of watching to another and gave a guilty undertow to the emotions. The *Challenger* launch was certainly the most memorable and, in a terrible way, the most exciting of all the shuttle launches. This is the case precisely because shuttle launches previous to it were renowned for being so dull, for being always delayed and postponed, and then for providing us, when they finally happened, with a dull repetition of all the other dull launches. What the *Challenger* disaster did was suddenly, momentously, shift modes from the "real" mode of an actual launch to the "SFX" mode of a film. In SF films, spaceships explode all the time and it is exciting. When the *Challenger* exploded, the moment collapsed these two modes of perception. That was one reason why, apart from being so terrible, it was so unsettling. Ever since that moment, culture has striven to separate space travel from SF, to emphasize the dullness and routine-ness of the former in a way that turns people thoroughly off from the reality. At the same time, the Culture Industry has churned out brilliantly realized images of space travel that people turn *on* to in increasing numbers. These pathways continue to diverge and that is the death-knell for real space travel—because if people don't want it then politicians won't spend money providing it. The future isn't real; it is better-looking than that.

I have seen the future and it doesn't work. It produces glittering images of pretend-working instead, and that is what we prefer. *Star Trek*, and its ilk, has been just too good at what it has set out to do.

Adam Roberts has been writing science fiction novels for many years, an activity he combines with being professor of nineteenth-century literature at the University of London. He's very sorry if the "science fiction novel writing" thing has contributed, in howsoever small a degree, to the decline of the actual Space Race. Very sorry indeed. He *had* hoped to be the first professor of nineteenth-century literature on Mars, but that looks increasingly unlikely now.

Melissa Dickinson

Alexander for the Modern Age: How Star Trek's Female Fans Re-invented Romance and Heroic Myth

Star Trek has always had a special relationship with its fans. It was, after all, a letter-writing campaign by fans that saved the show from early cancellation, and it was another such campaign that resulted in the first space shuttle being named *Enterprise*. Given how proactive the show's fans have always been, it's perhaps not surprising that they cheerfully went where no devotees of other programs had ever gone before in creating new fiction about their beloved characters. From the outset it was a controversial practice, in large part because these writers often wrote of romantic liaisons, particularly between Kirk and Spock. Here, Melissa Dickinson, well known in fanfiction circles under a pen name, explores the origins of *slash*.

IF STAR TREK IS THE TELEVISION SHOW that would not die, then Star Trek fanfiction is the life support system, still going strong and showing no signs of fading.

In 1975, Jacqueline Lichtenberg, Sondra Marshak and Joan Winston wrote a book called *Star Trek Lives!* about the life of *Star Trek* after its premature cancellation, and the tremendous cultural phenomenon of Star Trek fandom. The last chapter of this book was an in-depth look at amateur fan-written stories and teleplays based on the show. A fitting choice, as it turned out; thirty years later, it seems that fanfiction will likely prove itself the most long-lived of all forms of fannish expression. Don't believe me? Try Googling "Kirk,"

"Spock" and "fanfiction," and see what happens. I'll give you a hint: if you've never experienced fanfiction ("fanfic" for short), you're about to get an education, and fast.

Then again, if you've never experienced fanfic, you've probably never spent more than five minutes on the Internet.

Star Trek was, from the beginning, much more than a television show. It pioneered prime-time TV in more ways than half a dozen books could fully express, presenting relevant political and social commentary, breaking ground and shaking things up for the whole science fiction genre and galvanizing its millions of viewers to a degree that did not become fully apparent for years after it was canceled. Its vivid and complex ideas, themes and characters seized hold of the imagination in a way that no television show had before, touching so many chords in viewers that, it turns out, forty years of analysis by a host of really smart and insightful people haven't exhausted our discussions about *why*. Why, for thousands of fans, were three years of episodes and six movies not enough? Why did they find it necessary to continue the story—even if it meant writing it themselves?

I would not disagree with those who point to the significance of *Trek*'s idealistic vision of the future, much needed in the volatile political and social climate of the '60s. Nor would I debate the fairly common notion that there are some clear reasons why women science fiction fans of the '60s and early '70s—many of whom held advanced science and engineering degrees—might have connected powerfully with *Star Trek* (and specifically with Spock) as an expression of their own alienation among peers. The latter idea is particularly significant because it was, for the most part, women fans who organized the infamous letter writing campaigns, who published many of the letterzines and who wrote and continue to write the vast majority of the fanfic. Men have traditionally participated in Star Trek fandom in other ways, sometimes very creative ways. But it is a predominantly female art and obsession, this drive to create new *Star Trek* where the original episodes and movies left off. Almost before the show ended, women fans were quietly—and not so quietly—writing their own stories for no other motivation than love, and a powerful need to keep the characters and ideas of *Star Trek* alive.

Fanfic is now an institution as widespread as fandom itself, and literally millions of pages of it exist in thousands of small-run publications known as fanzines (or "zines") and on thousands more Web pages and mailing lists and online archives. Written about everything from *The X-Files* to *Pirates of the Caribbean,* from *Xena: Warrior Princess* to *House, M.D.*, the stories multiply faster than you can say "summer hiatus." But *Star Trek* fans were the first. Why? What was it about *Star Trek* that sparked this particular brush fire? And why, after forty years, is original series fanfic still burning steadily through copier toner and down fiber optic pathways alongside all those newer fandoms, capturing whole new generations of young fans born long after *Star Trek* aired?

Because those who write fanfic defy categorization in terms of age, ethnic background, career, family situation, sexual orientation and nearly every other criterion, it's very difficult to make any kind of generalization about them. The one commonality that's certain and almost certainly significant is the one previously mentioned: with few exceptions, the vast majority of fanfic writers are female. Less clear are the reasons why that's true, though some common threads have been teased out by observation. In particular, women seem to interact with text in a way that is perhaps fundamentally different from the way men do, bringing to it an intimate context that seems to be intrinsically understood by those who read and write fanfic. In this context, fictional characters who are seen to exhibit emotional complexity become somewhat akin to the readers and writers themselves—in other words, the very act of speculating about a character's motivations, needs and desires breathes life into the character and makes them, to a certain extent, *more real* than fictional characters who lack such complexity. This vibrancy creates in the would-be fanfic writer a desire to know more about the characters, to increase her intimate knowledge of them and their world. Exploring new narrative territory with familiar characters is an ideal path to such knowledge, as the fanfic writer can use her own storylines to ask herself how the characters she loves might react, and tease out new depths of their personalities and experiences in ways that the episodic television format rarely permits.

Fanfic also tempts minds that love a puzzle. For many writers, part of fanfic's appeal lies in the challenge of working with the jigsaw pieces that a given show provides, combining them in different and perhaps unexpected ways to make a new picture. The stories resulting from such endeavors often answer *what if?* or *what then?* questions about the show. For example, whatever happened to those pesky Iotians after McCoy left his communicator behind? Where, exactly, did V'Ger go after it joined with Decker and Ilia? What if it encountered the Borg in its travels? What if it *was* the origin of the Borg? Because fanfic writers love the show and know it intimately, because they are emotionally involved with the characters, sometimes these questions can originate from a single unresolved moment onscreen and cover more purely emotional territory. What kind of parents, for example, could create a James Kirk? Why did he never mention them onscreen? Did Uhura ever try to flirt with Spock again after "The Man Trap" (1-1), perhaps with more success? These are but two of the many routes by which fanfic writers approach their unique brand of storytelling, but may provide a glimpse into the different ways fanfic writers relate to the characters they write about.

If it's difficult to neatly and definitively answer the question *why fanfic?* then perhaps we can answer, *why Star Trek?*

Many erudite pages have been written about the fact that, at the most basic level and in the manner of all literary classics, *Star Trek* touched and engaged people because it concerned itself with the big questions. It wasn't afraid to confront us with the greatest philosophical dilemmas of the human condition, nor to force us to examine our own natures by reflecting them back at us in unexpected ways. It didn't give us obvious bad guys for our heroes to triumph against in clear conscience week after week. Instead it introduced us to a wounded mother so desperate to save her children she has learned to kill ("The Devil in the Dark," 1-25); an awkward, painfully isolated boy whose unique abilities and desperation for human contact made him fatally unsuited for society ("Charlie X," 1-2); an alien, enemy starship captain who was us ("Balance of Terror," 1-14). Even more significant for television, it regularly left us with more questions than it answered, often expressed in the nuanced language of some of science fiction's strongest writers. Add to this powerful mix a cast of characters as heroic and heroically flawed, as ambitious and complex and archetypal, as any figures of popular myth, and you get something unprecedented—something legendary, in fact, with all the connotations that implies.

What differentiates a story from a legend? Both can be retold and inspire new creations. But what do you have to do to tell a story that can inspire millions of people and sustain its power for decades, across generations with significantly different cultural experiences? Popular media has offered us many compelling, well-written stories, but I would suggest that what propelled the original *Star Trek* from story into legend, and made it different than anything else that came before it, were two essential qualities. First, it showed us a vision of human achievement so ambitious that we can only just conceive of the possibilities it suggests. This is the romance of *Star Trek* in the original sense of the word; like the legends of Alexander and King Arthur and the *Iliad*, it offered powerful inspiration by suggesting that man is limited only by his ability to envision his reality. Second, at the heart of that vision, it gave us a compelling personal drama that examined the most important questions of every human life: questions of honor, of individual choice, of identity and the search for self, of the hunger to overcome our essential isolation and find acceptance, intimacy, love, meaning. The Arthurian legend compels and moves us because it encompasses all levels of human striving. It's not just about the shining vision of Camelot; it's also about the love and betrayal and grief at the heart of the tale. The *Iliad* is not just about a city that dared to defy all of Greece, but about the honor of one man whose love for his family compelled him to war, and the wrath of another, from whom love was taken.

The original *Star Trek* contains elements of dozens of myths and legends, and the Camelot analogy has been drawn before. But perhaps even more closely, it bears striking parallels to the Alexander romance, written around the third century A.D. One of the earliest prose novels in existence, the semi-fictional story of Alexander turned out to be one of the most successful works in Western literature, eventually told in over twenty-four languages. By the seventeenth century, over eighty versions of the story existed, and within these tales can be found the origins of many of our most popular myths. The echoes of specific key elements of the tale can be found in so many *Star Trek* episodes that one could easily write a book comparing the two, beginning with the basic structural similarity between Alexander's travels in the East and his encounters with fantastical peoples and animals inhabiting distant lands—new life and new civilizations, indeed. In one tale, he discovers the Fountain of Youth, but declines to drink; how well would he have understood Kirk's rejection of paradise in "The Apple" (2-5)? When he faced the giant Porus in single combat, I'm sure he would have been glad to find some bamboo and the makings for gunpowder lying around. (I'll restrain myself from an essay paralleling Bucephalus and the *Enterprise.*)

How many of those echoes were intentional, and how many reflect the simple pervasiveness of those symbols and ideas in the whole genre of romantic adventure, it would be difficult to determine; what's significant is that *Star Trek* appropriated a great number of the most powerful symbolic images and myths available in our literary heritage and wove them together into a new narrative for modern audiences.

But like other great legends, the story of Alexander is more than a story of ambition and grand adventure; it is also a story about a legendary friendship, forged between two great warriors whose loyalty to each other was an example for the Macedonian-Persian troops, and the lynchpin upon which all of Alexander's successes depended. One of the most enduring and powerful elements of the true story of Alexander the Great is his crippling grief and extreme reaction to the sudden death of Hephaistion. We know that Alexander did not long survive the death of his childhood friend and that many of his contemporaries doubted his sanity after that loss because of the extremity of his reaction. He refused to leave Hephaistion's body for over a day and tried to exalt his fallen companion to godhood. In short, he was bereft, and he reacted as a man who had lost the better part of himself.

> The death of Spock is like an open wound. It seems that I have left the noblest part of myself back there, on that newborn planet.
>
> —Kirk, *Star Trek III: The Search for Spock*

So, we come to the heart of the matter. If it was *Star Trek*'s daring vision of humanity's future that engaged the imaginations of millions of viewers, it was the daring vision of personal loyalty, trust, intimacy, celebration of difference and strength through unity shown to us in the characters of Kirk, Spock and McCoy, and to a lesser degree in their companions, that struck the deep emotional chords necessary to compel its fans to pick up pen and keyboard. For the first time, a story with all the essential elements needed to create myth reached a whole generation at once. (If the Alexander romance could have reached twenty million people simultaneously, perhaps it, too, might have inspired tens of thousands of amateur spin-offs, instead of just eighty. Then again, perhaps not—women didn't write for public consumption in the third century A.D.)

I include McCoy here because he is an essential part of the equation, but to much the same degree as Odysseus is essential to the *Iliad*. He is a nuanced and fascinating character in his own right, and the story would be much changed without him, but his primary dramatic strength lies in his role as counterpoint to Kirk and Spock. He is not the star of this particular legend, though certainly a rich enough character to merit his own—as many fanfic writers recognized. But in terms of the vast body of original *Trek* fanfic, it becomes quickly evident that the phenomenon would not exist were it not for the two primary heroic figures of the series: Captain Kirk and, most particularly, Mr. Spock.

Spock is very possibly the single most original creation of Gene Roddenberry's inventive mind, as the staggering audience response to the character proved and continues to prove forty years later. Created as an embodiment of the conflict between human passion and human reason, between compassion and alienation, between civilized peace and animal violence, he is such a powerful, dramatic figure that it's difficult to fully measure his impact. Here was a character whose inner struggle was so vividly portrayed and so universal in theme, how could we fail to identify with him? And how could we not be drawn to his cool demeanor, his self-control, his dry wit, his supreme competence, his intelligence, his mysterious and sometimes superhuman abilities?

A perfect, superhuman being doesn't stay interesting for long, though, as *Star Trek*'s creators knew well, and Spock, we soon learned, had two fatal vulnerabilities. The first was his Vulcan physiology, which would betray him every seven years by sending him into a deadly rut cycle that would strip away all his hard-won self-control before eventually killing him if he did not surrender to its demands. And his second vulnerability, for which he would repeatedly risk his life and even those of his shipmates, was his personal feelings for his captain.

What kind of man must Kirk be, to merit such particular loyalty and devotion from a being of such immense value? *Star Trek* didn't just tell us that these two men were friends, but showed us over and over again how profoundly unified they were in purpose despite their seemingly vast philosophical differences, and how deeply they had come to trust one another's judgment and friendship. It showed us that Spock's weaknesses were Kirk's strengths, and vice versa, so that it became difficult to imagine one without the other. It showed us that Kirk was a man of deep morals and convictions, of personal charm and many talents, worthy of love and respect from a man like Spock. More, it showed us that, to James Kirk, Spock's differences were not something to merit suspicion or mistrust, but rather something of great value, to be respected and defended—to the death, if necessary.

If you read a certain passion in my descriptions above, that is intentional, for it is exactly this kind of emotional response which grabs hold of you and refuses to let you go, which even seventy-nine episodes and six movies cannot satisfy. Certainly, the ideal vision of a future where beings of all colors, genders and talents can coexist in peace and seek knowledge together is an appealing, inspiring one. But it's virtually impossible to imagine fanfic springing fully formed from the heads of a thousand Athenas, without a personal attachment to those exceptional and powerfully compelling characters and their unique story. Despite their differences, despite the inherent dangers and risk of loss associated with the lives they'd chosen, these characters chose to care about each other, to value and respect each other, and, in return, fans cared, too. A lot.

In all those thousands of fan-written Star Trek stories, it is possible to find a great many that don't focus on Kirk and Spock or their particular connection. Whole zines have been devoted to Scotty or McCoy or the Romulan Commander; whole Web sites offer stories about Ensign Chekov or Nurse Chapel or Spock's parents, Sarek and Amanda. Many more center around action-adventure plots or ensemble dramas (or comedies), and some take episodic form, though that is a tradition that does not seem to have persisted into recent decades. Plainly, it was not only the show's stars that demonstrated this depth of character or inspired the fannish need for *more,* but a huge percentage of the great volume of Star Trek fanfic does center around either Kirk or Spock or, more often, the two of them. And for many of Trek's most impassioned and prolific fanfic writers, that relationship was (and is) the key motivator, the primary *raison d'écrire.*

A fanzine published in 1988 prints this letter from a reader:

> Until very recently I was a bookstore casualty. I devoured mainstream [*Star Trek*], searching for every moment of closeness or friendship between our two heroes. I really didn't know what I was looking for specifically, but I knew I wasn't getting it.... About six months ago, I bought my first zine of any kind....I was instantly hooked. After a while, even though some of the stories dealt with a much deeper friendship than I had ever seen before, it wasn't enough....

To those who read or write a particular kind of Star Trek fanfic, this story is so familiar as to be ubiquitous.

Star Trek was full of precedents. The *Enterprise* gave her name to a space shuttle. Captain Kirk and Uhura gave us our first televised interracial kiss. Spock gave us the concept of the Vulcan mind-meld and took the idea of intimacy to a new level.

The meld is a terrible lowering of personal barriers, a deeply personal thing. How could it not be? One touches the other's mind, knows his thoughts, his feelings. More, it requires the physical intimacy of touch, the most sensitive part of the fingers touching the face. There's an undeniably seductive appeal in the idea, too—one that speaks to our deepest need to be understood and loved anyway, to be known without the need for words. What would it feel like, to let someone see your innermost thoughts and feelings and to know that they trusted you that way in return? In the course of the series, Spock melded with Kirk more often than any other, and we can hardly doubt Kirk's statement that he was "closer to the captain than anyone in the universe" ("Turnabout Intruder," 3-24). Even without the mind-meld, we know that there is something unprecedented between them. In "Amok Time" (2-1), Kirk voluntarily risked death to save Spock; later, Spock confessed that his grief at believing Kirk dead was powerful enough to break through a physical state of rut that McCoy himself pronounced fatal. Spock's alienness was an X-factor in the series that time and again crossed the traditional lines of fictional (and real world) male friendships, and introduced something new into the mix...something that defied categorization.

The connection between Kirk and Spock was so unique, so powerful and so difficult to categorize within the bounds of male relationships as our culture recognizes them that Gene Roddenberry himself created a new word to describe it. This word appears in his novelization of *Star Trek: The Motion Picture,* when Spock, at Gol, thinks of Kirk as his *t'hy'la*—a Vulcan word that Roddenberry tells us in a footnote can mean friend, brother or lover. Later in the same book, Roddenberry shows us a Spock so overcome with emotion at seeing Kirk again that he must lock himself in a private alcove as he attempts to master his emotions. Finally, when Spock mind-melds with V'Ger in an attempt to understand how it has achieved such purity of thought, he is ultimately brought to emotional crisis, culminating in an impassioned, intimate moment of confession where he clasps hands with Kirk and admits that without that simple feeling, his life has no meaning.

Is it any wonder that fans who loved these characters, who had been moved time and again by Spock's lifelong struggle to accept his own nature and by the forced isolation of Kirk's choice to command, should find themselves sharing their moment of obvious joy, and understanding implicitly that this moment of intimacy and confession is the most heartfelt and significant connection that either man has experienced? Certainly, we saw nothing close to it in the series, not even between Kirk and Edith Keeler. We can't imagine Spock, in his right mind, holding hands with Nurse Chapel and confessing that he chooses his feelings for her above total logic.

With this movie, *Star Trek* simply reinforced what a great number of fans already knew. It is Kirk that Spock valued more than any other companion, even more than his Vulcan ideals. It is Spock that Kirk could not live without and whose absence created a man who doubted himself and his command, who could not function as the confident starship captain we had seen in the series. While their younger analogs, Decker and Ilia, choose spiritual union over the physical, Kirk and Spock unequivocally choose the more fundamental connection of touch, of simple, human emotion. Spock doesn't name the feeling he's describing. But can we doubt, seeing their faces and the way they hold on to each other, that the emotion is profound?

Now, then, we have all the pieces of the Star Trek fanfic phenomenon: the power and familiar symbology of myth combined with heroic, yet human, archetypal characters about whom much is left unanswered; compelling philosophical and fantastical storylines that stimulate the imagination; the intimate drama of those heroic characters devoted to one another in the face of all dangers, willing to risk their lives, even set aside a lifetime's belief, to affirm their particular connection. Add to that the last ingredient: thousands of female fans deeply invested in that powerful combination, interacting with the original text of the show in their thoughts, identifying with the characters, exploring ideas about their lives and asking that irresistible, perennial question, *what if?*

For these fans, the question was a doorway through which they found they could use a text they loved, that they connected with personally and emotionally, to explore the Romantic aspects of a common mythology in great and immensely creative detail. I use "Romantic" here in the literary sense of Romanticism:

> Its chief emphasis was upon freedom of individual self-expression: sincerity, spontaneity and originality became the new standards in literature, replacing the decorous imitation of classical models favoured by 18th-century neoclassicism. Rejecting the ordered rationality of the Enlightenment as mechanical, impersonal and artificial, the Romantics turned to the emotional directness of personal experience and to the boundlessness of individual imagination and aspiration. Increasingly independent of the declining system of artistocratic patronage, they saw themselves as free spirits expressing their own imaginative truths....[1]

---

[1] Baldick, Chris. *The Concise Oxford Dictionary of Literary Terms*. New York: Oxford University Press, 1991.

This is a description that fits *Star Trek*, and particularly Star Trek fanfiction, most aptly indeed. Individual emotional expression is the key element in the vast majority of fanfic, and "imaginative truths" a resoundingly accurate common thread. The most memorable and popular fanfic stories explore a wide range of themes, but with a heavy emphasis on the emotional, the personal; where the show often ventured into philosophical territory, detouring now and then into straightforward action or science fiction or farce, fanfic is much more likely to concern itself with the emotional lives of the characters. The crises faced by Kirk, Spock and company are likely to be those we face in our own day-to-day lives: crises of identity, intimacy, alienation, sexuality, honesty, selflessness, trust, fear of loss. Writing about familiar characters, rather than ourselves, gives us a common language and an imaginative venue. We choose characters who are larger than life, idealized embodiments of the best of ourselves. In large part, we write specifically for other female fans. To a great degree, when we write and read fanfic, it is our own emotional landscapes we are exploring—and this, perhaps more than any other aspect of fanfic, is what makes this literary phenomenon unique. It may also offer a clue as to why a particular *what if?*, arising from subtextual cues in aired *Star Trek*, sparked an idea that spread so quickly, it became a phenomenon in its own right.

What if the deep emotional bond between Kirk and Spock could transcend all barriers and bring them both the ultimate personal fulfillment that the canon text seemed to perpetually deny them?

For some, the cognitive leap from observing the characters' profound closeness to speculating that Kirk and Spock might in fact be lovers is a very great one indeed. But for many female fans, it proved barely more than a slight tilt of the head or a blink of the eye. And thus *Star Trek* set another precedent, creating the first "slash" fandom—so named for the mark of punctuation that divides the names "Kirk/Spock" to signify the genre. (More commonly, Kirk/Spock fiction is referred to as "K/S" by the large and active subset of fans who read and write it.)

The genesis of this idea dates almost ten years before the release of *Star Trek: The Motion Picture*, likely even before the series was canceled. It circulated underground for a number of years before appearing in zine publications, and for that reason, it is difficult to pinpoint exactly when and where the first K/S story was written. Zine publisher, convention organizer and passionate K/S fan Jenna Sinclair writes,

> It seems that the idea of K/S came from England in the late '60s—when the show was just being canceled in the United States. The concept of Jim Kirk and Spock loving one another and translating that love into a sexual relationship was passed around in the UK through small groups of interested fans for several quiet years. The story "The Ring of Shoshern" was published in the K/S zine *Alien Brothers* in 1987, but the introduction to the story in that zine dates it to 1975. My personal information from contact with the author dates that story several years earlier, to 1968 and possibly slightly before that. (Source: email with the author, who referred to her original dated manuscript.) "Amok Time," the episode that most explicitly deals with Spock's Vulcan sexuality, aired in the U.S. in 1967, so K/S gained life just about as soon as it was possible for it to do so.

Rather ironically, she goes on to note, the first line of the very first printed K/S story is a line of dialogue: "Shut up... we're by no means setting a precedent." On the contrary, as Sinclair observes, the idea eventually permeated many fandoms that followed and continues to affect a great many lives.

The writing and sharing of slash fanfic, though once an extremely exclusive, underground activity, still managed to grow and thrive throughout the decades after *Star Trek* left the air, spreading to other fandoms and finding expression in thousands of fanzines. But its level of visibility virtually exploded with the use of the Internet. Mailing lists, newsgroups, online journals and Web archives served to connect thousands of slash fans who might never have become active participants in fandom on their own. They've also served to make fanfic and slash visible to the general public—so visible that it's become nearly mainstream, and the subject of dozens if not hundreds of news articles, television and radio segments and academic papers.

Nearly all of them, at some point, ask that same perennial question *why?* Why spend countless hours reading and writing homoerotic stories about TV characters for no profit, when you could be inventing your own worlds and characters, reading "real" literature—heck, edging the lawn or scrubbing your bathroom grout, for that matter? What's the motivation? And nearly all slash fans will tell you, journalists and academics seldom get it right. Or at least, they don't tell the whole story.

That's because if it's impossible to answer the *why fanfic?* question, *why slash?* is even more slippery—not because there is no answer, but because just as with fanfic writers in general, for every slash fan in existence, it's almost certain there's a different one, and very likely several. For some, it's a way to explore questions of importance to them, particularly regarding intimate relationships between equals. For others, sexual politics, gender politics, are part of the reason. Erotic fantasy most certainly plays a role, as women often find the idea of two attractive men together as appealing as some men find the reverse. For many K/S fans in particular, the answer to the question is quite simply unimportant, because the premise itself seems to be a logical extrapolation of the Kirk and Spock we saw onscreen. As one slash fan blogged recently in frustration, "So, here's a little 'if: then' for you. *If* your thesis paper on 'why slash' isn't about how slash fans defy any attempt to categorize their reasons for being there, *then* your thesis paper sucks." Eloquently put—though it brings us no closer to understanding why *Star Trek* inspired such a unique fan response in the first place.

I would suggest that it's more enlightening to ask, instead, what K/S was not. If we look at the canon text of the show, and the weekly romantic interests (I hesitate to use the word relationships) it provided for our complex, heroic, flawed characters, it becomes very quickly apparent that they lack two essential things: intimacy and equality. Those same bright, imaginative, educated female fans who identified with Spock, who admired Kirk for his ideals and courage (or vice versa), found it impossible to reconcile their admiration for the characters with the idea that Kirk could seriously fall in love with a pretty, emotionally vacant android in about fifteen minutes, or that Spock would get high on spores, leave his work and abandon his loyalty to Kirk for the vacuous Leila Kalomi, who so plainly didn't get him at all. Such "love interests" didn't match up with any image of ideal intimate partnership they could envision—no more than the relationships in genre romance novels did. Even Edith Keeler, who came closest to representing a true equal for Kirk, was so idealized as to be unsatisfactory. She might as well have been a slum angel Madonna, untouchable and virtuous, hardly a realistic choice for Kirk.

These passionate fans weighed the popular 1960s images of romantic love and found them wanting. Instead, they wanted for Kirk and Spock what they wanted for themselves: an emotional unity based on shared ideals, equality, intimacy and trust. They were busy throwing off the roles that society had tried to impress upon them—why should Kirk and Spock not do the same? K/S writers have seldom felt the need to portray Kirk and Spock as gay men. Rather, the details of physical attraction might be overcome, subverted or simply ignored, because the ideal romance would find beauty wherever it could. What would it matter what you looked like, if someone could see your thoughts and find them beautiful? In that idealized image of true intimacy, appearance—even gender—was secondary. And given those requirements, only one relationship in *Star Trek* fit the bill.

Derivative art enjoys a long and varied history, as does the tradition of shared stories as a language of cultural connection. Writers of the Hellenistic era wrote a good deal of what we might call *Iliad* fanfic, in which much textual and extratextual debate about the nature of the relationship between Achilles and Patroclus ensued. Similar speculation continues today, both in fiction and in scholarly writing, about whether Alexander and Hephaistion were lovers, or only passionate friends. Perhaps the real question we should ask is, why should *Star Trek*, as powerful and complex a mythology as any we have devised in recent centuries, be any different?

Melissa Dickinson is a professional graphic designer and aspiring writer. She and her husband own a consulting company that specializes in custom Web development and intranet business solutions, but they are hoping to shift gears into restaurant ownership very soon. Her *Star Trek* story "Triptych" appeared in *Strange New Worlds, Volume II*.

Paul Levinson

HOW STAR TREK LIBERATED TELEVISION

Paul Levinson is a renowned communications theorist at Fordham University, and he says *Star Trek* started a trend: a new way of presenting episodic television that ultimately led to a complete rethinking of how a TV show might end up being seen, and how it might turn a profit. These days, a movie can do lackluster box-office business and still be a financial success thanks to DVDs, but in the past, no one knew that there were ways other than a single prime time, weekly showing to make a hit out of a TV series—until *Star Trek*, quite accidentally, went where no television program had gone before... into syndication. Of course, it's impossible to say what went on behind the closed doors of network executives, but no one can doubt that *Star Trek* did it first, and the example of the "seventy-nine gems" clearly still looms large in Hollywood.

> Minerva's owl begins its flight only in the gathering dust....
>
> —G. W. F. HEGEL

HEGEL WAS TALKING ABOUT how the greatest writings of the classical world—those that would have the most lasting impact on our popular culture—took shape as the civilizations around them started to decline. He was thinking about Socrates and Plato in Athens, Cicero and the Roman Republic, Augustine and the end of the Empire.

Let's think about *Star Trek* and the decline of network television.

The twenty-first century has not been kind to traditional network television in America. Overall viewership has been falling for more than a decade. The premiere of *The Sopranos* several seasons ago drew more viewers than any program on the networks. A mere handful of millions separates Fox News on cable from network news on free TV. Although the Nielsen ratings in the fall of 2005 show more people watching television than ever before, it's often not the networks they are watching.

It wasn't always so. Television entered the 1970s at the height of the networks' oligarchic power. CBS, NBC and ABC accounted for ninety percent of the prime-time audience back then, which watched television on some 36 million TV sets. This translated into more than 100 million people. In contrast, the four major networks today (ABC, CBS, Fox and NBC) often have trouble attracting more than half that number of viewers in total.

The competition back then was as fierce as it is now. In order to attract the top advertising dollar, networks had to field a reliable thirty-percent share—a consistent third of all network viewers. Programs that achieved less lived on short leashes, regardless of their quality and the passion of their audiences. The original *Star Trek* on NBC was such a program. It was one of the best series I had ever seen on TV. And it was canceled in 1969, after just a three-year run. The reason: its ratings were slipping. Even worse: the majority of its viewers were children and teenagers, not the kind of audience that advertisers were looking for in the 1960s. In those days, kids didn't have much purchasing power. And they spent what they had on products not advertised on prime-time TV.

I was one of those kids (well, I was nineteen when *Star Trek* debuted on NBC TV in 1966). I was furious and heartbroken when it was canceled.

We all know what happened afterward to *Star Trek*. How it first returned in the afterlife of syndication, on local, unimportant stations throughout the country, at midnights on Sunday on Channel 11 in New York City, at after-school hours and other decidedly non-prime-time showings in other cities. How it inspired a following that generated four subsequent television series and ten motion pictures, and propelled *Star Trek* into the popular culture zenith inhabited by the creations of Homer, Shakespeare and Dickens.

This is the story of how that syndication not only launched *Star Trek* into mythic levels in our popular culture, but signaled the beginning of the end for the network domination of television. *Star Trek*'s success in syndication was the first time a television program called the shots in popular culture from a position on the sidelines, off the networks. In doing this, *Star Trek* opened up a cascade of rips and holes in the ABC-CBS-NBC curtain of TV control. From *The Sopranos* to HBO's *Rome*, from MTV to CNN and Fox News, to the Discovery and the Sci-Fi Channels, all that we see on cable today is the result of *Star Trek*'s amazing voyages beyond the networks.

SYNDICATION AND STAR TREK

Syndication before *Star Trek* was an afterthought for viewers. The pleasures it afforded were akin to those you got when you drove a friend's jalopy, or enjoyed food you took home from a fine restaurant the night before.

Other enormously successful reruns had only a fraction of *Star Trek*'s impact. "To the moon, Alice, to the moon!" is no doubt recognizable to countless viewers around the world who have seen *The Honeymooners* in reruns since its CBS prime-time debut on a Saturday evening in 1955. So is the theme music from *Bonanza*. But only one movie has been made of *The Honeymooners*—with Cedric the Entertainer in 2005—and no movies have been made of *Bonanza*.[1] No further series carried forth the story of *The Honeymooners*, and *Bonanza* had one failed "prequel," *The Ponderosa* on cable TV in 2001. *Lost in Space*, on CBS from 1965 through 1968, did manage a movie adaptation, but it and the original series have had little to no effect on our popular culture.

I Love Lucy is the high-water mark of this kind of syndication. The show began filming for CBS in 1951, continued for twenty-three years in one or another version, and soon was syndicated all over America and the world. By 1974, Viacom had 179 syndicated episodes of *Lucy* in the field. In New York City alone, you could see reruns of *Lucy* on three different local TV networks—in fact, twice a day on one of them. Lucy is as hilarious today as she was in the '50s,

[1] There was one TV movie in 1988, *Bonanza: The Next Generation*.

and you can see her in a fair number of old movies, too. But of course there can be no new *Lucy* series, nor are there any sections in bookstores stocked with paperbacks that tell the story of her further or alternate adventures.

What did *Star Trek* have that all these other shows did not? It was not only the storyline. It was the specific way in which *Star Trek* broke into syndication. It fit none of the patterns. It broke all of the molds. Unlike *Lucy* and *Bonanza*, which were huge successes throughout much of their original prime-time runs, *Star Trek* was a ratings disappointment. Indeed, *Lucy* and *Bonanza* were still riding high in prime-time network television during their syndications—which of course far outlived their original lives—but *Star Trek* was dead and all but buried when its syndication began in 1970. Thus its success in syndication was a slap in the face of network television and its ratings logic from the very beginning.

But *Star Trek*'s syndication also came along at just the right time in the history of television.

DIVERSIFICATION OF MEDIA

The history of media shows a very interesting pattern that has repeated itself many times. When new mass media start out, they attempt to please everyone. They create entertainment and report news in a way that is designed to appeal to as many people as possible. They are the most "mass" of mass media at these outsets.

But sooner or later, this changes. The first modern American magazines that rolled off the printing presses in the 1840s were intended for all readers. *Harper's* had something for men, women, children, outdoors types, bookworms—everyone. A hundred years later, a hundred different magazines on newsstands beckoned to fisherman, gardeners, coin collectors, doll collectors, businessmen, housewives and almost every conceivable taste and interest. Radio underwent a similar, if faster, development. Stations in the 1920s and 30s broadcast news, talk, sports, all kinds of music, and soap operas and mystery shows, to boot. By the 1960s, we had stations devoted entirely to rock 'n' roll, country and Western, classical music, or talk.

Television from its inception did everything faster than every other medium. It was in ninety percent of American homes by the end of the 1950s—a decade after its commercial introduction—a record for adoption still not exceeded by personal computers and cell phones.

Although few people realized it, television's sped-up evolution made it ready for diversification by the early 1970s. Certainly the network executives had no idea what was coming. They had pulled the rug out from under Hollywood and the neighborhood movie theater in the 1950s—Hollywood moguls had hugely underestimated the appeal of staying at home and watching TV—and the network execs in turn made the same kind of mistake about cable. They overlooked the public's appetite for specialized choices in TV viewing and how cable could feed it.

Star Trek in syndication provided the first example. It gave viewers something they wanted. If this was not precisely at the times they wanted—which is the great dividend of on-demand TV today—it was still something that some people wanted which the networks had taken away. *Star Trek*'s success in syndication was the first example of the people choosing not what the networks offered, but what the networks had specifically chosen not to offer.

In retrospect, a science fiction show was an ideal vehicle for this maiden voyage.

Although the 1950s is known as the "golden age" of science fiction, the sales of its leading authors, Isaac Asimov, Robert Heinlein and Arthur C. Clarke, were far from golden back then. On television, *Captain Video and His Video Rangers* ran on the third-rate DuMont TV network from 1949 through 1955. Actually, DuMont was fourth-rate—always struggling, limping far behind the big three networks. Tim Brooks and Earle Marsh kindly describe it as "perpetually impoverished" in their 1979 *Complete Directory to Prime-time Network TV Shows*. *Captain Video*'s budget was so pinched that it provided the grand total of $25 per week for props! (That's right—twenty-five dollars. I didn't leave off any zeros.) *The Twilight Zone* had considerably more success in its original thirty-minute format on CBS from 1959-1962, but failed to make the transition to an hour-long show.

Given this ambiguous status of science fiction—the mixed signals it gave to the popular culture of intense fan interest but unreliable mass following—it is entirely understandable that NBC first took a chance with *Star Trek*, and then was quick to cancel it. NBC execs took a chance because they thought they could cash in on the space program and the gleaming new, final frontier of science fiction. But they dropped the show like a hot potato when consistently high ratings failed to materialize, with the failures of the hour-long *Twilight Zone* and other science fiction on television as their guide.

What happened afterward to the networks is also understandable, but only now with the wisdom of hindsight.

THE TIME AND THE PLACE: GUERRILLA TELEVISION

How can TV—how does any medium—cater to a specialized taste? How can it satisfy that appetite in a way that invites the rest of the public to join the party? What is the best time and place for such presentations?

The thing about syndication is that it had no time and place—nothing appointed for everyone at the same time, at least not nationally. It was off or under the radar. It went totally contrary to the mainstream miracle of network television in which everyone in the country, or at least 30 or so million viewers, watched the same show at the same time. In its heyday, network television reveled in everyone arranging calendars and making a point of staying home at a particular time to watch a hit show.

Even locally here in New York City, *Star Trek*'s schedule in syndication was sketchy. It was on midnight on Sunday, but sometimes it was also there on Saturday.

I remember calling my girlfriend Tina, long since my wife. "Did you see 'City on the Edge of Forever' last night? I tuned in in the middle and didn't want to wake you."

"When will be it on again?"

Who knew? Maybe a year, maybe next week, if you took into account the Saturday schedule, but who knew what that was or how long it would be in effect?

The people at Channel 11 presumably knew, though come to think of it, maybe not. I'm sure I saw "The Trouble with Tribbles" at least three times in syndication in one year, and "Spock's Brain" twice ("You'll get nothing more from her, Jim—hers is the mind of a child!"). Where was the sense in that?

It didn't make much sense but that was its charm—and its power.

Marshall McLuhan's celebrated 1960s distinction between "hot" and "cool" media explains part of it. Hot media lay everything out clearly and precisely. But once we get it, hear it, read it—like a newspaper—we have little further interest in it. We already know its stories. We know what to expect. Cool media are more low-profile, ambiguous, imprecise. We therefore can never get enough of them. We can't get our fill because we can never imbibe them completely. *Star Trek*'s banishment from the networks immersed it in a dark, cool pool of our memories. The vagaries of syndication brought it a lot closer—yet still somehow always just a bit beyond our calendar and reach. You couldn't really make a plan or precise appointment with yourself to see it. But you also knew that it was somehow always there, anyway. Like some ubiquitous, invisible being, it was everywhere and nowhere at the same time. Many people worship such beings. *Star Trek*'s fans felt that way about *Star Trek* in syndication. The fact that it was about the coolest thing in the universe—the universe itself, the ultimate ambiguity—only added to its attraction. *Star Trek* in syndication was thus the perfect marriage of medium and content—cool medium presenting cool science fiction "where no man has gone before" content. (*I Love Lucy* and *The Honeymooners* never could have gone there. They made us laugh because we knew their jokes only all too well.)

But *Star Trek* was just one program. And syndication, even galvanized by *Star Trek*, was too old a system, with too much second-hand baggage, to lead an uprising in television. *Star Trek: The Next Generation* and other original programming would certainly make a big impact in off-network programming in the years that followed. But the real revolution that *Star Trek* in syndication had started would take place on cable.

DuMont Avenged!

Ironically, cable was introduced in State College, Pennsylvania, in the 1950s, as a way of providing TV network programming to people beyond broadcast range. The town of State College is located right smack dab in the middle of that wide state, too far from Philadelphia in the east and Pittsburgh in the West to receive their signals via air. But it is a big college community, and the television networks and their advertisers wanted to reach it. The answer was cable. Like FM radio when it was first introduced in the 1940s, cable was thought of as an adjunct, an extra channel, for mainstream broadcasting.

This did not change until the early 1980s, when CNN, MTV and HBO began offering programs not available at all on the networks. This was less than a decade after *Star Trek* in syndication had shown the good sense of providing a program no longer available on network TV. Cable was the brain-child of many people, all of whom were aware of the success of *Star Trek* in syndication. Only a TV exec confined to a planetoid around Alpha Centauri could not have been. But at least one of the great pioneers of cable in the 1980s had a more explicit connection: *Star Trek* reruns had been a big hit on Ted Turner's WTBS television station in Atlanta in the 1970s. He had seen firsthand, in his profit-and-loss columns, that there was not only life but spectacular impact beyond network TV. You need only to hear Darth Vader as the voice of CNN to appreciate how deeply Ted Turner was tuned into science fiction and its power in the real world.

Of course, cable was by no means the only contender tugging at the throne of network TV. When a medium begins to falter, it has no shortage of would-be successors seeking to topple it further. Videotaping technology was also invented in the mid-1950s, and soon replaced the feeble kinescope, which at first was the only way of making copies of television shows. Among the early successes of video was the taping of the 1959 Nixon-Khrushchev "Kitchen" debate for broadcast on NBC. But these Ampex videotape devices were used by the networks to enhance their programming—like cable TV in those days, videotaping was just an adjunct of network TV, not a stand-alone medium—and the taping devices were in any case not available to the general public. An Ampex recorder had a price tag of $45,000 in 1958.

Sony came to the rescue of videotape and television viewers starved for diversity and more control over their television in the mid-1970s—just as *Star Trek* was beginning to make a name for itself in the backwaters of syndicated television. VCRs introduced by Sony were intended for the viewing public, and cost less than one-tenth of the 1958 Ampex. As demand quickened, prices dropped to below $2000 per device. Still no bargain, but affordable to the upper middle classes. Soon VCRs would be in reach of everyone, and become standard gear for television.

When the television networks finally realized what was happening, they were horrified at the prospect. People were watching rented movies rather than prime-time shows on their TV screens. Even worse, viewers could tape a program, play it back and speed past the commercials. So upset were the networks about this possibility that they went all the way to the Supreme Court—in 1984, as cable was first beginning to flex its muscles as an independent medium—in an attempt to make it illegal for viewers to videotape television shows. (So much for corporate network support of the First Amendment when it can hurt their pocketbooks.) The Supreme Court, in a rare display of good judgment about the media in the twentieth-century, wisely decided not to give the networks what they wanted.

Today, TiVo and similar technologies, as well as "on-demand" cable, are making the VCR obsolete, and the networks along with it. V-casts and mobisodes are debuting on cell phones. How much longer commercial television can endure with viewers effortlessly able to delete commercials, or watch programs by subscription on cable and cell phone with no commercials to begin with, is anyone's guess. But the successful assault on network hegemony began in 1970, on the date that *Star Trek* went into syndication.

The feature shared by all of these developments—*Star Trek* in syndication, the rise of cable TV and VCRs, and now TiVo and its siblings—is the assertive viewer, the basic human desire to see and hear our entertainment when we want it, rather than wait passively for a network to dole it out.

The Internet probably has been the least injurious of new media to the traditional television networks. We can look on the Web for additional information about our favorite network shows. And we can "stream" or download a missed episode of a current network series—or simply see one we want to view again. But these very benefits of the Web cater, again, to our hunger for entertainment on *our* schedule rather than someone else's, and in the long run only expose the rigidity and unresponsiveness of traditional network TV to our needs.

The Internet as a medium for first military and then scholarly work goes back to the 1960s. The personal computer as a device at hand for everyday people was introduced in the 1980s and its connection to the Web took wings about a decade later. Once again, the transformation from corporate and administrative to personal satisfaction took place just a few years after *Star Trek* debuted in syndication on Channel 11 in New York City, Ted Turner's WTBS in Atlanta and local stations across America. Coincidence? Well, one could argue that the impulse to satisfy our entertainment needs on our own schedule was so strong, and the networks so inept in fulfilling it, that the revolution would have happened anyway, with or without *Star Trek*. Certainly the technology of cable and the Web, and the daring of innovators like Ted Turner, would have been there anyway. But revolutions need a first shot, a Paul Revere, to signal their onset. And *Star Trek* in syndication provided that.

It is probably also worth noting that David Gerrold, author of the acclaimed "Tribble" episode and one of the editors of this book, also contributed to the digital revolution with a column about personal computing in *Profiles*, a magazine devoted to the Kaypro "CP/M" computer in the 1980s. In fact, so did my friend Rob Sawyer, the other editor of this book. The roots of the revolution fomented by *Star Trek* run wide and deep.

HUMAN-FASHIONED FUTURES

The evolution of television toward greater satisfaction of viewer tastes and choices is no coincidence. Along with the diversification and specialization of mass media, the empowerment of the viewer points to a crucial truth about the human relationship to technology: in the long run and the last analysis, we control our technology and media, not vice versa.

You wouldn't know this given what most critics of media say. Those who pass judgment on our popular culture often depict us as creatures of our media, which increasingly dictate our tastes, schedules and lives. In fact, the liberation of television begun by *Star Trek* shows just the opposite.

It is entirely appropriate that science fiction in general and *Star Trek* in particular led this charge. At its best, science fiction shows human rationality struggling with and triumphing over a chaotic, hostile, dangerous universe. Mainstream media such as the *New York Times* confine most reviews of science fiction to columns on page thirty-eight or the equivalent in which three or four novels are accorded a paragraph or two each of review—almost literally on the margins. This may in fact help science fiction, by keeping it suppressed and edgy, but it misses how science fiction is the quintessential storytelling of our time, uniquely capturing the human connection to the cosmos: our capacity to first know it and then reshape it to our own specifications. (Not only does science fiction get short shrift in the *New York Times*. So does mystery. And romance novels are not reviewed there at all. The genres are apparently too popular to merit the *Times*' attention. If it's not about a dysfunctional Southern family, the "newspaper of record" has little interest in reviewing it. But that's a story for another time.)

More than any program in the history of television, *Star Trek* exemplified these highest ideals of science fiction. Kirk, Spock, McCoy, Scotty, Sulu and the rest were standard-bearers for our human encounter with the cosmos, for the unique mixtures of passion and logic that we bring to our encounters with everything.

Back here on Earth, in the 1960s, the program failed. But its lessons and thrills were far more profound than could be contained in any decade or network. It was and is a story for the centuries and the millennia, and its appropriate medium could therefore never be just network television, or indeed any single means. Its proper vehicle is, instead, every possible kind of communication at hand, which today includes books, television, motion pictures and the Web.

Who back in the 1960s could have predicted such pollination, which broke through network TV like an explosion of dandelion seeds, invigorating half a dozen media and transforming television in the process? Not even Harlan Ellison, author of "City on the Edge of Forever" (in my and many other people's estimation the best script and episode in the original *Star Trek* series), who told the *Washington Post* in 1972 that in his opinion *Star Trek* was "dead."[2]

In those days, after all, gone was pretty well gone on television.

---

[2] Thanks to David Alexander's 1994 biography of Gene Roddenberry—*Star Trek Creator*—for salvaging Ellison's comment from the historical dustbin.

Like an enemy of the state who had been declared a non-person in Orwell's *1984*, with all images expunged from the public record, a television show once canceled was invisible, unattainable. It wasn't like an old book that stayed on the same shelf, in the same library, for years and years. Its exile was far worse than yesterday's newspaper, which you at least could keep around to wrap fish. For that matter, last year's and earlier newspapers were available on microfiche in the library, for anyone who wanted to peruse them.

It was into the pit of such programmed, televised amnesia that NBC and just about everyone assumed *Star Trek* was headed after its cancellation. Instead, when NBC canceled the series, it actually was taking the first big step in canceling itself and the two other networks as the mighty triumvirate that once dictated everything new that we saw on television.

The twenty-first century revolution in media had begun.

Paul Levinson's *The Silk Code* won the 2000 Locus Award for Best First Novel. He has since published *Borrowed Tides* (2001), *The Consciousness Plague* (2002), *The Pixel Eye* (2003) and *The Plot to Save Socrates* (2006). His science fiction and mystery short stories have been nominated for Nebula, Hugo, Edgar and Sturgeon Awards. His eight nonfiction books, including *The Soft Edge* (1997), *Digital McLuhan* (1999), *Realspace* (2003) and *Cellphone* (2004), have been the subject of major articles in the *New York Times, WIRED* and *Christian Science Monitor*, and have been translated into eight languages. He appears on *The O'Reilly Factor*, *The CBS Evening News*, *Scarborough Country* and numerous national and international TV and radio programs. He is professor and chair of communication & media studies at Fordham University in New York City.

Howard Weinstein

BEING BETTER

In 1986, William Shatner appeared in a *Saturday Night Live* skit lampooning Star Trek conventions. He told the show's loyal fans to "get a life," and declared, "For crying out loud, it's just a TV show!" But is it? Or is *Star Trek* something more, something even its brave captain didn't grasp, back then, on the twentieth anniversary of the series? Now, on the fortieth anniversary, even Bill Shatner seems to have recognized that perhaps he was part of something very special indeed. Here, Howard Weinstein, author of the animated *Star Trek* episode "The Pirates of Orion," places *Trek* in its historical context and explains why it was indeed more than just a TV show.

IT'S IRONIC TO BE CELEBRATING *Star Trek's* fortieth anniversary when, for the first time since *Star Trek: The Next Generation* began in 1987, there'll be no new *Trek* TV episodes. Sales of *Trek* books from Simon & Schuster have dwindled. No new movies since 2002, no *Trek* comic books for years. Frankly, *Star Trek's* outlook hasn't been this bleak since the original show's demise in 1969. And even though I come to praise *Star Trek*, not to bury it, it's reasonable to wonder (with apologies to Monty Python): has *Star Trek* passed on? Ceased to be? Expired and gone to meet its maker? Is *Star Trek* an ex-parrot?

Does *Star Trek* have anything relevant left to *say* after forty years?

Star Trek and I go way back. I was twelve when the voyages began on NBC in 1966, and the 1968 book *The Making of Star Trek* (by Stephen Whitfield and Gene Roddenberry) was what got me interested in writing for television. My first pro writing gig was a 1974 script for NBC's animated Saturday morning *Trek* revival. I've been writing *Star Trek* in various media ever since, including six novels, sixty comic-book issues, story-development contributions to *Star Trek IV: The Voyage Home* (my favorite of the movies), articles for *Starlog Magazine* and a *Deep Space Nine* anthology short story. I attended the very first Star Trek convention as a fan in 1972, and I've been a guest speaker at *Trek* conventions every year since 1976.I still recall being a teenager and negotiating with my mother for the right to watch dinnertime *Trek* reruns, and dismissing maternal admonishments that "the world doesn't revolve around *Star Trek*." Not all of it, Mom, but a lot of my life has indeed revolved around *Star Trek*.

I mention this to establish that I've had a long time (and good reason) to ponder and appreciate *Star Trek's* humble beginnings and surprising longevity. Somehow, after barely lasting three TV seasons, nurtured by a ragtag fandom, *Star Trek* puttered along until it found the fast lane, became a dynasty, spanned four decades and spawned enough profitable spinoffs to rewrite the rules of show biz.

In today's cable age, we're accustomed to 24/7 science fiction. But during television's first twenty years, speculative fiction was limited to occasional anthologies (like *The Twilight Zone* and *Outer Limits*), juvenile series (like *Lost in Space*) or low-budget kiddie shows. While science fiction authors had been using the futuristic format to comment on contemporary society in print for decades, Gene Roddenberry did something unique and daring for television.

Had *Star Trek* arrived a few years earlier or later, it might have come and gone without a ripple. Whether through luck, genius or some combination, Roddenberry's space opera reached the right place at the right time. But can a creature of one era adapt for others? Is there a future for the future as *Star Trek* portrayed it? How did it appeal to at least three generations of viewers? Before exploring those questions, we need to remember that the world of 1966 was very different from today's.

Only two decades had passed since World War II, when American and Allied troops literally rescued civilization from evil. For adults (who'd also lived through the Great Depression), memories of a world in flames hadn't faded. For us postwar baby-boom kids, the heroic exploits of WWII were quickly integrated into pop-entertainment, in '60s movies and TV shows (like *Combat, Rat Patrol* and even *Hogan's Heroes*). We kids didn't only play cowboys and Indians, we also played army with toy soldiers and plastic guns—and sometimes with real helmets, canteens and medals brought home by our fathers and uncles as service souvenirs.

In 1966, our main international enemy, fondly known as "godless communism," was embodied by the sinister (though ultimately sclerotic) Soviet Union. Understandably, Americans were a tad jumpy about the threat of global domination by yet another implacable foe. We and the Soviets threatened each other with nuclear annihilation, locked in a dance of death in which no one dared pull the trigger—a strategic doctrine called Mutual Assured Destruction, which formed the appropriately Strangelovian acronym MAD. It was madness, but it actually did help prevent an all-out World War III. Neither side really wanted to start a war no one would be left alive to win.

Guided by moral certitude, America became the self-styled international Defender of All Things Good. But matters on the home front were a little less definitive. For Americans of all walks of life, WWII had opened the floodgates of change. Millions of Americans from different backgrounds, religions—and races—had enlisted or were drafted, and many left their hometowns for the first time, to be thrown together in Uncle Sam's service. For some, these encounters confirmed prejudices; for others, they expanded horizons.

Women went to work in place of the men who went to war. And African Americans from the old South—descendants of slaves liberated less than a century before—headed north in search of factory jobs. Blacks and women learned skills and earned paychecks in realms once reserved for white men. The war had opened up possibilities never before imaginable. All this new social mobility started reshaping America at an unprecedented pace.

Gene Roddenberry lived through those changes. Born in El Paso, Texas, in 1921, he grew up during the Depression, piloted bombers in the war, flew Pan-American airliners from New York to Calcutta, moved to Los Angeles, became an LAPD cop and, finally, became a writer—all by 1951.

By 1961, the Soviets had put the first satellite, dog and human into orbit, while NASA's fledgling test rockets blew up on the launch pad with dismaying regularity. We awoke to the specter of Soviet domination of space and the possibility of enemy ICBMs raining nuclear destruction down from the heavens. American schoolchildren endured not only fire drills but air raid drills, too. Even in first grade, huddled under our desks or against the cool-tiled corridor walls, I wondered how this would help if a bomb hit the building.

But, unlike today, when our feckless leaders react to crises by cutting our taxes and crossing their fingers, President John F. Kennedy responded to the challenge of his era with a call to glory. Summoning our will and skill, setting the goal of reaching the moon by the end of the decade, JFK said: "There is no strife, no prejudice, no national conflict in outer space as yet. Its hazards are hostile to us all. Its conquest deserves the best of all mankind, and its opportunity for peaceful cooperation may never come again. But why, some say, the moon? Why choose this as our goal? And they may well ask, why climb the highest mountain? Why, thirty-five years ago, fly the Atlantic? . . . We choose to go to the moon in this decade and do the other things, not because they are easy, but because they are hard, because that goal will serve to organize and measure the best of our energies and skills, because that challenge is one that we are willing to accept, one we are unwilling to postpone and one which we intend to win."

If you're looking for a blueprint for *Star Trek*, there it is. As Kennedy set our course, Roddenberry was already working on the ideas which would become *Star Trek*. In spite of the MAD-ness, *Star Trek* was energized by can-do optimism, personified by the first president of a new generation, leading a country which had emerged from the ashes of the Depression, won World War II and become the most powerful nation in human history.

Roddenberry also heard Martin Luther King Jr.'s dream, ringing out from Lincoln's memorial on that historic August day in 1963: ". . . One day this nation will rise up and live out the true meaning of its creed: 'We hold these truths to be self-evident: that all men are created equal.'"

And as blacks (and many whites) united to realize the promise of true racial equality, still unfulfilled a century after the Civil War, women also sought equal opportunity. Daughters of the women who'd worked during the war (and waited a hundred and fifty years for the right to vote) wanted more options than an "MRS" degree.

Roddenberry stirred all this idealism into *Star Trek*. The starship *Enterprise*, with its integrated crew of humans (and aliens), flew the flag of the United Federation of Planets, the logical extension of the United States and United Nations. After centuries of strife, Roddenberry's future Earth had evolved into a peaceful world ready to join with other enlightened civilizations scattered through the cosmos.

In order to sell his series, Roddenberry was savvy enough to know he'd have to pitch it in terms any network executive could grasp: *It's* "Wagon Train *to the Stars," with lasers instead of six-guns!* And he loved the idea of using the science fiction format as a prism through which to view humanity's foibles and potential. Reflecting the man who created it, and the life and times of a country poised for greatness, *Star Trek* told morality tales only thinly disguised by their futuristic setting. While the show could be corny and heavy-handed, it regularly encouraged us to think, feel and dream.

Back in the real world, however, early-1960s idealism had a short shelf life. By *Star Trek's* premiere in September 1966, John Kennedy had been assassinated. Decaying inner cities burned during summer race riots. Our military force in Vietnam ballooned into a misled legion of a half million, and Vietnam became the first "living room war." Harrowing footage of combat and death dominated the evening news—in stark contrast to government assurances of "light at the end of tunnel." By the time *Star Trek's* final original episode faded out in June 1969, Martin Luther King Jr. and Robert Kennedy had been murdered, cities were still burning, college campuses and political conventions had exploded with anti-war passion and anarchy seemed a greater threat than the Russians. Yet, in the face of all that, *Star Trek* remained resolute in portraying a better future.

Though Roddenberry didn't write every episode, he had ultimate script approval (for the first two seasons, at least), and he established the humanistic template for the show's other writers to follow. Quite a few stories dealt with a conflict between ideas which have proved frustratingly incompatible: the impulse to enlighten the benighted vs. the desire to be tolerant of alien cultures. Historically, the more technologically advanced societies usually deemed themselves the more worthy, with an unfortunate result: colonial powers force-feeding "modern" values and standards to "primitive" peoples, a process which all too often devolved into subjugation or genocide. By the 1960s, many Americans were ready to face up to the disgraceful degradation white hubris had heaped upon black and native Americans (not to mention various immigrant groups).

Star Trek said there had to be a better way of dealing with difference. Right from the start, it acknowledged that mere mortals don't have the wisdom or the right to interfere with the normal development of other cultures, and mandated noninterference through the Prime Directive. The catch, of course, was one innocuous word—who gets to define *normal*?

As *Trek* fans know, Captain James T. Kirk managed to find numerous justifications for bending the Prime Directive. In many cases, as in "The Apple" (2-5), it was because his ship and crew were endangered by what Kirk regarded as bad decisions by the aliens they'd encountered. Or Kirk would conclude that a planet's status quo was anything but normal and had to be changed for the good of the downtrodden inhabitants. Still other times, Kirk would determine that a planet's normal development had already been altered by outside meddlers (either diabolical aliens, or well-meaning but misguided humans) and he and his crew had to set things straight. Whatever the specifics, *Star Trek* made us think about thorny dilemmas: does might make right? On interpersonal or interplanetary scales, do we have the right to force others to conform to our standards? Are we secure enough to accept diversity as a strength and not a weakness?

As *Star Trek's* second season began in September 1967, American involvement in Vietnam faced growing opposition. The episode "A Private Little War" (2-19), written by Roddenberry, tackled Vietnam head-on. In an odd quirk of timing, this show (shot months earlier) first aired on February 2, 1968—right in the middle of the Tet offensive, when Viet Cong guerrillas and North Vietnamese troops temporarily overran American strongholds in South Vietnam and exposed our tenuous hold over supposedly safe territory.

The *Enterprise* visited a planet where the Klingons had armed one group of primitive villagers with flintlock rifles, unleashing increasing aggression against the hill people led by Kirk's old friend Tyree. McCoy was stunned when Kirk decided to even the odds by giving Tyree's people equivalent weapons. "Jim," McCoy snarled, "that means you're condemning this whole planet to a war that may never end."

Kirk actually referred to Vietnam, in case anybody missed the point, recalling "the twentieth-century brush wars on the Asian continent. Two giant powers involved, much like the Klingons and ourselves. Neither side could pull out."

"It went on bloody year after bloody year," McCoy said.

"What would you have suggested, that one side arm its friends with an overpowering weapon? Mankind would never have lived to travel space if they had. The only solution is what happened back then. . . ."

"And if the Klingons give their side even more?"

"Then we arm our side with exactly that much more," Kirk said, "a balance of power—the trickiest, most difficult, dirtiest game of them all, but the only one that preserves both sides."

I've wondered if Roddenberry regretted writing an episode endorsing U.S. intervention in Vietnam. Had he known it would coincide with growing anti-war sentiment, would he have had Kirk make a different choice?

No matter. The point was, *Star Trek* regularly mixed futuristic action-adventure with timeless ethical questions. In "The Devil in the Dark" (1-25), elegantly written by Gene L. Coon, the subject was fear of the unknown. The *Enterprise* was summoned to kill a rock-eating monster which was attacking and killing mining colonists on Janus VI. Kirk halted the hunt when Spock discovered the "monster" (called the Horta) was not only intelligent, she was a mother trying to protect her unborn offspring inside their eggs, which the mining operations had been destroying.

"It wasn't just a monster," Roddenberry said in *The Making of Star Trek*. "It was someone. And the audience could put themselves in the place of the Horta . . . identify . . . feel! That's what drama is all about. And that's its importance, too. . . . If you can learn to feel for a Horta, you may also be learning to understand and feel for other humans of different colors, ways and beliefs."

Star Trek actually respected the intelligence of its audience, a rare quality at a time when network TV wasn't very sophisticated, and there weren't a lot of dramatic series addressing weighty topics. While early *Star Trek* may not have been subtle, Roddenberry and his writers bucked the prevailing winds every time they did stories that encouraged viewers to ponder important issues. Frankly, when it came to attracting thoughtful adults, as well as younger viewers eager to change the world for the better, the show had little competition.

By the time the original series ended, reality was getting even more ugly. The early 1970s brought us more of the worst: the killing of four students by young National Guardsmen during anti-war demonstrations at Kent State University, Nixonian paranoia leading to Watergate and the resignation of the disgraced president, and national divisions along racial, gender, political and generational lines. Cynicism reigned supreme.

In that bleak landscape, *Star Trek* became an oasis of optimism, and a surprise hit in syndicated reruns. In that pre-Internet era, fans connected through photocopied fanzines, communal televisions, campus clubs and the first of the *Trek* conventions. And it wasn't just because we liked the show or loved science fiction. *Star Trek's* main characters spoke to its audience—especially geeky young people in search of an identity—in a way few other TV characters did. Spock made it okay to be cool and smart. McCoy made it okay to be sarcastic, cranky, cautious and caring. And Kirk made it okay to stand up for what's right (and to speak... like... *this*). Their archetypal traits became part of us.

Long before *Star Trek*, poet Emily Dickinson wrote: "Hope is the thing with feathers that perches in the soul." For us, hope was the thing with warp-drive nacelles and we wanted to beam aboard for the ride. Sure, we wanted to escape from repulsive reality, but it was more than that. *Star Trek* attracted a quirky group of misfits who weren't ready to bail on idealism, and it offered an affirmative blueprint for a better future to those foolhardy enough to think it might be possible.

Did Roddenberry really believe in the perfectibility of human nature, that the essence of who we are would change so radically by the twenty-third century that we'd no longer be the frantic, violent, fearful, greedy species we've always been? On the surface, *Star Trek* appeared to fold that romantic notion into an entertaining confection of starships and Shakespearean allusions, and we bought it. Who wouldn't want to believe that it's possible to transcend the worst and become the best? Back then, that's what I thought Roddenberry was trying to tell us.

Now, after forty years of observation and experience, I think fear, greed and violence are too deeply embedded in our DNA to ever change. It's no accident that scientists see similar motives and instincts in the unexpectedly complex societies of chimpanzees, our closest genetic relatives. So maybe human nature is fatally flawed, and utopian peace and brotherhood are pipe dreams.

To today's twelve-year-olds, the world of 1966 is ancient, nearly incomprehensible history. We now face new perils that make the threat of nuclear Armageddon seem quaint by comparison. As we ponder where we *were* forty years ago, where we *hoped* to be by the twenty-first century and where we actually *are*, how can we not be disappointed by this mess of a world? *What happened to our dreams? Why are we going backwards?*

While it might be tempting to dismiss Roddenberry as a starry-eyed dreamer, we shouldn't be so hasty. Thanks to the dubious benefits of experience and disappointment, I see things in *Star Trek* I didn't see back then—including a healthy subtext of cynicism. For instance, in the overwrought (yet curiously satisfying) episode "The Omega Glory" (2-23), Roddenberry wrote a memorable line for McCoy. As Kirk was about to begin yet another fight to the death (this time against the demented Captain Tracy), McCoy muttered to Spock, "Evil usually triumphs, unless good is *very, very careful*."

The swashbuckling Kirk and brainy, logical Spock get most of the attention. But maybe it's McCoy, the cynical romantic (or is that romantic cynic?), who most speaks for Roddenberry. While I can't pretend to read Roddenberry's mind, I can get into McCoy's misanthropic head after watching him for forty years and writing him for thirty. McCoy *knows* human nature is fatally flawed, and utopian peace and brotherhood are poppycock. He expects that Abraham Lincoln's "better angels of our nature" will always be mugged by the evil thugs of our nature. He is a pessimist—but not without hope. Viewed through McCoy's eyes, Roddenberry's message becomes more cautionary. *Star Trek* said we'd reach that brighter day, but never said the trip would be easy. There was that nasty little eugenics tiff with Khan, and the millions of dead to which Spock refers in Terran wars after WWII. Even in *Star Trek*'s "present," there's plenty of evil to go around.

So, if human nature is hopeless, how do we escape self-inflicted doom? *Star Trek* had an answer: *our hard-wired nature is what it is—but our behavior is what we choose.* The distinction is *crucial.* If we blame all our sins on the limits of our nature, we can shrug our shoulders and—*Voila!*—we're absolved of responsibility. But if we accept the premise that we possess the power to control and alter our behavior, then we have no excuse for failing to do so.

That debate formed the core of the first-season episode "A Taste of Armageddon" (1-23), written by Robert Hammer and Coon. An innocent diplomatic mission to Eminiar VII exposed the *Enterprise* to a thousand-year war between Eminiar and its neighbor, Vendikar, worlds which had decided, after centuries of increasingly destructive fighting, that the only way to avoid annihilation of their entire civilizations was to replace actual attacks with computer-simulated ones. Citizens classified as "casualties" willingly reported to disintegration chambers. As Eminian council chief Anan 7 explained, the people die but the civilizations live on. Unfortunately, while Kirk and his landing party were on Eminiar, the *Enterprise* was "hit" and Kirk's crewmembers declared "dead." Proving that lunacy is in the eye of the beholder, Kirk destroyed the Eminians' war-management computers—thus breaking the treaty with Vendikar.

"Do you realize what you've done?!?" Anan shouted at Kirk.

"Yes," Kirk replied. "I've given you back the horrors of war.... The next attack they launch will do a lot more than count up numbers on a computer. They'll destroy your cities, devastate your planet.... Yes, councilman, you have a real war on your hands. You can either wage it with real weapons—or you might consider an alternative. Put an end to it. Make peace."

"There can be no peace," Anan hissed. "Don't you see? We've admitted it to ourselves. We're a killer species. It's instinctive. It's the same with you...."

"All right, it's instinctive," Kirk admitted. "But the instinct can be fought. We're human beings with the blood of a million savage years on our hands. But we can stop it. We can admit that we're killers, but we're not going to kill today. That's all it takes, knowing that we're not going to kill, *today*."

After five centuries of sanitized warfare, the Eminians couldn't even conceive of an alternative. But, faced with the big bye-bye, they accepted Federation mediation and began peace talks with the Vendikans.

The Big Idea that infuses all of *Star Trek* is right there in Kirk's words to Anan 7: *"The instinct can be fought.... We can admit that we're killers, but we're not going to kill today. That's all it takes, knowing that we're not going to kill,* today."

Flawless characters who automatically do the right thing are dull. *Star Trek's* characters were intriguing (and remain so) precisely because they are imperfect beings who wrestle with conflict and *choose* to do the right thing. They do what good fictional (and real-life) heroes should—inspire us to be better than we'd otherwise be. We humans exercise our capacity for conscientious choice all too rarely, which makes it all the more extraordinary when we do. Consider this:

In 1947, Brooklyn Dodger Jackie Robinson became the first black player in major league baseball when America was an openly racist society. Some of Robinson's own teammates implied they'd rather be traded than play with a "nigger." Team leader and shortstop Pee Wee Reese, who grew up in the Jim Crow South, was described by *New York Times* columnist Bob Herbert as a man who "had never so much as shaken hands with a black person." All season, Reese saw opposing pitchers throw at Robinson's head, runners try to spike him when he played first base, and fans pelt him with spit, garbage and racial epithets. One day, as jeers rained down on Robinson in Cincinnati, Reese called time, walked across the diamond and put a hand on Robinson's shoulder. In that small but monumental gesture, Reese overcame human nature and a heritage of hate when he decided "his own" were wrong and he reached out to "the other."

And this: For eighteen years, an anti-technology lunatic known as the Unabomber spread terror on college and research campuses by mailing explosive devices which killed three people and injured twenty-nine. He said he'd end his bombing campaign if major newspapers would print his manifesto against the evils of technology, which the *New York Times* and *Washington Post* did in 1995. Law enforcement authorities hoped someone would recognize the language—and David Kaczynski did. He suspected it was written by his reclusive older brother Ted, who lived in an isolated shack in rural Montana. Imagine David's quandary: turn in his own brother, knowing Ted might get the death penalty if found guilty, or don't turn him in, knowing more innocent victims might die. It's an ugly characteristic of human nature that indiscriminate loyalty often takes precedence over integrity, and we reflexively resist turning on "one of our own"—perhaps because we're praying we'll get the same free pass if we commit some shameful act.

Pee Wee Reese and David Kaczynski *chose* integrity and responsibility, and their real lives illustrate *Star Trek's* premise that human *behavior* can be improved, even if human *nature* can't. It's a deliberate choice we're all capable of making—and too few of us do. Harry Chapin, the late folksinger-activist who devoted much of his brief thirty-eight years to alleviating world hunger, wrote: "If a man could take his time on earth, and prove before he died what one man's life could be worth, well, I wonder what would happen to this world?"

The twenty-third century is a long way off. We current occupants of Planet Earth won't be around to see how it turns out. When your DNA is stamped with an expiration date, getting discouraged about the present is understandable.

So: does *Star Trek* have anything relevant left to say about *today's* world? Yes, and here it is: *"Here's who we are now (boooo) . . . and here's who we might someday be (yaaay!)."*

That dissonance between the actual now and the potential tomorrow energizes a basic human survival strategy—having aspirations. It's so straightforward and universal, the wonder isn't that *Star Trek* caught on, and held on for so long; it's that hardly anybody other than Roddenberry has believed this thread is worth weaving into commercial entertainment. Those privileged to work in the arts have an obligation not only to entertain, but also to provoke audiences to think and feel.

Humans have always had aspirations (although early desires revolved around not getting stomped or eaten by big animals). But the dream of a materially better future seems quintessentially American, and modern. After all, America was the first country to officially declare the concept: "*We hold these truths to be self-evident, that all men are created equal, that they are endowed by their Creator with certain unalienable Rights, that among these are Life, Liberty and the pursuit of Happiness.*"

The original *Star Trek* often reiterated simple verities about human aspirations. So did the original-series movies, and (in more subtle undertones) *The Next Generation* and *Deep Space Nine*. But I think *Voyager* and *Enterprise* muted the message; *Star Trek's* audience no longer heard the call that first brought them into the tent, and drifted away. Maybe the later writers and producers thought viewers had grown too sophisticated for the old message. Or maybe they thought the message had become so self-evident that it could be reduced to nearly imperceptible subtext.

But here's the thing about self-evident truths: eventually, they no longer are. We develop amnesia, and they blend into the background noise. If they really were perpetually self-evident, the world would be in a lot better shape. Apparently, we flawed humans need somebody to grab those self-evident truths and whack us over the head with them every so often. That's what *Star Trek* did.

These days, we long for the good ol' days, when our biggest worry was Soviet missiles. At least we knew who and where the enemy was. Nowadays, it's not so simple. And thanks to our defective nature, every time one old conflict is doused, another flares. (This mindless determination to repeat the same senseless battles was a recurrent *Star Trek* theme.) As long as true believers of many stripes are more determined to annihilate than coexist, then we need *Star Trek*'s message of hope and tolerance more than ever—to remind us that we are not prisoners of our nature: "*The instinct can be fought.... We can admit that we're killers, but we're not going to kill,* today."

When NBC canceled *Star Trek* in 1969, I wrote a letter of protest and got this letter in return: "We too believe that *Star Trek* is an attractive show with a fine cast. It was for these reasons that it found a spot in our schedule in the first place *but, unfortunately, the pro-*

gram failed to develop the broad appeal necessary for keeping it in our schedule next season. . . " (my italics).

Au contraire. The chord struck by *Star Trek* forty years ago still resonates today. And I hope *Star Trek* will rise again, reinvigorated by writers willing to go "back to the future," back to the plain truth that captivated us in 1966: *we can be better.*

Star Trek has always been, by turns, flawed, optimistic, hammy, sublime. *Star Trek* is *us.* When it's done right, it's about something universal and fundamental—aspiring to be better than we are.

The human adventure is just beginning.

Howard Weinstein sold his first story at age nineteen (the animated *Star Trek* episode "The Pirates of Orion"). His fiction credits include six *Star Trek* novels, three *V* novels, sixty *Trek* comics and "Safe Harbors" in the *Deep Space Nine: Tales of the Dominion War* short story anthology. His non-fiction books include *Puppy Kisses Are Good For The Soul & Other Important Lessons You & Your Dog Can Teach Each Other* and a biography of New York Yankees baseball star Mickey Mantle. Howard has written articles and columns for the *New York Times*, *Baltimore Sun*, *Newsday* and *Starlog Magazine.*

APPENDIX: EPISODE REFERENCE

Season # Episode #	Episode Title	Writer(s)
(by airdate)		(teleplay/script, if applicable)
0-0	The Cage	Gene Roddenberry
SEASON 1		
1-1	The Man Trap	George Clayton Johnson
1-2	Charlie X	D. C. Fontana/Gene Roddenberry
1-3	Where No Man Has Gone Before	Samuel A. Peeples
1-4	The Naked Time	John D. F. Black
1-5	The Enemy Within	Richard Matheson
1-6	Mudd's Women	Stephen Kandel/Gene Roddenberry
1-7	What Are Little Girls Made Of?	Robert Bloch
1-8	Miri	Adrian Spies
1-9	Dagger of the Mind	S. Bar-David
1-10	The Corbomite Maneuver	Jerry Sohl
1-11	The Menagerie, Part 1	Gene Roddenberry
1-12	The Menagerie, Part 2	Gene Roddenberry
1-13	The Conscience of the King	Barry Trivers
1-14	Balance of Terror	Paul Schneider
1-15	Shore Leave	Theodore Sturgeon
1-16	The Galileo Seven	Oliver Crawford and S. Bar-David/ Oliver Crawford

Season # Episode #	Episode Title	Writer(s)
(by airdate)		(teleplay/script, if applicable)
1-17	The Squire of Gothos	Paul Schneider
1-18	Arena	Gene L. Coon/Fredric Brown
1-19	Tomorrow Is Yesterday	D. C. Fontana
1-20	Court Martial	Don M. Mankiewicz and Stephen W. Carabatsos/Don M. Mankiewicz
1-21	The Return of the Archons	Boris Sobelman/Gene Roddenberry
1-22	Space Seed	Gene L. Coon and Carey Wilber/ Carey Wilber
1-23	A Taste of Armageddon	Robert Hamner and Gene L. Coon/ Robert Hamner
1-24	This Side of Paradise	D. C. Fontana/Nathan Butler and D. C. Fontana
1-25	The Devil in the Dark	Gene L. Coon
1-26	Errand of Mercy	Gene L. Coon
1-27	The Alternative Factor	Don Ingalls
1-28	The City on the Edge of Forever	Harlan Ellison
1-29	Operation: Annihilate!	Stephen W. Carabatsos
SEASON 2		
2-1	Amok Time	Theodore Sturgeon
2-2	Who Mourns for Adonais?	Gilbert Ralston
2-3	The Changeling	John Meredyth Lucas
2-4	Mirror, Mirror	Jerome Bixby
2-5	The Apple	Max Ehrlich
2-6	The Doomsday Machine	Norman Spinrad
2-7	Catspaw	Robert Bloch
2-8	I, Mudd	Stephen Kandel
2-9	Metamorphosis	Gene L. Coon
2-10	Journey to Babel	D. C. Fontana
2-11	Friday's Child	D. C. Fontana
2-12	The Deadly Years	David P. Harmon
2-13	Obsession	Art Wallace
2-14	Wolf in the Fold	Robert Bloch
2-15	The Trouble With Tribbles	David Gerrold

Season # Episode # (by airdate)	Episode Title	Writer(s) (teleplay/script, if applicable)
2-16	The Gamesters of Triskelion	Margaret Armen
2-17	A Piece of the Action	David P. Harmon and Gene L. Coon/ David P. Harmon
2-18	The Immunity Syndrome	Robert Sabaroff
2-19	A Private Little War	Gene Roddenberry/Jud Crucis
2-20	Return to Tomorrow	John Kingsbridge
2-21	Patterns of Force	John Meredyth Lucas
2-22	By Any Other Name	D. C. Fontana and Jerome Bixby/ Jerome Bixby
2-23	The Omega Glory	Gene Roddenberry
2-24	The Ultimate Computer	D. C. Fontana/Laurence N. Wolfe
2-25	Bread and Circuses	Gene Roddenberry and Gene L. Coon/John Kneubuhl
2-26	Assignment: Earth	Art Wallace/Gene Roddenberry and Art Wallace
SEASON 3		
3-1	Spock's Brain	Lee Cronin
3-2	The *Enterprise* Incident	D. C. Fontana
3-3	The Paradise Syndrome	Margaret Armen
3-4	And the Children Shall Lead	Edward J. Lakso
3-5	Is There In Truth No Beauty?	Jean Lissette Aroeste
3-6	Spectre of the Gun	Lee Cronin
3-7	Day of the Dove	Jerome Bixby
3-8	For the World Is Hollow and I Have Touched the Sky	Rik Vollaerts
3-9	The Tholian Web	Judy Burns and Chet Richards
3-10	Plato's Stepchildren	Meyer Dolinsky
3-11	Wink of an Eye	Arthur Heinemann/Lee Cronin
3-12	The Empath	Joyce Muskat
3-13	Elaan of Troyius	John Meredyth Lucas
3-14	Whom Gods Destroy	Lee Erwin/Lee Erwin and Jerry Sohl
3-15	Let That Be Your Last Battlefield	Oliver Crawford/Lee Cronin
3-16	The Mark of Gideon	George F. Slavin and Stanley Adams

Season # Episode # (by airdate)	Episode Title	Writer(s) (teleplay/script, if applicable)
3-17	That Which Survives	John Meredyth Lucas/ Michael Richards
3-18	The Lights of Zetar	Jeremy Tarcher and Shari Lewis
3-19	Requiem for Methuselah	Jerome Bixby
3-20	The Way to Eden	Arthur Heinemann/Michael Richards and Arthur Heinemann
3-21	The Cloud Minders	Margaret Armen/David Gerrold and Oliver Crawford
3-22	The Savage Curtain	Gene Roddenberry and Arthur Heinemann/Gene Roddenberry
3-23	All Our Yesterdays	Jean Lissette Aroeste
3-24	Turnabout Intruder	Arthur H. Singer/Gene Roddenberry

ACKNOWLEDGMENTS

SPECIAL THANKS to Earl Green of *theLogBook.com* (http://www.thelogbook.com) and Sheryl Franklin (http://www.sherylfranklin.com/startrek.html) for their assistance with this manuscript.